Christmas

To Ron Brown

From Scanton

SERVICE AMERICA IN THE NEW ECONOMY

SERVICE AMERICA IN THE NEW ECONOMY

Karl Albrecht and Ron Zemke

McGraw-Hill
New York   Chicago   San Francisco   Lisbon   London
Madrid   Mexico City   Milan   New Delhi   San Juan
Seoul   Singapore   Sydney   Toronto

Library of Congress Cataloging-in-Publication Data

Albrecht, Karl, 1941–
    Service America in the new economy / by Karl Albrecht and Ron Zemke — Rev. ed.
      p. cm.
    ISBN 0-07-137722-0
    1. Service industries—United States—Management.   2. United States—Economic
conditions—1981. I. Zemke, Ron. II. Title

  HD9981.5 A43   2001
  658'.00973—dc21

                                               2001031718

McGraw-Hill

A Division of The McGraw·Hill Companies

1 2 3 4 5 6 7 8 9 0 AGM/AGM 0 9 8 7 6 5 4 3 2 1

ISBN 0-07-137722-0

This book was set in Times New Roman by Patricia Wallenburg.

Printed and bound by Quebecor World/Martinsburg.

McGraw-Hill books are available at special quantity discounts to use as premiums and sales
promotions, or for use in corporate training programs. For more information, please write to the
Director of Special Sales, Professional Publishing, McGraw-Hill, Two Penn Plaza, New York,
NY 10121-2298. Or contact your local bookstore.

 This book was printed on recycled, acid-free paper containing a minimum of 50%
recycled, de-inked fiber.

CONTENTS

PART 2
SERVICE AMERICA II:
DOING BUSINESS IN THE NEW MILLENNIUM

PREFACE

A
S THE LONG-RUNNING "customer service" movement faded from the business scene, seminar manuals and conference notebooks gathered dust on managers' bookshelves, videotapes and handout materials migrated toward the back of the training departments' storerooms, and the Internet became the Next Big Thing. Of course, service, by and large, still stinks. Did we improve anything, gain anything, or learn anything?

Airline profits have hit record highs in recent years, and yet customer confidence in that industry—at least in the United States—is near an all-time low. Heavy investments in digital technology for flight scheduling, booking, pricing, and resource allocation have driven down costs, while the treatment of customers as compliant cattle has driven loyalty almost to zero.

Hospitals and doctors benefit from an amazing array of medical technologies, including the best of digital electronics, and yet the American medical industry continues to lose over 100,000 patients per year by mistakes in diagnosis, treatment, and medication. HMOs are routinely vilified for placing their concern for profit far above their concern for human life and well being.

Banks are rushing to "digitize" their customers in order to cut labor costs and achieve economies of scale. Yet consumers in general have less regard for banks as service businesses than ever. People seeking loans for various purposes are flocking to cut-rate Internet sources because they see no added-value premise in going through their banks or mortgage brokers.

Many of the largest corporations have abandoned any pretense of serving the public. It's impossible to call a big company and talk to a human being. You get a telephone menu, and you're lucky if you recognize the solution to your problem in any of the options offered you by the maddeningly cheerful "radio" voice. The mindless use of digital technology to depopulate the customer interface will turn out to be one of the biggest mistakes many companies will ever make.

This "digital moat"—the defensive wall of electronic technology that keeps customers out of contact with real, living, breathing people who can be of service to them—creates a commoditized sameness among competitors, makes competitive differentiation virtually nonexistent, and eliminates all possibility of emotionalizing or dramatizing the customer's experience of value. In the end, it's merely a battle between software routines, and that battle will always end in a draw.

The phenomenal popularity of dot-com businesses (i.e., Web sites trying to impersonate real businesses) is testimony to the distaste many technical people have for the messy task of interacting with real human beings. What a wonderful way to do business: All you have to do is sit at your computer all day and tinker with your Web site, and the money just pours in—presumably. You don't have to talk to customers—put up with their questions, demands, complaints, quirks, and special problems. Just let the computer handle them. Of course, you have to rationalize all this by telling yourself that your "CRM" system, alias customer relations management software, will tailor the response to each customer and make him or her happy in his or her own unique way.

The reality, however, is far removed from the fantasy. Web-based businesses, so far at least, have probably set back the state of the art in delivering customer value by at least 10 years. And even the best of them have simply transformed their businesses into virtual vending machines. When a business offers a choice between interacting with a software algorithm and interacting with a sullen, indifferent, incompetent, and ill-informed service employee, we'll take the software every time. But for some kinds of services, we'd really rather have a pleasant, helpful, well-informed person who's authorized to think. A computer may save the customer's time, but it can never make him or her feel special; only a human being can do that. To paraphrase science philosopher Arthur C. Clarke's classic remark about computers replacing teachers, "Any service worker who can be replaced by a computer should be."

As management consultants, we have watched with considerable amusement as the techies have suddenly discovered business. The German philosopher Wolfgang Goethe said, "There is nothing so frightening as ignorance in action." In record time, the invading cyber-Vikings created their own business ideology and vocabulary, which, they take great pains to emphasize, owe nothing to the "traditional" thinking process of commerce. By characterizing established businesses as "old economy," or "bricks-and-mortar" enterprises, they authorize themselves to reinvent business. "After all," they smugly pronounce, "the Internet changes everything. The old rules no longer apply, so why bother to learn them?"

Actually, information technology will evolutionize business, not revolutionize it. In fact, it is more than likely that the companies who take best advantage of online technology will be the established leaders in the so-called old economy—retailers, publishers, catalog marketers, banks, and all the rest. Procter & Gamble and Wal-Mart have linked their computer systems together—B2B, or business to business as it's called in the current jargon—for well over a decade. As early as 1989, Hewlett Packard had decided to "wire" the entire company, putting over 90,000 employees in regular contact.

E-commerce will go down in business history as the big failure story of the first decade of the new millennium. Successful companies will, of course, continue to use online technology to simplify and integrate their operations, interlocking their systems more and more with those of suppliers and partners. And most established companies will extend their market reach through Web technology. However, the heart of the e-commerce story, as promoted by the press, namely the Internet-only company, will eventually be chalked up as virtually a total failure.

In *Service America!: Doing Business in the New Economy*, we predicted that delivering customer value would become more and more important as the years progressed. We stand by that prediction. As the business world's intoxication with all things digital wears off and we understand better how to tame technology and focus it for the achievement of worthwhile human goals, we will once again see the concepts of service, value creation, and sensible business practices in their proper perspective. And the return to a human-values focus will feel good for most of us; it will feel right. It will be like coming home to a place we've always known, but now understand better and appreciate better, and from which we have the confidence to take on the ever more complex challenges of the true new economy.

In this book, we've tried to renew, revalidate, and extend the principles set forth in the first edition. We believe its basic message is timeless and still as relevant today as it was a decade and a half ago when we wrote it. We take great satisfaction in building upon it.

ACKNOWLEDGMENTS

Ron Zemke wishes to thank the following people for their assistance and support: PRA partners Chip Bell and Tom Connellan, who both encouraged the author and added to the tone and tenor of this new version and updated vision of service in America. Jill Applegate, the PRA theme park expert, kept the Minneapolis team focused on the right ends and kept us from using the same stories and examples ad nauseum. She also made sure we finished on time, without whining. David Zielinski, whom I worked with at *The Service Edge* newsletter from 1988 to 1997 and who has come to be an integral and irreplaceable part of the PRA writing team, once again came to the line, even when that line had shifted as far south as Guatemala. And I thank Chris Lee, our long-time *Training* magazine colleague, who brought her eagle eye to bear in the revising and modernizing of several of the chapters. Last but not least, my thanks to Susan Zemke, who remembered well the angst of the first edition but nonetheless embraced this second edition and was even more supportive and supporting.

SERVICE AMERICA
IN THE NEW ECONOMY

Introduction: Service Management Update

> "And how am I to face the odds of man's bedevilment, and God's? I, a stranger and afraid in a world I never made."
>
> —*A. E. Housman*
> *Last Poems*

FOLLOWING THE RELEASE IN 1985 of the first edition of this book, the business world embraced the concept of *service management* as a competitive weapon with remarkable enthusiasm. There were books, articles, conferences, seminars, training programs, videos, newsletters, and even professional societies and academic research programs aimed at making customer focus a critical and permanent part of Western management thinking. Consulting firms sprang up to implement these new ideas. Even the established management gurus, who had made their names on other topics, were moved to declare the primacy of customer value. Virtually every training consultant and motivational speaker had to add "customer service" to his or her repertoire of topics. Even university extension catalogs sprouted offerings aimed at transforming businesses.

The wave of interest lasted for quite some time, and it spread well beyond the United States. The first edition sold over half a million copies and was translated into a number of other languages. Both authors were called upon to lecture about service management around the globe. About 4 years after the appearance of the first edition, the publishing category was getting saturated. As management movements go, customer focus had an unusually long run—nearly 10 years.

Yet the wave didn't last. The service revolution apparently got hijacked somewhere along the road to victory. Like so many other management movements before it—management by objectives, human relations training, behavior modification, participative management, productivity, and the quality revolution—customer focus became the object of intense flirtation by many firms, but ultimately the infatuation faded. The same fate befell several other revolutions such as total quality management (TQM), reengineering, and ISO 9000, which presented a system of documenting all work processes. E-commerce, hailed by many as the revolution of all revolutions, had the same fate in store for it.

Some years down the line, we now have a rare opportunity to look back upon the history of this particular management fad, movement, or theory— whichever you choose to call it—and analyze its development. And in thinking about the anatomy of the service movement, we see the prototypical anatomy of all such movements. We can best understand and extend the service management approach by studying it in the context of the process by which business concepts come into—and go out of—fashion.

Before proceeding with this discussion, we vigorously assert that we do not believe that the ideology of service management has failed. Indeed, it has succeeded remarkably well in the hands of those who have applied it intelligently. We have always emphasized the distinction between service management (the concept we elaborated in the first edition) and the various incarnations created by those who sought to popularize "customer service." In the first edition of the book, we recognized explicitly that only about 10 percent to 15 percent of businesses would fully grasp the implications of a strategic, customer focus and would commit the proper energy and resources to make it a permanent way of managing. Most of the rest, we predicted, would mistake it for an employee motivation program, an advertising proposition, or a reason to rewrite the corporate rule book.

Our prediction was essentially correct, but like most movements before and after it, the customer movement left behind some significant traces of permanent change. The lexicon of customer focus and customer value became more firmly embedded in business discourse. Outstanding service companies like Disney, Federal Express, and Nordstrom became obligatory cases for study in countless seminars, conferences, and college courses. Some would claim that consumers, particularly in the United States, have become more acutely aware of service quality and more demanding of those who provide it. Even the U.S. federal government, as well as other national governments, has embraced many of the elements of the service management model. The U.S. Congress has held unprecedented hearings on the practices of various service industries, particularly the airlines.

While we celebrate the beneficial effects of the service movement, we remain convinced that the real value and potential impact of the service management model is yet to be realized. At the same time, we are coming to a stage in business—worldwide, not just in America or the West—in which we will need its principles more than ever before. We believe that Western management philosophy has lost its way somewhat in recent years, particularly with the mindless infatuation with all things digital, and that it has wandered into an intellectual house of mirrors. We believe there is a deep-lying need, only partly articulated, for a return to some of the most basic and timeless precepts of leadership, management, and enterprise thinking. And we still believe that the service management model offers a road back to sanity.

In order to fully understand the premise and the promise of service management for this millennium, it is necessary to understand the hijacking of the service movement. Who hijacked it? How? And why? And at what cost to those who might have capitalized on its possibilities?

THE CURRENT STATE OF SERVICE MANAGEMENT

Two primary factors, we believe, led to the fade-out of the customer focus movement. One was the aggressive promotion of competing management methodologies, particularly TQM, as solutions for the problems of service quality. The other was the "too hard" factor; that is, the disappointment and disillusionment felt by many executives when they realized that "customer service" was not the panacea or the quick fix they'd been led to believe it was. When they discovered that it involved such distasteful realities as financial investment, long-term commitment, constant attention to detail, service-oriented leadership, culture-building, perpetually listening to customers, and even changing the business design, many of them signed off.

TQM, of course, and its companion ideologies such as ISO 9000, faded from the management spotlight at about the same time the service movement began to fade. They suffered from the same terminal disease: The results fell short of the promise.

In 1989, Florida Power & Light, a gas and electric utility covering the central region of the state of Florida, won the legendary Deming Prize from the Japan Union of Scientists and Engineers (JUSE) for its outstanding TQM program. It was, and still is, the only non-Japanese company to win the award, which is based on the systematic application of statistical techniques to improving quality all across a company. Within 6 months of winning the award, the company dismantled its entire TQM program, having decided it was far too costly in comparison to the results it delivered. A near-mutiny by the employees led the new CEO and management team to reexamine the program. Employees were saying, "We're spending so much time on quality meetings, task forces, measurement programs, and reporting, that we can't get our real work done. We thought the purpose of a quality program was supposed to be to do the work better and make more profit."

Indeed, the Florida Public Utilities Commission, the state body that oversees utility companies, declared that the prize-winning TQM program contributed little, if anything, to the value received by FP&L's customers (also known politically as "ratepayers"), and it prohibited the company from including the costs of the program in its rate structure. The firm was forced to cover the multimillion dollar cost from its profit account, not from its customer revenues.

The FP&L incident delivered a shock to the TQM movement in the United States, and probably even in Japan, on a number of levels. Even though the company spun off its quality group as a commercial quality consulting firm, which marketed its methods to other firms, the incident seemed to mark the turning point in the fate of TQM.

For one thing, it called into question the "numbers neurosis" that many TQM practitioners seemed to embrace as a core ideology. Slogans like "If you can't measure it, you can't manage it" became the official coin of the theoretical discourse. Service management fans, suspicious of the applicability of statistical process control (SPC) methods to human interaction, replied with a quotation from Albert Einstein: "Not everything that counts can be counted; and not everything that can be counted counts." The proposition of *subjective measures of quality*, as a worthy companion to objective measures of quality, appealed to some and appalled others.

Nevertheless, for a period of about 5 years, the aggressive promotion of the TQM ideology by a host of writers, consultants, and conference organizers made it the method of choice for many firms. It seemed to us that many executives and leadership teams, when faced with the task of setting out an ideology for change in their service quality efforts, tended to respond to either the "numbers" ideology or the "people" ideology, but rarely both. Even with its heavily statistical orientation, TQM seemed to offer a comfortable familiarity to many executives, particularly males, who had been trained all through their careers to think of management in terms of command and control. The idea of "50,000 moments of truth," as Scandinavian Airlines CEO Jan Carlzon expressed it, seemed to many managers to hint at a loss of control and a feeling of impotence. The command model held a much stronger appeal for many than the enablement model.

The ISO 9000 movement, an offshoot of the TQM worldview, offered a similar appeal. Most of its more enthusiastic promoters, however, were consultants who wanted to help companies implement it. ISO 9000, a specification document published by the International Standards Organization in Geneva, Switzerland, offered a procedure for documenting all the work processes in a business leading up to its ultimate product or output. Typically, an internal task force or a consulting firm would diagram and describe in detail the flow of work events from product design through engineering, testing and evaluation; production planning; physical production; shipping and delivery to the customer.

Once the task force or consultants had thoroughly documented the firm's processes, including the whole range of support activities, they would call in an independent auditing firm to examine their processes to confirm that they were following the procedures they had written. If they passed the examination, the firm would receive an official certification as an "ISO 9000 compliant" organization.

As with TQM, this highly mechanistic worldview turned some executives on and turned others off. One of the more zealous promoters of the ISO approach asserted, "You should document your processes so thoroughly that you could replace your entire workforce with all new people, and the new people would be able to operate the systems perfectly." Another consultant, eager to extend the ISO ideology to the service sector which, after all, far overshadows the manufacturing sector in size, particularly in the United States, confidently advised, "Just go through the ISO 9000 specification, and wherever you see the word 'product' just substitute the phrase 'product or service,' and it will apply just as well to a service organization as to a manufacturing organization."

We believed at the time, as we do today, that the attempt to overlay or force-fit a numbers-based, command ideology such as TQM or ISO 9000 onto a service business represents a profound misunderstanding of service enterprises. It also represents a failure to grasp even the most rudimentary truths about customers, service workers, and work cultures. Further, it represents a willingness to settle for far less than might be achieved by a cultural, leadership-based approach to service excellence.

Yet TQM and ISO 9000 had their run on the stage of management theater, and, to be sure, some business leaders succeeded in applying them skillfully and effectively. But we consider it unfortunate that, as competing ideologies, they distracted attention from the subtle perception of the real opportunities offered by the strategic customer focus concept.

And we said so, frequently and emphatically. In March 1992, during the very peak of the worldwide popularity of the TQM movement, and particularly its zenith in America, Karl Albrecht stood on a platform in London in front of 1200 quality experts and declared, "TQM will be dead within three years." Although some of the participants threatened the intellectual equivalent of lynching, the prediction came true. He made similar assertions in a number of articles, particularly in one of the quality industry's leading publications, *Quality Digest*.[1]

In 1991 Ron Zemke came under fire for an article in *Training* magazine[2] that explored in some depth the argument that the quality movement had become something of a hybrid between a beauty contest and a consultant's gold rush. Though written as a tactful exploration of both sides of the argument, it led to some stinging rebuffs and attacks. About a year later, Tom Peters made the point a bit more directly and bluntly—as only Tom Peters can—declaring TQM "a full employment act for quality professionals."

The second major factor in the fade-out of the service movement, the "too hard" factor, ultimately took the largest toll of corporate "customer service" programs. One organization after another launched its latest top-down initiative, complete with motivational seminars, task forces, slogans, notepads, and prizes, only to let it wither and die. Employee cynicism, characteristically high in large organizations, fed on the high "fizzle factor" of these programs. Each new "This time we're serious" program and every "We really mean it" communication campaign was apt to collide with a "wait and see" attitude. More often than not, management's failure to follow through proved the more cynical employees correct in their pessimistic predictions.

A surprisingly large number of executives and top teams displayed a remarkable lack of understanding of the dynamics of change and the realities of selling a big idea throughout an organization. Many had little or no grasp of the need for preparation and culture-building—or cultural repair, in many cases—before launching their enthusiastic all-hands programs. Many utterly failed to grasp the relationship between service workers and service systems: the notion that even the most enthusiastic workers cannot deliver superior customer value if they don't know what it is or don't have the resources or support systems to enable them to do it.

Still others failed to grasp the role of leadership in the service quality equation. Too many chief executives got the idea that they could simply write a check for a service quality program and then turn their minds to other business. For them, it never sank in that service quality *was* the business.

However, for many executives, probably the most discouraging realization of all was: Nothing lasts. Or, as hotel pioneer J. Willard Marriott put it, "Success is never final." It began to dawn on them that the all-hands training program would have to be repeated, if not next year, then certainly the year after that. High turnover of customer-contact employees—typically among the lowest-paid people in most organizations—steadily drained away the knowledge, commitment, and spirit aroused by the training programs and work projects. Pretty soon, a large fraction of the workforce had not had the medicine. Over time, this pollution of the motivational level by newcomers tended to drag down the morale and commitment of the veterans.

An associated realization, also devastating to many executives, was "The employees don't think we really mean it when we talk about serving customers." Saying it once or twice or even ten times, they discovered, is simply not enough. Once you stop saying it, employees conclude that it's no longer important to you and that they can stop worrying about it until or unless you bring it up again. When the CEO stops talking about it, the vice presidents stop talking about it, and then the middle managers stop talking about it. Finally the supervisors, ever watchful to see what spin top management is applying lately, stop emphasizing it to their people. And once the people stop hearing about it, it fades and dies.

More than one executive we've worked with has learned a humbling lesson: Big ideas are damned hard to sell in organizations, and it's even harder to keep them sold.

At about the same time the TQM, ISO 9000, and service quality movements were fading (about 1995), U.S. business began to feel the pressure of a more primitive shift in emphasis. American enterprises, and to a lesser extent firms in other countries, began to move into a reconstruction phase. An unprecedented period of mergers, acquisitions, and dramatic growth on the part of retail giants got mixed in with demergers, spin-offs, and an intensive movement toward delayering, outsourcing, and partnering. A healthy, growing economy, coupled with low unemployment rates and a remarkably flexible workforce, enabled U.S. firms to rearrange themselves to maximize their strengths.

Key phrases such as "core competencies," "strategic partnering," and "supply chain management" replaced the terminology of "service," "quality," and "customer value." Thus began a deep-running ideological drift in American management thinking, toward *resource-based competition* rather than *value-based competition*. A large banking corporation finds it difficult to win more customers by adding value or reinventing its service package, but it's easy to find profit growth by buying up its smaller competitors. After all, why have two competing branch banks on opposite sides of the street? Let's just buy out the other bank, close its branches, and add its customers to our inventory.

Why should a large airline try to offer better service, when all airlines have conditioned their customers to make their choices solely on the basis of price? Why not buy up, or force out, the smaller airlines and relieve the pricing pressure? Why mess with customer service programs that just fizzle out anyway?

Why should a megafirm such as McDonald's try to gild the lily with service training for its employees, when the evidence shows clearly that most people won't pay a few cents extra for a better dining experience? It's vastly better for cash flow to simply open another restaurant in a less well-served area than to try to inch up the revenues of existing ones with questionable customer care programs.

This is not to suggest that no companies are interested in service quality as a competitive factor: Surely firms like Disney and Federal Express are still in a class by themselves. However, the example set by the giant firms, namely buying their competitors and kidnapping their customers, has drawn more attention in recent years. The business press seems particularly fond of adventure stories about megafirms like Exxon-Mobil and AOL-Time Warner, and high-profile executives like Bill Gates and Al "Chainsaw" Dunlap, than in the struggles of middle-of-the-pack firms to deliver value.

THE SECOND COMING OF SERVICE?

But perhaps the stage is set for another shift in management thinking and priorities. Maybe the capital-intensive approaches to competition used by the megafirms aren't the answer for midsize and smaller firms. Although most of the coverage in the business press centers on large enterprises, it pays to recall, as futurist John Naisbitt points out, that the 500 largest firms in the United States—the Fortune 500—contribute only a bit more than 10 percent of the country's gross domestic product. All the rest still need a good answer to the basic question of success and growth.

Will there be a second coming of interest in service and customer value? Is customer focus the real home base we all must return to? Have executives and managers been distracted in recent years by cost management, restructuring, and information technology, to the neglect of the basic value package itself? Have they been allowing their companies and brands to become ever more homogenized and commoditized, drifting toward a state of bland sameness with no real differentiation? Have our biggest companies lost their personalities? Once the economies of scale are mostly harvested, how does a large firm maintain its growth pattern?

It's easier to predict the demise rather than the rise of any management movement, but a second coming of service does seem to have possibilities. That's why we agreed to update and extend the service management model we presented in the first edition.

We have retained the structure and most of the content of the original book because we believe they are still relevant and we don't think we could say it any better. Readers of the original will see a familiar conceptual foundation. We have chosen to simply modernize the examples and cases that illustrate the key concepts, and then extend the model into the new business environment of globalism, hypercompetition, and technology.

Service management, if it is to endure and remain relevant, will have to rest on a contemporary platform of business in the new millennium. Some things have changed radically, and some things have remained the same. Information technology in particular has presented new opportunities and threats, and it has radically rearranged priorities. More complex and diversified organizational structures have led to different ways to compete, cooperate, and deploy resources. Many firms are having to reinvent their value packages as customer priorities change and customer choices proliferate.

It is imperative that we see through this maze of change and opportunity, and discern the new truths of business success. At the same time, we need to focus our attention ever more closely on the timeless truths, those immutable principles that can help leaders guide their enterprises skillfully through ever more challenging times.

SERVICE AMERICA I: DOING BUSINESS IN THE NEW ECONOMY

C H A P T E R

THE SERVICE IMPERATIVE

"McDonald's has more employees than U.S. Steel. Golden arches, not blast furnaces, symbolize the American economy."

—*George F. Will*

W

E LIVE AND WORK in a service-centered, service-sensitive economy. In the United States, nearly 74 percent of the gross domestic product and 79 million jobs are derived from the performance of services, rather than the production of product.[1] Equally important, as manufactured products become more commodity-like, it is increasingly the quality and variety of the accompanying service that makes the critical difference between success and failure in the marketplace. According to the Strategic Planning Institute of Cambridge, Massachusetts, organizations that emphasize and deliver high-quality service see a greater increase in market share and have a higher return on sales than those for whom service is a secondary or low-priority concern, poorly provided.

Trend analyst John Naisbitt marked 1956 as the beginning of the service economy, when, "For the first time in American history, white-collar workers in technical, managerial, and clerical positions outnumbered blue-collar workers. Industrial America was giving way to a new society." Naisbitt labeled this new era the "information society." The emergence of the Internet and World Wide Web as global instruments of commerce, marketing, and information warehousing, confirmed that appellation. Earlier still, Harvard sociologist Daniel Bell noted the same events and trends, and he declared that we have entered into the "postindustrial society." Call it what you will, the fact remains that we live in an America—indeed, in a world and time—dominated by enterprises that perform rather than produce.

According to the U.S. Department of Commerce, the forecast for the foreseeable future can be summed up in four words: *more of the same.* There will be continued fast growth in service industries and service jobs, high-tech and information technology (IT) skills, and hospitality leading the way. Service is no longer an industrial by-product, a sector that generates no wealth but "simply moves money around," as economists once scoffed. Service has become a powerful economic engine in its own right—the fast track of the new U.S. economy. *Newsweek* columnist George F. Will summarized the look of this new economy succinctly when he observed that "McDonald's has more employees than U.S. Steel. Golden arches, not blast furnaces, symbolize the American economy." We would add but one sentiment to Will's observation: How well those employees are equipped to serve can and will determine the fate of the organization.

Let's be clear here. We aren't suggesting that U.S. Steel must convert its factories into laundries to survive or that Ford should consider abandoning automobile manufacturing for condominium management. As Wharton School management professor Russell Ackoff has argued, this shift to a service-centered economy does not mean that fewer goods will be produced and consumed, "any more than the end of the agricultural era meant that fewer agricultural products were produced and consumed. *What it does mean* is that fewer people will be required to produce manufactured goods."[2] To us, that implies that the economic gold and the growth are in more and better services. That's where the jobs are; that's where the energy is; that's where the opportunities will continue to be. We understand that the preoccupation of the 1990s has been with technological plays, particularly e-commerce, retail, and business-to-business. But however important, that narrow preoccupation obscures an important reality. Almost every new technology venture, be it dot-com, network management, or software development, successful or failed, is at its heart a service venture.

The fabric of our economy and the way we do business are changing. This change in thrust, this transformation from a marketplace focused on goods to one focused on services, this phenomenon that Ackoff called the "second industrial revolution" and Naisbitt refers to as the "beginning of the information society," is real and important. It is our new competitive edge, both domestically and in the world at large. Already 30 percent of the world's need for services—be they medical, technological, entertainment-driven, or conceptual—are filled by American exports. It is only a beginning.

We contend, however, that this shift from products to services, if it is to be fully leveraged as a driving force, requires a parallel transformation in the way organizations are conceptualized, structured, and, most importantly, managed. We contend that organizations that place a premium on the design, development, and delivery of services are as different from traditional industrial organizations as the factory is from the farm. The distinction applies not only to organizations that market pure service products (the traditional service industries) but also to manufacturers of goods and commodities which place a high strategic value on service and treat it as an integral part of their product offerings. Whether service is valued simply because it is a useful strategy for product differentiation or because service is an ingrained organizational belief, the result is the same. In those organizations service isn't a function or a department. To them, *service is product.*

SERVICE IS ...

What do we mean by service? Several things. Bureaucrats and economists traditionally have talked about the *service sector* and defined it as consisting of "industries whose output is intangible." To the U.S. Department of Commerce, that definition covers organizations that employ just over 61.4 percent of all the people employed in the United States, and applies to four broad segments of the economy[3]:

1. Transportation, communications, and utilities.
2. Wholesale and retail trade.

3. Finance, insurance, and real estate.

4. Services—the fastest growing part of the service sector, which includes business services such as accounting, e-commerce, engineering, and legal work; personal services such as housekeeping, barbering, and recreational services; and most of the nonprofit areas of the economy.

All four of these groups offer service in the classic "help me" sense: Help me with my taxes, help me get from point A to point B; help me find a house; help me pick out a new pair of shoes. There is nothing intrinsically wrong with this traditional approach to defining who is and who isn't in the service business. Indeed, today's time-pressed, two-income family—that's two-thirds of us—would be lost without an ample selection of "help me" services. It does, however, mask the full impact of service in today's marketplace.

Management expert and social scientist Peter Drucker is even more emphatic that the term *services*, as used to describe the largest portion of our contemporary economy, is a singularly unhelpful description. In a mid-1980s column in *The Wall Street Journal*, he surveyed the world economy, manufacturing, commodities, and services, and concluded:

> We may—and soon—have to rethink the way we look at economics and economies, and fairly radically. "Information" is now classed as "services," a 19th-century term for "miscellaneous." Actually it is no more services than electrical power (which is also classed under services). It is the primary material of an information-based economy. And in such an economy the schools are as much primary producers as the farms— and their productivity perhaps more crucial. The same in the engineering lab, the newspaper and offices in general.[4] (January 9, 1985)

Drucker could not have been more prescient. The "new economy" is indeed a service economy. We heartily agree with Drucker's argument that service, as we know it today, is very much a primary product. It is, indeed, this argument that service is not a single-dimensioned "thing" that is at the core of our contention that service is as much a commodity as an automobile, and therefore as much in need of management and systematic study.

Harvard Business School professor Theodore Levitt has argued persuasively that the service and nonservice distinction becomes less and less meaningful as our understanding of service increases. "There are no such things as service industries. There are only industries whose service components are greater or less than those of other industries. Everybody is in service," he wrote. At Citigroup, 180,000 employees work in back rooms, never seen or heard by the public. They spend their time writing letters of credit, opening lockboxes, processing transactions, and scrutinizing everything done by those who deal with customers on the front lines. Is Citigroup any less a manufacturer than General Motors? And is GMC, half of whose 388,000 employees deal with the public, any less a service provider? Service is everyone's business.

"FIX IT" SERVICE

The second dimension after "help me" service is "fix it" service. It sometimes seems we are a nation of broken toys. The car is in the shop, the cell phone is out of order, and this software upgrade somebody sold me isn't working all that well. Service in this sense is underaccounted for in the economy and marketplace, but seldom undervalued in the eye of the contemporary consumer.[5] The quality of a company's "fix it" service is already a significant factor in its marketplace success. The capacity of a Dell Computer, a General Electric (GE), or a Caterpillar Tractor to deliver high-quality, "fix it" service as a matter of routine—while others offer excuses, complex requirements, or failure—sets each apart in its industry and in the marketplace as a whole. We are not suggesting, of course, that manufactured goods have never before needed fixing. Far from it. But the abundance of products too complex for users to repair and maintain on their own has accentuated the need. For example, when was the last time you tried to fix the crippled hard drive on your desktop? At the same time, consumers have come to expect—to demand really—that a manufacturer's obligation to guarantee the performance of a product should extend further beyond the point and date of purchase than ever before.

Such changes in consumer needs and expectations can be both a bane and a blessing. It is the growing demand for fast and effective service in the desktop computer business, for example—a plea that fell on the deaf ears of most dealers and manufacturers, that's behind the success of companies like SunMicrosystems, the Computer Doctor Inc., and The Geek Squad, which specialize in electronic products systems support. The same demand is enticing manufacturers into the development of aggressive, third-party service subsidiaries and Web site-based, self-service options.

And what an opportunity it is! Every day, thousands of iMacs come rolling off the Apple Computer assembly lines in Cupertino, California, while an even greater number of Dell, Compaq, and Gateway PCs flood the marketplace. If we add "orphaned" personal computers and computer peripherals in this country (gear manufactured by companies that no longer exist but owned by users who do) then the need for quality "fix it" service in the computer area alone is staggering.

According to the U.S. Census Bureau, the repair of information processing, telecommunications, and other diverse electronic products, dubbed the "electronic products service business," bills $35 billion annually. This figure should more than double by 2007.[6] Yet few manufacturers of high-tech gear are interested in the opportunities presented by this obvious void. This is so despite the fact that a well-run service operation can contribute as much as 30 percent to a manufacturer's revenues.

This naiveté about the bottom-line value of service among producers of hard goods may be glaringly obvious in the desktop computer world, but it is hardly unique to that world. Automobile manufacturers, machine tool builders, and any number of consumer-product makers have suffered the same malady in the past. The attitude plainly has been, "This would be a great business if it weren't for all the damned customers wanting things fixed." Such an attitude almost always proves to be a costly error in judgment, but it's becoming a more deadly mistake every day. Service, it increasingly turns out, can play a significant role in the economic well-being of an organization that produces hard goods. When *your* food processor is distinguishable from the competition's food processor by only a bit of detailing and a small increment on the price tag, your customer service and service reputation become a critical discriminator. The GE commercial that promises, "We don't desert you after we deliver it" plucks a heartstring in a million frustrated consumers. You can count on GE.

An unusually incisive set of studies of consumer complaint behavior was carried out for the U.S. Office of Consumer Affairs in the 1970s and 1980s, and was expanded upon in the late 1990s by the company formerly known as TARP (Technical Assistance Research Programs Inc.), now rebooted as e-Satisfy.com of Arlington, Virginia. These studies spoke volumes about the bottom-line benefits of delivering first-class service. According to their findings, manufacturing organizations that don't just "handle" or process dissatisfied customers but go out of their way to encourage complaints and quickly remedy them reap significant rewards.[7]

Among e-Satisfy's key findings:

- The average business never hears from 96 percent of its unhappy customers. For every complaint received, the average company has 24 other customers with problems, 6 of which are serious problems.
- Complainers are more likely than noncomplainers to do business again with the company that upset them, even if the problem isn't satisfactorily resolved.
- Of customers who register a complaint, between 54 and 70 percent will do business again with the organization if their complaint is resolved. That figure goes up to a staggering 95 percent if the customer feels that the complaint was resolved quickly.
- The average customer who has experienced a problem with an organization tells nine or ten other people about it. Thirteen percent of people who have a problem with an organization relate the incident to more than 20 people.
- Customers who have complained to an organization and had their complaints satisfactorily resolved tell a median of five to eight people about the treatment they received, depending on the industry.
- Customers who have a bad experience trying to resolve a problem will tell 8 to 16 other people about their negative experience.[8]

If automobile industry studies are correct that a brand-loyal customer represents a lifetime average revenue of at least $140,000 to the company, then the image of a manufacturer or dealer in a bitter dispute with a customer over an $80 repair bill or a $40 replacement part is plainly ludicrous. Similar logic holds for almost every business sector. In banking, the average loyal customer represents $156 per year in profit.[9] Appliance manufacturers figure brand loyalty is worth $2800 profit per customer over a 20-year period. Your local supermarket is counting on you for $4400 this year and $22,000 for the 5 years you live in the same neighborhood. Clearly, it makes far more sense to spend your dollars on retaining these loyal customers than on the more costly and exacting exercise of trying to find replacements.

As e-Satisfy founder John Goodman put it in an address to the Nippon Cultural Broadcasting Company in Tokyo:

> The fundamental conclusion [of our studies] is that a customer is worth more than merely the value of the purchase a complaint concerns. A

customer's worth includes the long-term value of both the revenue and profit stream from all his purchases. This becomes particularly important if the customer could potentially purchase a range of different products from the same company.[10]

The Japanese, by the way—world leaders in product quality—were slow to see service as important *and* problematic. Decades of concentration on manufacturing defect-free products and exporting finished goods left customer service basically unattended to. The tendency in Japan was, as it had been in the United States, to equate service only with servitude and face-to-face attention rather than with customer-centered management.

The pattern of consumer behavior e-Satisfy uncovered and others have since verified is as true for industrial sales as for retail sales. There really is no mystery, then, as to why a heads-up company like Procter & Gamble prints an 800 number on all of its 300-plus products. Each year, P & G, the nation's largest producer of consumer products (Ivory soap, Folger's coffee, Crest toothpaste, Pamper's disposable diapers, Tide detergent), answers more than 1 million phone calls, e-mails, faxes, and letters from customers. One-third of these contacts deal with complaints of all kinds, including those about products, advertisements, and even the plots of TV soap operas sponsored by the company. If only half of those complaints are about a product with a 30-cent profit margin and a minimum of 85 percent are handled to the customer's satisfaction, the benefit to the company in the year, according to a formula developed by e-Satisfy, could exceed half a million dollars. Such a sum represents a return on investment (ROI) of almost 20 percent.

The "fix it" dimension of service is most surely an important economic force in its own right.

VALUE-ADDED SERVICE

The third service dimension shaping the way we do business is the most intangible of all. "Value-added" service has the feel of simple civility or caring when delivered in a face-to-face context, but it is more than that. When it shows itself in such an ingenious and successful product as the American Express Platinum Card or the FedEx Same Day parcel delivery service, it looks far more like perceptive marketing.

Value-added service is more easily understood in experience than in definition; you know it when you see it. Because a cabin attendant pushing the drink wagon on the New York to London flight is out of loose change, she gives you back three one-dollar bills from a five for a $2.50 drink. In response to an offhand comment you made, a calling officer from Wachovia Bank, who pitched factoring services to you last week, sends you an article on how to use limited trusts to help put your kids through college. An InFocus LCD projector dealer setting up a seminar on how to use the projectors in sales presentations stays to help one of your salespeople rehearse for a next-day presentation. All these people are practicing the fine art of value-added service.

Each variation on the same theme is an example from, and an integral part of, the service revolution. The common thread is customer-focused service. None of these examples represents a new definition of what service means. It is rather the value and power they have in the marketplace that is new.

John Naisbitt's "high-tech/high-touch" concept has a lot to do with the development of this need. As new technology is introduced into our society, there is a counterbalancing human response. For example, Naisbitt points out, "The high technology of heart transplants and brain scanners led to a new interest in the family doctor and neighborhood clinics." In that same vein we have noticed that the advent of automated tellers in banking gave rise to a countermand by many for access to a personal banker. The more retail e-commerce Web sites there are, the more consumers desire live, human contact with the company as a value-added option. The more we are faced with high tech, the more we want high touch. At the same time, the fewer contacts we have with the *people* of an organization, the more important the *quality* of each contact becomes. All contacts with an organization are a critical part of our perceptions and judgments about that organization. The impressions of the *people contacts*, however, are often the firmest and most lasting.

Russell Ackoff sees another dimension to the demand for value-added service: a shifting focus from concern for one's standard of living toward a concern for the quality of life. If some aspects of this phenomenon represent a shift away from materialism and the "I-can-have-it-all" credo, as some claim, other factors that fall under the quality-of-life umbrella certainly signal that with a secure standard of material life, the accessories become more important. A young person's need for a car gives way to a desire for the right kind of automobile. Access to discretionary funds sufficient to support frequent air travel gives way to a desire for first-class seating and the best possible amenities. The total experience of obtaining a product or service becomes integrated into a real and palpable quality of the product or service itself. Managing the total customer experience, from parking lot, to purchase, to successful use, is the order of the day.

The trend toward consumerism, the changing competitive climate, and the current roller-coaster economy all have forced companies to reexamine their relationships with customers. As a result, customer service has become a strategic tool. It used to be regarded as an expense. Now it is seen as a positive force for increasing sales and for reducing the cost of sales.

The constant quest for improvement in the quality of life is not a new phenomenon, only a new mass phenomenon. In the early industrial era of this country, only the wealthy few played tennis, summered in the mountains, or wintered in the tropics. Today these are mass cultural experiences. Our parents and grandparents were tickled to have a paid week off once a year. The paid vacation was a great labor victory. Plenty of us now consider a 2-week vacation in Hawaii or Europe a birth right. As the mass demand for a product or service increases, the ability to deliver it effectively, efficiently, and dependably is taxed. It must be managed. Thus we find ourselves hip deep in the service management era, the age of *systematically* designed, developed, and delivered services.

SERVICE AS A MANAGED ENDEAVOR

Historically, the terms *service* and *management* haven't coexisted comfortably. Service delivery was something most self-respecting business school graduates shunned, with the exception perhaps of rising young bank officers. The concept of management seemed to encourage an orderly image antithetical to service in the traditional reactive "help me" sense.

Ronald Kent Shelp, former vice president of American International Group (a New York-based multinational insurance company) and chairman of the federal advisory committee on service industries, attributes those perceptions to a confusion of *personal services*—such as those provided by housekeepers, barbers, and plumbers—with the concept of *service as the provision of intangible products in general*. Consequently, service has been misperceived as always involving a one-to-one relationship between provider and receiver, as labor-intensive, and as having productivity characteristics not readily increased by capital and technology.

Characterizing service in today's economy as servitude is like calling Ronald Fromm, CEO of the Brown Shoe Company (the $1.6 billion retail chain that started out as Buster Brown) a shoe clerk. Today two-thirds of the U.S. gross national product results from service production; and at the same time, personal service in the traditional sense accounts for less than 1 percent of all service jobs. Here is how Shelp sees it:

> While personal-service jobs were declining, industrialization was calling forth a whole range of new services. Some of these were the result of newfound affluence, as more and more people could afford more and better health care, education, amusement, and recreation. Other services were needed to increase the productivity of production, wholesale trade, information processing, financial services, communications. These services and others like them (engineering, consulting, retailing, and insurance) became highly productive when modern technology supplied them with computers, satellite and other rapid communications, and systems analysis.
>
> Thus service jobs moved away from the low end of the economic spectrum toward the other extreme. Much of the service-oriented job growth in advanced nations has taken place in professional, managerial, administrative, and problem-solving categories. Increasingly, education became the name-of-the-game in service jobs.[11]

This change in the nature of what a service is now places many different kinds of activities under the economic umbrella of "service and service-related industries." Shelp sorts these into the following five types and suggests that each developed in response to a set of stages and parallel economic conditions through which Western society has passed and through which many developing countries are now passing[12]:

- **Unskilled personal services.** Housekeeping services for females, military conscription for males, and street vending for both sexes are the primary type of service activity in traditional societies. Historically, these kinds of jobs have provided opportunities for the essentially unskilled. Though unskilled labor exists today, it is on a very different scale. People plying the trades of housekeeping, street sweeping, janitoring, and the like do exist, but it is more likely than not that the services they provide are through a corporation like ServiceMaster International or Sodexho and not on a freelance basis. It is also most likely that these organizations call on technology and mass-production techniques to assist in the delivery of the service rather than on simple brute labor. But automated or not, it is a good bet that the effort is more effectively managed now than it used to be.

• **Skilled personal services.** As productivity increases in agricultural societies and production exceeds subsistence levels, industrialization and trade begin to develop. Opportunities open for the kinds of services provided by skilled artisans, shopkeepers, wholesale and retail merchants, repair and maintenance people, and clerks. The need arises for complex government and government services to support both industry and the burgeoning urban population. This is the first stage of what we describe above as service in the traditional sense. Yes, these services are also very much with us today, but as is the case for unskilled services, they are now organized and managed. Retail e-commerce is very much an enclave for skilled personal services. The small company in Marblemount, Washington, that markets specialty wood chips for barbecue and smoker enthusiasts over the Internet reaches a national audience, just as the cheesemaker in Pienza, Italy, reaches a transnational audience for his farm-made pecorino, Parmigiano reggiano, and taleggio cheeses.

• **Industrial services.** As an industry becomes competitive, the need for marketplace support services arises. Industrial services are really organized groups of highly skilled specialists. Their services are, by and large, those that cannot be provided by individual contractors. They are the services offered by legal and accounting firms, banks and insurance firms, real estate brokers, and trading companies. We traditionally called such services "the professions" and did not consider them amenable to innovation and productivity improvement. But all that is changing. The marketing and management of "professional services" are becoming hot topics. The creation of accounting, health, and legal franchise operations has, in effect, industrialized the industrial services.

• **Mass consumer services.** As the wealth of a population increases so, too, does discretionary purchasing power. This gives rise to a consumer service industry able to enjoy economies of scale while accommodating a growing consumer demand for discretionary services. The demand for travel has promoted growth in airlines, hotels, and auto rental companies. The demand for dining (in the United States, an average of nearly two meals a day is now consumed outside the home) both fancy and fast has led to a highly variegated restaurant industry. And the demand for entertainment has created a broad base of services from movies to video/DVDs to computer games and professional sports. A significant increase in the health and wellness industries can be attributed to the growth of discretionary income as well.

- **High-technology business services.** The introduction of microchips, lasers, satellites, bioengineering, and the like creates opportunities for large advances in both the invention of new services and the streamlining of existing ones. The automation of goods production, data processing, and hydroponics are creations of the special services of the knowledge worker, which fosters a demand for new, highly technical, narrowly focused services. The creation of industrial robots threatens production line jobs; at the same time, a need for skilled robotic technicians arises. Of course, it is not a one-for-one swap. Not every job lost to automation is replaced by a skill or technology servicing job. All the same, every job that can be done by a robot will at some point be replaced.

Another kind of business service specialist created by the new technology is the knowledge consultant. Management consultants, university researchers, Web page designers, and software developers are examples of such service providers. The tasks performed by each of these specialists are highly organized, integrated, and managed. This is service in its most vital and modern sense.

From this perspective it is obvious that as a society increases in sophistication and wealth, the demand for services outweighs the demand for commodities. As discretionary time and money make their presence felt in the marketplace, the ways in which one can satisfy basic needs are most likely to increase, not the basic needs themselves. Thus the railroad has seen first the automobile and then the airplane rival it as a method of fulfilling travel needs. This means that competition for the funds of travelers and shippers has increased both within and across industries. And *increased competition*, as Shelp notes, leads to an *increased demand* for services that create efficiencies which are the basis of effective competition. At every stage of the evolution of service, we see an increase in competition among service providers as well as an increased need to effectively and efficiently deliver such services. Increased also is the awareness that a service is managed differently from a commodity.

The idea that service is a unique product that has to be understood and managed differently from a manufactured commodity isn't exactly cutting-edge news. As far back as 1984, *Business Week* heralded "service as a marketing edge" and chronicled the upgrading of service from an onerous corporate chore to an important organizational strategy. Although the article focused primarily on the value-added dimension of service and not on service as a product per se, the message of the headline has echoed through the economy ever since.

That same year, Louis V. Gerstner, Jr., the then newly-named president of American Express, called service his "most strategic marketing weapon." The 1984 tab for the communications lines, computers, data banks, salaries, and training that went into AmEx's service centers ran to $150 million, and that service-first focus has remained a critical factor in the organization's success. AmEx, along with companies like Dell, FedEx, USAA insurance, and Whirlpool, continue to see service as an advantageous marketing tool. Such companies are learning that aggressive service programs effectively allow them to discover the demographics and needs of their marketplace and niche, unearth problems with new products or service performance, determine the life expectancies of products, and gain insight into the ability of consumers to make their own repairs.

At Procter & Gamble, the customer-service unit working the end of the toll-free number not only acts as a problem solver and value-added service to consumers but is also an effective data trap for information that can lead to other service improvements. During the 1960s, for example, P & G noticed that the average household's weekly laundry increased from 6.4 to 7.6 loads. At the same time the average wash temperature dropped 15 degrees. Closer investigation revealed that the cause of this was a multitude of new fabrics, especially synthetics, that required closer sorting and control of the weekly wash. The upshot for P & G was the creation of the All-Temperature Cheer laundry detergent, a product especially developed to solve another of consumers' ever-evolving needs.

Over the years P & G's call centers gathered information that has led the company to develop many value-added services. On the basis of such hot-line data, the company now includes special cooking instructions for Duncan Hines brownies that are prepared at high altitudes. It has added instructions for turning the average white cake into a wedding cake and developed guidelines for defrosting Downy liquid fabric softener, which sometimes freezes in snow-belt states. G. Gibson Carey, a P & G advertising executive, has an explanation for the company's "knock-yourself-out-for-the-customer" approach to service that tells us something about both P & G and value-added service in general: "There is a whole lot of enlightened self-interest involved."

Managers in mature industries such as machine tools, chemicals, consumer durables, and electronics as well as purveyors of formerly regulated services such as banking, communications, utilities, and air transportation are facing challenges that require them to take a new look at the service dimensions of their products. As we write this, airlines, for example, are taking a terrible beating from customers on everything from flight schedules and delays to onboard treatment from cabin personnel. The inability to respond effectively to the complaints and criticism is costing the industry untold hours of labor in response to customer complaints and governmental inquiries—as well as years of damage to customer esteem. Traditional goods purveyors are finding that the classic market differentiation strategies of price, quality, and special features are not enough to ensure either customer satisfaction or repeat business.

Theodore Levitt likens the relationship between today's buyer and seller to a marriage. He observes that if the act of selling someone something was once a simple, "time-discrete, bare human interaction." It is most certainly not that today. Today's buyer, whether a purchaser of industrial or consumer products, expects significantly more from the seller than a "take-the-money-and-run" attitude. Levitt's exposition reflects a logic and perceptiveness that easily foreshadows today's customer relationship management (CRM) trend by 15 years.

> Buyers of automated machinery (for example) do not, like buyers at a flea market, walk home with their purchases and take their chances. They expect installation services, application aids, parts, post-purchase repair and maintenance, retrofitted enhancements, and vendor R & D to keep the products effective and up to date for as long as possible and to help the company stay competitive.
>
> Thanks to increasing interdependence, more and more of the world's economic work gets done through long term relationships between sellers and buyers. It is not a matter of just getting and then

holding onto your customers. It is more a matter of giving the buyers what they want. Buyers want vendors who keep promises, [and] who'll keep supplying and standing behind what they promised. The era of the one-night stand is gone. Marriage [between buyer and seller] is both necessary and more convenient. Products are too complicated, repeat negotiations too much of a hassle and too costly. Under these conditions, success in marketing is transformed into the inescapability of a relationship.[13]

Service, in the context discussed by Levitt, is an ongoing relationship between buyer and seller that focuses on keeping the buyer happy with the seller after the sale. This is a relationship undertaken not for vague public image purposes, but for vital economic ones. The buyer-seller relationship is not a simple contract of trust between two individuals but a promise of continuing contact between two economic entities for mutual benefit. In Levitt's words:

> During the era we are entering the emphasis will be on systems contracts, and buyer-seller relationships will be characterized by continuous contact and evolving relationships to effect the systems. The "sale" will be not just a system but a system over time. The value at stake will be the advantages of that total system over time.[14]

Levitt's point is made in simpler terms in a story we heard told by Bill Gove, a motivational speaker. Gove told of a likely fictional businessman named Harry, the owner of a small general-appliance store in Phoenix, Arizona:

> Harry is accustomed to being price-shopped by young couples looking for their first new refrigerator or washer-dryer or air conditioner. When a young couple comes into the store, pen and paper in hand, asking detailed questions about prices, features, and model numbers, Harry is pretty sure that their next move will be to trot off to a nearby discount appliance dealer to compare tags. When, after spending half an hour with such a couple and patiently answering all their questions, Harry suggests an order, he usually gets a firm, "We want to look around some other places."
>
> His rebuttal is to nod, smile, move up close, and deliver this little speech: "I understand that you are looking for the best deal you can find. I appreciate that because I do the same thing myself. And I know you'll probably head down to Discount Dan's and compare prices. I know I would. But after you've done that, I want you to think of one thing. When you buy from Discount Dan's, you get an appliance. A good one. I know because he sells the same appliances we do. But when

you buy the same appliance here, you get one thing you can't get at Dan's: You get me. I come with the deal. I stand behind what I sell. I want you to be happy with what you buy. I've been here 30 years. I learned the business from my Dad, and I hope to be able to give the business over to my daughter and son-in-law in a few years. So you know one thing for sure: When you buy an appliance from me, you get me with the deal, and that means I do everything I can to be sure you never regret doing business with me. That's a guarantee." With that, Harry wishes the couple well and gives them a quart of ice cream in appreciation for their interest.

Now [Gove asks his audience,] how far away do you think that young couple is going to get, with Harry's speech ringing in their ears and a quart of vanilla ice cream on their hands, in Phoenix, in August, when it's 125 degrees in the shade?

Yes, it's a salesman's story, where the salesman gets cute and gets the order. But the point is exactly the same as Levitt's and the core message of customer relationship management. Today the buyer-seller relationship is more than a fleeting, face-to-face encounter. The product purchased isn't simply an item with a set, intrinsic value the buyer is invited to take or leave. It is rather a *bundling* of the product, the seller, the organization the seller represents, the service reputation of the selling organization, the service personnel that will handle postsale questions, the buyer, the organization the buyer represents, and both organizations' images in the marketplace.

Service is a key differentiation in such a marketplace, especially when the choice is among products and services distinguishable along no other dimension that is meaningful to the customer. Let's assume that you tell us that your laptop computer is better than the competitor's laptop because yours has a 1 Ghz microprocessor. If we don't know a microprocessor from a food processor and you don't do anything to help us see why that just might be important, then we are left not having the faintest idea why we should buy from you instead of the competitor. Or worse yet, if you tell us that your laptop has a 1 Ghz processor and that *everyone's* laptop has a 1 Ghz processor, you merely convince us that there is no valuable difference between your product and the competitor's. Let's assume you tell us that should anything go wrong—heaven forbid—with your computer, a technician will be on the spot in less than 2 hours to remedy the problem. By way of contrast, if something happens to the competitor's computer, you as the customer will be forced to put it in a box and mail it back to the factory. If you then add that their factory closed last week, you will have told us quite a lot about your computer that differentiates it from the competitor's.

Service is not a competitive edge; it is *the* competitive edge. People do not just buy things and services; they also buy expectations. One expectation is that the item they buy will produce the benefits the seller promised. Another is that if it doesn't, the seller will make good on the promise. When a company picks Ricoh over Minolta as a photocopy machine supplier, many considerations go into the decision. One is the dependability of the "fix it" service reputation that accompanies the Ricoh name. If the technician providing the "fix it" service maintains the machine in line with the buyer's expectations and does so in a way that gives an impression of competence and friendliness, the relationship is solidified along two additional dimensions. Should the technician prove to be either incompetent or offensive to the buyer's employees in the fulfillment of his or her duties, the relationship may be short-lived despite the fact that the initial conditions of the decision have not changed.

Let's consider why express package senders use FedEx or United Parcel Service (UPS) when the U.S. Postal Service (USPS) is so much less expensive, and supplies a similar service—the movement of letters and packages from point A to point B across the face of the earth. To answer this question, we have to go back to the young couple at Harry's appliance store in Phoenix. If they can afford the purchase, they will return to Harry's to buy their air conditioner. When you buy from Harry, you buy from the best. And if anything goes wrong, you can rely on good old Harry. In the same way, when you buy from FedEx or UPS, you don't just send a package. You get FedEx's and UPS's renowned reliability with the deal, a value of considerable weight in any purchase decision. If the buyer buys and the package doesn't arrive, there is no second guessing: "Hey, what more could we do? We went with FedEx." FedEx doesn't just deliver the product; it puts its prestige behind the "absolutely, positively anytime" guarantee just as loudly and as often as it can. And we get the message.

While many business schools teach an approach to management and management science more appropriately described as industrial management, this situation is changing today. The stunning success of corporations like Disney, FedEx, ServiceMaster Industries, Midwest Airlines, and AOL—all companies whose products are almost purely services—has caused academics, entrepreneurs, and eager business school graduates to look at service industries with a new respect. Those organizations, which are among the fastest growing and most profitable in the world, could never have achieved the results they have achieved without highly competent, sophisticated management. Managers in such companies, as well as in financial services organizations like American Express, Citicorp, Charles Schwab & Co., Fidelity, and Dun & Bradstreet, and retailers like Wal-Mart, Kohl's, Nordstrom, Southland, Lucky Stores, and Target Corp., are proving that service is both big business and a challenge to the most seasoned of management minds.

THE SERVICE MANAGEMENT CHALLENGE

Economics and sociology have conspired to change the competitive landscape. Carl Sandburg's "Stormy, husky, brawling, City of Big Shoulders," Chicago, which was America's "hog butcher for the world, tool maker, stacker of wheat, player with railroads" is but a romantic memory today. Service is now the business of business in America, and increasingly in all developed economies.

The capacity to serve customers effectively and efficiently is an issue every organization must face. No one can evade this challenge: Manufacturers and traditional service providers, e-commerce operators, profit-making and nonprofit organizations, private-sector and public enterprises must all face the task of responding effectively and efficiently to customers and consumers who expect quality and service as part of every purchase. Some organizations are well aware of this need and have responded to it. For others, the need to be customer-focused and service-preoccupied continually comes as a rude surprise. But it cannot be ignored; it is not a momentary fad that will suddenly go away. It is the standard customers and consumers have come to measure organizational performance by for the past 15 years. The marketplace has opted to do business with those who serve, and over the long term it has declined involvement with those who merely supply.

Organizations concerned with honing a competitive edge in this new century must continue to develop two new capacities. The first is the ability to think strategically about service and to build a strong service orientation around and into their organizational visions. The second capacity, which is perhaps more difficult to develop, is the ability to effectively and efficiently manage the design, development, and delivery of experiences. In our view the ability to manage the production and delivery of a service differs from the ability to manage the production and delivery of a commodity. It requires a familiarity with the idea of something intangible having economic value and a deftness in conceptualizing *intangible* outcomes. It requires a tolerance for ambiguity, an ease in dealing with lack of direct control over every key process, and a finely tuned appreciation for the notion that the organization is equally dependent on soft (people-related) skills and hard (production-related) skills. Last but not least, it requires a tolerance for—perhaps even an enjoyment of—sudden and sometimes dramatic change. The only constant in service is change.

Not all individuals and organizations are up to this challenge, and there are plenty of head-in-the-sand managers who deny its importance. Many cross their fingers and proclaim, "That service fad's all over. Isn't it?" Yet others take to it like ducks to water. In between are those individuals and organizations who can, and eventually will, master the art and science of managed service delivery. It is our hope that what follows—our account of how others have met and mastered the challenge, and the principles we have extracted from their success—will make this mastery easier.

C H A P T E R

THE EVOLVING ART OF SERVICE MANAGEMENT

"We have 50,000 moments of truth out there every day."

—Jan Carlzon

SERVICE AMERICA I: THE BEGINNING

ASIDE FROM OUR OWN YEARS of work with service-centric organizations, two major influences led to the first edition of this book. Those were *In Search of Excellence*—the book—and Scandinavian Airline System (SAS)—the airline. The 1982 best-seller that made Tom Peters and Robert Waterman icons in the business world was based on McKinsey and Company research designed to pinpoint the attributes of "excellent, innovative" companies.

The McKinsey study was done at a time when all things good seemed to be happening someplace other than the United

States. Peters, Waterman, and their McKinsey colleagues came to the conclusion that eight factors characterized successful American companies and, if focused on, could be successfully adopted by any organization. Those factors were:

- A bias for action—the "just do it" factor.
- Close to the customer—the customer-centric, customer service element.
- Autonomy and entrepreneurship—risk taking and creativity.
- Productivity through people—empowering people to take action.
- Hands-on, value-driven—management by personal presence and vision.
- Sticking to the knitting—doing what you do best and doing it better all the time.
- Simple form, lean staff —uncluttered organizational structure.
- Simultaneous loose-tight properties—push responsibility and accountability to the line level.

We were heartened to see these characteristics lauded—characteristics we saw in abundance in the best managed service-centric companies. The authors' assertion that "far too many managers have lost sight of the basics, in our opinion; quick action, service to customers, practical innovation, and the fact that you can't get any of these without virtually everyone's commitment," really rang bells for us. It was this tight focus and personal leadership energy, combined with certain fundamental techniques, that we viewed as core to the emerging art of service management.[1]

The second major influence was the Scandinavian Airline System (SAS).

THE SAS STORY

Although Peters and Waterman had pointed to an abundance of organizations practicing what *In Search of Excellence* preached, it wasn't until we came upon Scandinavian Airline System (SAS) and its charismatic president, Jan Carlzon, that we were able to see the potential of a broad-based, service management focus.

Although SAS is no longer the high-visibility darling of the European airline business, the service management lessons we learned from it are still critical and valid for any of today's organizations seeking a service advantage.

In 1981, SAS was struggling with a severe downturn in business. A worldwide recession had cut deeply into the airline industry, and companies were bleeding money from every pore. During that year SAS posted an $8 million loss, a disastrous amount for the time.

The multinational board of directors of SAS was understandably concerned. The company president resigned, and the board promoted a rising young star, Jan Carlzon, to that position. An energetic, flamboyant man of 39, Carlzon had been managing one of the company's subsidiaries. He had a strong marketing orientation, which became his strongest asset in the turnaround struggle that was to come.

While most other airline companies were whittling back their expenditures with an energy bordering on desperation, Carlzon decided to go in exactly the opposite direction. He embarked on a death-or-glory expedition to turn SAS around, and his strategy revolutionized the company's attitude toward its customers. What followed was a spectacularly successful turnaround maneuver in which SAS went from the $8 million loss to a *gross profit of $71 million* on sales of $2 billion in a little over a year. SAS was voted airline of the year and laid claim to being the most punctual airline in Europe. The company strove for, and largely achieved, recognition as "the businessman's airline."

Naturally, more than a few people were curious to know just how Carlzon had managed to pull off that stunning maneuver. Carlzon did not attribute his success to such conventional tactics as advertising, rate cutting, and cost reduction, or even to his own leadership. He credited most of the improvement to the effects of a deceptively simple philosophy: *Make sure you're selling what the customer wants to buy.*

Of course, Carlzon did not attempt to reorient the organization singlehandedly. He drew upon the intellectual resources of several key people, two in particular. One was Richard Normann,[2] a Swedish management consultant, who was one of the first to suggest the metaphor of the "moments of truth," which became such a key part of the SAS service management philosophy. Normann contributed a number of key ideas during the early formation of the strategy. Another key architect was Jan Lapidoth, an exceptionally bright young executive on Carlzon's team. He served the role of conceptual shepherd, among others, in helping to formulate and articulate the overall theory of service management as it unfolded.

Carlzon believed that if he could teach SAS managers and employees to keep tabs on the kind of treatment the customer received at each of the critical stages of their dealings with the company, it would be possible to create a conscious impression of service quality for customers to carry away. By turning on the whole organization to the mission of service, Carlzon believed he could get the customer to recognize a significant difference between SAS and all other available transportation options. This would generate repeat business and goodwill that would result in a significant level of word-of-mouth business.

In Carlzon's view SAS had become an "introverted" organization which had lost its conceptual focus on the customers' needs as critically important to success. Front-line people tended to be preoccupied with their individual tasks. Managers were concerned about routine managerial duties, and administrative people preoccupied themselves with forms and reports. In such an organization, the prevailing attitude seemed to be, "If only the customers would go away and leave me alone, I could get my job done."

"Who," Carlzon asked, "is paying attention to the real needs of the customer?" He believed it was time to shift attention from the production process—the delivery system —to the market. "We must pay attention to what our customers are telling us with their behavior," he asserted. "The world is changing. Business is changing. And the needs of our customers are changing. Unless we become truly a customer-driven organization, we won't grow. We must formulate a viable concept for service." Carlzon contended that a constant preoccupation with the needs of the market would force attitudinal and structural changes throughout the SAS organization. This would mean a shift in the deployment of the delivery system so that it would be more in harmony with the customers' priorities. If that happened, Carlzon reasoned, the company's image would improve. As its image improved, its sales performance would improve, and the process would become self-reinforcing.

With the help of his key executives, Carlzon began to preach and teach the gospel of customer orientation energetically and persistently through the organization. Rather than cascading the message through the chain of command, Carlzon and his direct reports hand-delivered the new direction to the entire organization—personally, through a worldwide series of "all hands" meetings. The not-too-subtle message: This is important, and I'm here to make that point. Carlzon reasoned that such a new concept would require a radical redirection of the thoughts and energies of everyone in the organization, and would take a long time to catch on. He was convinced that the game would be over if he had to wait for the new gospel to "take" at its own speed, so he decided to take his message directly to the working people. He formed an implementation team consisting of consultants and hand-picked executives at the highest levels. He and his team embarked on an aggressive campaign to change the thinking of some 20,000 people.

Carlzon followed through with an intensive campaign to demonstrate a philosophy he referred to simply as "visible management." He and his executives personally shouldered the task of evangelism. All executives were expected to devote a substantial portion of their time to spreading the word. In particular, they were instructed to use their personal clout as well as formal authority to direct the attention of managers at all levels to Carlzon's new gospel. The most energetic and hard working of all the executive evangelists was probably Carlzon himself, who personally visited front-line people throughout the SAS system. In Sweden, Denmark, and Norway he preached his gospel of service, creativity, and finding a better way. He staged theatrical presentations and used highly provocative methods to put his points across.

Carlzon and his team followed through with convincing evidence of their own commitment: they put *all 20,000 SAS managers and employees* through a 2-day training program designed to help them grow as individuals and to fill them with a new and dynamic sense of the organization's purpose. There was also an intensive internal program of employee communications, aimed at constantly reinforcing the message.

The effort to indoctrinate managers was just as intensive as that directed at the front-line workers. In fact, before launching the massive training phase, Carlzon had hosted a 3-week gathering of the top 120 executives and 30 senior union representatives. Reviewing together the new approach, these executives and union representatives thought deeply about the philosophical and strategic issues involved in implementing it and discussed what would be required in various divisions of the company. Training for middle managers proceeded more or less in tandem with the front-line training. In many cases supervisors joined with performance-level people at large-group training sessions of 100 or more people.

Certainly, SAS did much more than merely train its employees. Out of the management meetings came a number of projects and programs for putting the SAS organization back into shape. These ventures great-ly helped create the public impression that something new was going on at SAS, even though Carlzon and his leaders attributed their ultimate suc-cess to a new way of thinking rather than to any specific business moves.

To strengthen the follow-through process, Carlzon set up an internal consulting group. He asked its members to work directly with managers all over the organization in an effort to find ways of overcoming obsta-cles and moving various projects ahead. Here, too, Carlzon personally took an aggressive lead in finding new ways to serve the customer. One of his brainchildren became known in-house as the BMA project, the businessman's airline. He decided that, rather than try to be all things to all people when, in fact, the company hadn't been much of anything to anybody, SAS should have a "best-known-for" feature. Its best bet was to become famous for catering to the needs of day-time business travel-ers moving regularly about Scandinavia and the Continent. This led to the creation of the highly successful Euroclass service. Even for rela-tively short flights, a business traveler could partake of a somewhat higher level of comfort and service than tourist class, and could sit in a separate curtained-off section of the cabin. In addition, business-class fares were stabilized and guaranteed. This normalization of fare struc-tures and service levels did a great deal for SAS's image in the minds of business travelers.

A second important change masterminded by Jan Carlzon was the "on-time departure" program. Seeking to score more points with busi-ness travelers, he decided to make SAS the most punctual airline in Europe. "Can we come up with a new plan in 6 months?" he asked his operating executives. "If so, how much do you think it will cost?" This challenge—which continues to vex airlines today—captured the imagi-nation of a number of key players, and it became a rallying idea.

The original estimate for the venture was that it would be a 6-month undertaking at a cost of about 8 million Swedish kronor, the equivalent of about $1 million. The project won so much support at so many levels that it took only 3 months for SAS to become the most punctual European air-line at a cost of only about 1 million kronor, which amounts to about $125,000.

Again, Carlzon's unwavering focus lent impetus to the effort. According to legend, Jan Lapidoth had a monitor installed in Carlzon's office showing the status of every flight in the SAS system. It was not unusual for an SAS pilot to land at his destination city and have someone hand him this message: "Mr. Carlzon would like you to call him." When the pilot called, Carlzon would say, "I just wondered why your plane took off late." Perhaps there was an acceptable reason beyond normal human control, but the effect was to keep the pressure on at all levels. Few SAS pilots looked forward to the prospect of explaining to the president of the company why they didn't get their customers in the air at the advertised time.

The Teachings of Chairman Jan.   Although Carlzon's high-profile turnaround strategy attracted considerable attention, few people understood immediately the real implications of what SAS had achieved under his guidance. What was not readily visible to the casual observer was that Carlzon had evolved, largely in an intuitive way, a unique approach to the company's management. This approach was characterized by an almost obsessive commitment to *managing the customer's experience* at all points in the cycle of service. Given this obsessive commitment as a starting point, the task became one of getting as many heads as possible turned in the right direction and helping them to see Carlzon's new vision of the company's place in the market.

Many management theorists in Sweden, and indeed all over Scandinavia, began to study this new management philosophy. Because of his flamboyant personality, Carlzon was seldom at a loss for words, and many of his one-liners reflected his own attitudes about the conduct of a service business. A Carlzon remark that caught the attention of many SAS people was, "There is nothing more rotten and useless than an airplane seat that leaves the ground empty." A more telling line that found its way into the lexicon of business executives all over Europe was, "We have 50,000 moments of truth out there every day." A *moment of truth*, by Carlzon's definition, is an episode in which a customer comes into contact with some aspect of the company, however remote, and thereby has an opportunity to form an impression.

The problem and the challenge, from this point of view, are that most moments of truth take place far beyond the immediate line of sight of management. Since managers cannot be there to influence the quality of so many moments of truth, they must learn to manage them indirectly, that is, by creating a customer-oriented organization, a customer-friendly system, and a work environment that reinforces the idea of putting the customer first.

An SAS Postscript.   In 1993, Jan Carlzon left SAS after 12 memorable years at the helm, yet his legacies remain—namely, a reputation for on-time flights, high-quality personal service, and fiscal caution. Prior to Carlzon, SAS had experienced regular periods of financial panic, usually accompanying the purchase of new equipment, which resulted in pendulum swings in attention to service and performance. Those days may be gone. Today SAS is building creative alliances throughout Europe and has pioneered regular service to former Warsaw pact countries as well as established Trans-European routes to the Far East.

SAS participated actively in the creation and development of Star Alliance, the world's largest airline alliance involving the partnership of SAS, Air Canada, Air New Zealand, Ansett Australia, British Midland, Lufthansa, Mexicana, Thai Airways International, United Airlines, Varig, All Nippon Airways, and a number of other airlines.

In the Scandinavian market, SAS offers an unbeatable nonstop network between capitals and economic centers in conjunction with its five regional partners. In addition, SAS is able, via Star Alliance, its regional partners, and Spanair and airBaltic (all three of which are partly owned by SAS) to offer more than 8000 departures daily to over 815 destinations in 130 countries. During 1998, SAS flew 21.7 million passengers to 101 destinations in 31 countries, 9 of which were outside Europe—6 in Asia and 3 in the United States. In 1998, the SAS group's operating revenue was SEK 40.9 billion and its income after financial items was MSEK 2829.

For a complete account of Carlzon's dramatic turnaround of SAS, track down Carlzon's own book, *Moments of Truth.*[3]

SERVICE MANAGEMENT: THE EMERGENCE OF A THEORY

As management experts of various stripes all over Scandinavia analyzed Carlzon's approach, they recognized the elements of a new paradigm. Word spread of this new approach to management of service organizations, and a new management theory was born: *service management*, a concept championed most visibly by Christian Grönroos, professor of international and industrial marketing at the Swedish School of Economics and Business Administration in Finland. Soon representatives of other service companies began beating a path to the door of SAS. "How did you do it?" they wanted to know. "What are the essential ingredients of service management, and how can they be implemented in our industry?" Books, articles, masters' theses, doctoral dissertations, and seminars began to appear. Service management was the new wave in Scandinavia. The term *service management* and the concept associated with it became so popular that Scandinavian management institutions and technikons began to offer concentrations in service management within the framework of business degrees. Service management became the most popular topic for top-management and middle-management seminars.

THE DIFFUSION OF SERVICE MANAGEMENT

It was late 1983 when we discovered SAS and service management and decided to extend the concept to the United States. Karl Albrecht was visiting colleagues in Copenhagen who related the SAS story and pointed out that the service management theory was rapidly gaining converts in Scandinavia. Albrecht had not previously heard of the concept, which to the best of his knowledge had not yet made an impact in America. Subsequent discussions with other management thinkers in Britain and continental Europe confirmed that they, too, knew nothing of it.

After Albrecht returned to the United States, we both set about exploring the possibility of applying service management concepts in our individual consulting work. As a result of many discussions and a great deal of further investigation, including visits to SAS, we concluded that service management was a story worth telling. And that led us to the decision to write the first edition of this book.

The fact that service management, as we first knew it, originated in Scandinavia is an interesting, but not critical, attribute of the story. What is important is that people in service businesses desperately needed—and still need—a model for thinking about service: The times called for it. Service management remains timely and is as germane to business now as it was in 1985. Of course, Scandinavian companies have no particular monopoly on service excellence or creative service management. A number of American firms have earned reputations for outstanding service and customer orientation as well. The Marriott hotel chain has invested enormously in building a service image, as has its sister company, Ritz-Carlton Hotels, the only company to twice win the Malcolm Baldridge National Quality Award.[4] The McDonald's fast-food chain embodies the high level of service expressed in its motto, "Quality, Service,

Cleanliness, and Value," making it the de facto standard of comparison for the whole fast-food industry. Walt Disney, the man who virtually invented the theme park, founded an organization that has made customer service seem so perfectly natural that experts have scrutinized Disney's employee and management training as if it might have magic incantations hidden somewhere within it. At least three books have been written on the Disney management magic.[5] The list of made-in-America exemplars of outstanding service management companies has grown impressively. Indeed, the list today is long enough that Ron Zemke has written a book celebrating 100 exemplary companies.[6]

All the service-focused firms we have investigated have at least one thing in common: a clear *model for service*. In each case, their leaders have arrived at a clear and communicable definition of excellence. This is the sine qua non—the essential first step. In each case, the individual organization has embarked on its own particular way of actualizing its service strategy, but all of them have clear strategies from which to work and have followed a path as intensive as that which Carlzon mapped out for SAS.

Service management makes inordinate sense in virtually any industry that deals in an intangible product or in any industry where products are relatively indistinguishable from one another. Examples that arise immediately are airlines, banks and savings and loan associations (S&Ls), hotels, restaurants, resorts, theme parks, hospitals, public utilities, financial management organizations, educational institutions, and government service agencies. Even organizations producing highly tangible products can benefit from certain elements of the service management point of view.

We believe service management is a *transformational concept*. It is a philosophy, a thought process, a set of values and attitudes, and sooner or later a set of methods. To transform an entire organization into a customer-oriented entity takes time, resources, planning, imagination, and an enormous commitment by management. The process is conceptually simple, but given the monolithic resistance to change displayed by most organizations, it is almost always a very tall order.

BETWEEN THEN AND NOW

Obviously, much has changed between 1985 and the writing of this second edition. New, exemplary companies have come to the fore, and old icons have faded. New customer expectations, new research, and new ideas have emerged. Following is a preview of the more prominent trends and ground breaking research that have and continue to invigorate the evolving art of service management. Three themes characterize these advances.

The dollars and sense of service.   In the first edition, we asserted that a service-centric focus had positive payoff in profits. It was as much an intuitive claim as one supported by empirical data. However, Robert Buzzell and Bradley Gale demonstrate in their book *The PIMS Principle*[7] that delivering quality customer service pays—and pays well. (See Figure 2-1.)

Their database demonstrates that businesses that deliver superior service quality (the top quintile of companies researched) earn an average return on sales (ROS) of 12 percent. Businesses that deliver inferior service quality (the bottom quintile) had an average ROS of 1 percent to 3 percent, lose market share, and have a lower price index.

Furthermore, a study by Harvard University's W. Earl Sasser and Bain & Company's Frederick Reichheld found that the longer you are able to retain a customer, the more profitable the relationship becomes. Working with data from a variety of service industries, they showed that profits climb steeply when a company reduces its customer defection

	High-Value Firms	Low-Value Firms
Return on Sales	12%	1–3%
Market Share	6%	12%
Price Index	110%	98%

Strategic Planning Institute

FIGURE 2-1   The economics of focusing on customer value

rate. Based on an analysis of more than 100 companies in two dozen industries, the researchers found that firms could improve profits by 25 percent to 85 percent by reducing customer defections by just 5 percent. Loyal customers generate more revenue for more years, and costs decline because the expense of acquiring new customers to replace defecting customers is less.[8]

What brings these customers back and back again? All those things that surround the core product or service—how well they are served and communicated with, how their problems are handled, and whether their experience is managed in a way that encourages a long-term relationship. (See Figure 2-2.)

Another study, conducted by Arthur D. Little, Inc., for a purchasing agent's group, analyzed the cost of service failures. The researchers asked purchasing agents, "What action do you take when a vendor lets you down?" (See Figure 2-3.) Of the purchasing agents questioned, 28 percent declared that they would immediately decrease the volume of business they do with that vendor. A whopping 18 percent said they would immediately sever all ties with that vendor.

Bracketing service expectations. In the aftermath of *In Search of Excellence*, businesses of every size and description claimed to make listening to customers a top priority. The listening had four purposes:

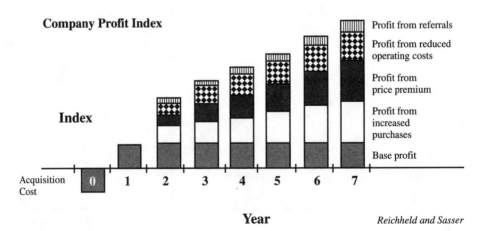

Reichheld and Sasser

FIGURE 2-2   **Length of a customer relationship**

Question: What do you do when a vendor lets you down?

Answer: • Decrease Volume   28%

              • Call on Carpet   26%

              • Sever All Ties   18%

Source: Arthur D. Little

FIGURE 2-3   Purchasing managers' action resulting from poor performance by vendor

- The first was to understand the customer's moments of truth and map the "cycle of customer experience" from the customer's point of view.

- Second, to keep tabs on the market's, and even individuals', changing wants, needs, and expectations. "Riding the customer's learning curve" is an IBM expression for this kind of listening, which is one of the mainstays of the market research business. As any restaurateur can tell you, it is critical to survival to know when the market is tiring of sushi and has begun to develop a lust for wild game or New Zealand home-style cooking. Customer relationship management (CRM), one-to-one marketing, data-mining, and micro-segmentation all owe their origin and impetus to the customer listening admonition.

- Third, to unearth and capture the unexpected ideas that customers and those who work with them offer that can lead to innovations in processes and products.

- Fourth, to involve the customer in the business. For example, when Embassy Suites managers buttonhole guests in the hotel to ask them about their stay, or someone at Longo Toyota in El Monte, California, calls up a new car buyer 6 months after a purchase to find out how the new wheels are working, they are enfolding the customer in the details of the business and heightening the customers' perception of their responsiveness.

In the 1990s books and courses dedicated to the "voice of the customer" became commonplace, and for the first time market research firms started taking service research as seriously as product research. Much of the focus of these educational programs and customer listening efforts derived from the work of the Center of Retailing Studies, College Station, Texas, and three dedicated researchers, Leonard L. Berry, A. "Parsu" Parasuraman, and Valarie Zeithaml. Their work, often referred to as the SERVQUAL research, found that 80 percent of the variance around approval ratings by customers could be attributed to five performance factors: reliability, assurance, tangibles, empathy, and responsiveness.[9]

- **Reliability.** The ability to provide what was promised, dependably and accurately.
- **Assurance.** The knowledge and courtesy of employees, and their ability to convey trust and confidence.
- **Tangibles.** The physical facilities and equipment, and the appearance of personnel.
- **Empathy.** The degree of caring and individual attention provided to customers.
- **Responsiveness.** The willingness to help customers and provide prompt service.

Quite a few corporations, nonprofit organizations, and even government agencies have used these five powerful factors as a foundation for their customer listening efforts. Other researchers have added to, and some have even taken issue with, these five core factors. But it is the research of Berry et al. that demonstrated that customer service expectations could be bracketed and studied categorically to help shape service strategies.

Managing the customer experience.   It's a fundamental concept that what happens in the parking lot and at the ticket window and at coat check are just as much a part of customer satisfaction and retention as is the performance on the concert hall stage. The concept of *experience management,* or taking care of those satisfaction shaping tangentials, is a critical part of contemporary service management and a growing focus for many organizations. For example, Southwest Airlines has a "director of customers" executive-level position. Move.com, Dell Computer Corp., and Charles Schwab and Co. all have directors of customer experience. The OnStar subsidiary of General Motors has a director of customer experience and enterprise customer management. Every Ritz-Carlton Hotel has an on-site director of quality management. The common mission: To ensure that everything surrounding the delivery of the core product or service—be it a room for a night or a 30-year financial investment—is as effortless and positively memorable as possible for the customer. If you've ever spent a fun day at a government agency trying to obtain a building permit or renew a commercial license, you know firsthand the antithesis of a positively managed experience. You'd never confuse it with a day at Walt Disney World or Universal Studios's Island of Adventure Theme Park.

Several books have been penned on the developing art/science of customer experience engineering and experience management, the most notable being *The Experience Economy: Work Is Theatre and Every Business a Stage*, by B. Joseph Pine and James H. Gilmore.[10]

Theme restaurants such as Chuck E. Cheese, Planet Hollywood, Hard Rock Café, and Rainforest Café are attempts to enfold the dining experience in a larger, more memorable, entertainment-oriented event. The Geek Squad, a Minneapolis-based computer office systems repair company, sets itself apart from the crowd by calling its service technicians "special agents" and dressing them in a way that makes them memorable, and emblematic of the company name. The techs wear white shirts and thin black ties, pocket protectors, and *Blues Brothers*–style dark glasses. Then carry badges and drive black and white VW bugs bearing the Geek Squad logo. But that distinct identity only works because Geek Squad service techs are carefully selected, continually trained, and likely to be as affable as they are technically proficient. The company's goal is to make a visit from the "computer guy" amusing and memorable as well as cost-effective.

Above all else, experience management is an acknowledgment of the importance of both seeing service in the broad context envisioned by the SAS pioneers and of managing customers' many moments of truth for a positive outcome.

SERVICE MANAGEMENT TOMORROW

In Chapter 12, we speculate about tomorrow's service world. How those predictions will turn out only time will tell. But one thing we are unequivocal about is that service management is continually developing and self-renewing. And this decade will see as much change—if not more—than the last.

3

THE SERVICE TRIANGLE

"To make a great dream come true, you must first have a great dream."

—*Hans Selye, M.D.,*
Developer of the Stress Concept

A NEW LANGUAGE FOR THINKING ABOUT QUALITY

AS WE ENTER THE TWENTY-FIRST CENTURY and we find that the human values of service and concern for people begin to prevail ever more strongly in business organizations, we need a vocabulary for a customer-centered, service-oriented way of doing things. Throughout this book we will be introducing a new vocabulary for the service management model—reasonable-sounding terms like customer value, value package, value model, value proposition, moments of truth, cycles of service, and service strategy. At the risk of seeming to insult the intelligence of those who read this, we'll start here by offering some definitions of some very basic terms. These particular definitions, however, signal a critical shift in our point of view about service, quality, and value.

Service
Work done by one person or group for the benefit of another.

From the standpoint of business, to work is to serve, no matter what the work involves. All work is service work. From the most microscopic level of one person's job, all the way to the macro level of the organization's delivery of value to its customers, service is what's going on. It no longer makes any sense to talk about "product" businesses or "service" businesses. The act of assembling a computer, or sewing a garment, or molding a chocolate bar is a way of serving others, just as much as the act of selling it to a customer or advising the customer how to use it. We need to get comfortable with the broadest possible connotation of the term service, to mean serving. It encompasses all of the work going on, everywhere, in business organizations. Next, we need a working definition of *quality* that goes beyond the usual "product-quality" terminology.

Quality
A measure of the extent to which a thing or experience meets a need, solves a problem, or adds value for someone.

Note the key word *measure* in this definition. Quality is a measure. It's not merely a feeling, a belief, a value, or a commitment. Nor is it an ethereal concept or a philosophy, although those are all parts of the way we must think about quality. Quality is a measure that reflects an ultimate judgment of value received. It necessarily includes both subjective and objective criteria. Nothing in this definition of quality confines it to any physical characteristics. The definition incorporates both tangible and intangible measures. Therefore, it is pointless to talk about quality and service as if they were two separate concepts. Service—total service — is everything we do in any organization, regardless of how tangible or intangible the outcomes are. So quality, by this definition, is the measure of value for total service.

Once we have defined service and quality, we can establish a definition for service management.

Service Management
A total organizational approach that makes the quality of service, as perceived by the customer, the number one driving force for the operation of the business.

Enough said—for now.

50,000 MOMENTS OF TRUTH

The metaphor of the *moment of truth* is a powerful idea for helping people in service businesses shift their points of view and think about the customers' experience. SAS president Jan Carlzon's one-liner, "We have 50,000 moments of truth out there every day," really hits home. In the spirit of keeping our definitions current, we offer this working definition of a moment of truth.

> *Moment of Truth*
> *Any episode in which the customer comes into contact*
> *with some aspect of your organization and gets an*
> *impression of the quality of its service.*

Case in point: A friend of ours was traveling alone in Japan on an extended vacation. At the train station he inquired, in his limited Japanese, which train he should take to go from Sapporo, where he was at the moment, to Tokyo. The man behind the counter wrote out all the information for him—times, train numbers, and track numbers. He even took the trouble to write it in both English and Japanese, in case our friend should lose his way and later need to show the note to some other Japanese person.

This was a moment of truth for our friend, one of many that happened that day. At that instant, he formed an impression of the train company, or at least of that one employee. He came away thinking, "What a nice experience. There's somebody who really takes the trouble to help people."

But the story doesn't end there. Pleased and gratified, our friend thanked the fellow at the information booth and walked down the corridor to the waiting area to wait for the departure time. A half-hour later, the information man come bustling through the waiting hall, searching the crowd. When he spied our friend, the man gestured for the return of the paper. He wrote something on it, gave it back, bowed quickly, and hurried back to his post. He had figured out a faster, more convenient sequence of trains, and came to correct the note!

Managing service well means getting it right. It means managing so that *all* the customer's moments of truth are positive. As consultant Donald Porter, former director of customer service quality assurance for British Airways, points out:

If you're a service person, and you get it wrong at your point in the customer's chain of experience, you are very likely erasing from the customer's mind all the memories of the good treatment he or she may have had up until you. But if you get it right, you have a chance to undo all the wrongs that may have happened before the customer got to you. You really are the moment of truth.

Each of us has a storehouse of moments of truth from our life experiences. We remember moments when it seemed that people or systems or both went out of their way to be difficult or unhelpful. And we recall shining moments when we felt appreciated, cared for, cared about, and genuinely valued.

From your point of view as the customer or as the receiver of the service, you experience the moment of truth as *intensely personal*. It's *you* standing there, not some faceless nonentity. You're thinking, "I am a person. I have an important stake in this situation, and I want to be treated properly." Most of us will forgive "system" malfunctions, even to a preposterous degree, so long as someone acknowledges our personal needs and makes an effort to set things right. The concept of managing the moments of truth is the very essence of service management.

GETTING HIGH GRADES ON THE CUSTOMER'S REPORT CARD

Every time a service organization performs for a customer, that customer assesses the quality of the service, either consciously or unconsciously. The sum of this customer's repeated assessments and the collective assessments of all customers establish in their minds an image of the organization's service quality.

Think of customers as carrying around a kind of report card in their heads, which is the basis of a grading system that leads them to decide whether to partake of the service again or to go elsewhere. As we shall see later, it is crucially important to find out as much as possible about this all-important but invisible report card. You can consistently score high grades on your customers' report cards only if you know what evaluation factors they are applying when they think about your organization and what you offer.

THE PRINCIPLE OF REGRESSION TO MEDIOCRITY

Why *don't* the trains run on time? Why is getting prompt service from an Internet services provider an impossible dream? Why do so many people consider "postal service" a contradiction in terms? Why did C. Northcote Parkinson, the originator of the famed Parkinson's law, claim, "If there's anything a public servant hates to do, it's something for the public"? Why is there so little perception on the part of T. C. Mits (The Celebrated Man-In-The-Street) of quality in service? Why is outstanding service so scarce when so many companies presumably thrive or perish on the satisfaction of their customers? The answers to these questions may suggest solutions to service quality problems.

Consultant Donald Porter tells a story about British Airways (BA) that supplies part of the answer. When BA wanted to upgrade its service image in the mid-1980s from that of a mediocre public utility to a customer-pleasing paragon, its first step was to find out how customers rated it in comparison with other airlines. BA conducted a market research study among airline passengers—both its own customers and travelers who had never flown BA—to try to find out. The study, Porter says, aimed at answering two questions: First, what factors did passengers really consider most important in their flying experiences? Second, how did British Airways stack up against the other airlines on those factors?

"After some extensive interviewing and data analysis, we discovered some very interesting facts," says Porter. "Of all the statements made by the air travelers we interviewed, four factors stood out from all the rest as being critically important. What took us aback was the fact that two of the four factors came more or less as a surprise to us—we hadn't really considered them consciously before."

According to Porter, the travelers BA interviewed seemed to be responding to four key factors as they moved through the chain of experience:

1. Care and concern on the part of public contact people.
2. Problem-solving capability of front-line personnel.
3. Spontaneity or flexibility in the application of policies and procedures.
4. Recovery, or the ability of front-line people to make things right when they have somehow gone wrong.

"'Care and concern' are fairly clear, I think," says Porter. "We weren't surprised to find this a key factor, although I think we'd have to confess that we couldn't claim a very high level of performance on it. Likewise, 'problem solving' was pretty clear. Customers thought our people should be skilled at working out the intricacies of problematical travel schedules, handling complicated logistics, and in general getting them on their way."

Porter continues, "The importance customers placed on spontaneity was a bit puzzling. Customers were saying, 'We want to know that your front-line people are authorized to think. When a problem comes up that doesn't fit the procedure book, can the service person use some discretion, find a way to jockey the system on the customer's behalf? Or does he or she simply shrug shoulders and brush the customer off?'"

But it was the fourth factor that truly surprised BA. "It had never really occurred to us in any concrete way," Porter says. " 'Recovery' was the term we coined to describe a very frequently repeated concern: If something goes wrong, as it often does, will anybody make a special effort to set it right? Will someone go out of his or her way to make amends to the customer? Does anybody make an effort to offset the negative effects of a screw-up? Does anyone even *know* how to deliver a simple apology?"

The market research led BA to some genuine realizations, Porter recalls: "We were struck by a rather chilling thought: If two of these four primary evaluation factors were things we had never consciously considered, what were the chances that our people in the service areas were paying attention to them? For the first time, we were really beginning to understand and come to terms with the real motivational factors that are embedded in our customer's nervous system."

At the same time, BA's study discovered some other interesting statistics. When the interviewers asked air travelers to rate British Airways in comparison with other airlines they had personally dealt with, about 20 percent of the respondents said they considered BA superior to other airlines they had used. About 15 percent considered British Airways inferior to others. The remainder expressed no strong opinions one way or the other. The initial reaction of company management to the figures was guardedly optimistic: "It seems like 85 percent of the people interviewed think we're OK." But as the implications of the data began to soak in, the attitude changed to one of concern. If 65 percent of respondents evaluated the company as just so-so in quality of service, they didn't see much difference between BA and other airlines. Because the company had failed to manage—indeed, had only recently become aware of—half the factors that air travelers said they considered key to a positive service experience, it had ample room for improvement.

From these cases, as well as our everyday experiences, we believe we can draw a conclusion, one that can be stated as a core *principle* of service management:

> ***When the moments of truth go unmanaged,***
> ***the quality of service regresses to mediocrity.***

"Just a moment," you might say. "Isn't it a little harsh to define an average level of service—neither poor nor outstanding—as 'mediocre'? Isn't just 'okay' okay?" Maybe. But to survive and prosper in a service industry requires differentiation. An effective service company must show evidence that it really does have something special to offer. Especially in industries where customers don't readily see important differences in the choices of service offered them, "average" really equates to "mediocre," at least in the mind of the customer.

CUSTOMER EXPECTATIONS ARE THE ONLY ONES THAT COUNT

The ante keeps going up because *customer expectations are progressive.* If you're accustomed to telephone service in the United States, not only will you be horrified at the average level of service in New Delhi but you will also tend to disapprove of shortfalls in U.S. service as well, even though it is better than most others in the world. As customers, we tend to expect at least the level of service we've become used to.

We also compare service providers across industries. We use FedEx for speedy delivery; we call on L. L. Bean for unfailingly gracious assistance; we visit Walt Disney World for a delightful family vacation. We have come to expect responsiveness, reliability, and careful attention to our needs from these organizations. When your competition is any service provider your customers come in contact with, it behooves you to understand what customers want from you and where they learned those expectations.[1]

In Search of Excellence authors Thomas Peters and Robert Waterman emphasized the importance of "staying close to the customer." By this they mean learning in intimate detail what really counts to your customer; what he or she likes and doesn't like; what your customer will and won't buy. Although the book was published in 1982, their advice is still apt. Some of the most dismal failures of organizations can be traced to losing their contact with the customer at the time when the customer's needs and motivations were changing.

SEEING SERVICE AS A PRODUCT

In addition to learning to understand the customer better, it's helpful to understand the concept of service itself better. Though a service is obviously different from a physical product, it is still a product. A service product—any incident of doing for others for a fee—can be distinguished from a commodity by one or more, usually several, of the following characteristics:

1. A service is produced at the instant of delivery; it can't be created in advance or held in readiness.
2. A service cannot be centrally produced, inspected, stockpiled, or warehoused. It is usually delivered wherever the customer is, by people who are beyond the immediate influence of management.
3. The "product" cannot be demonstrated, nor can a sample be sent for customer approval in advance of the service. The provider can show various examples, but the customer's own haircut, for example, does not yet exist and cannot be shown.
4. The person receiving the service receives nothing tangible; the value of the service depends on his or her personal experience.
5. The experience cannot be sold or passed on to a third party.
6. If improperly performed, a service cannot be "recalled." If it cannot be repeated, then reparations or apologies are the only means of recourse for customer satisfaction.
7. Quality assurance must happen before and during, rather than after, production, as would be the case in a manufacturing situation.

8. Delivery of the service usually requires human interaction to some degree; buyer and seller come into contact in some relatively personal way to create the service.

9. The receiver's expectations of the service are integral to his or her satisfaction with the outcome. Quality of service is largely a subjective matter.

10. The more people and processes the customer must encounter during the delivery of the service, the less likely it is that he or she will be satisfied with the experience.

Note please we are not suggesting that every service can or should possess all of these characteristics or that these are the only characteristics a service can have. Just the same, these characteristics paint a picture of a special kind of transaction between buyer and seller: the transaction we call service. The better your organization understands this transaction, the higher the grades it can earn on the customer's report card.

THE CYCLE OF SERVICE

One of the obvious places to start in thinking about the quality of an organization's service is to inventory the *points of perception*, that is, the moments of truth in that particular business. Think about your own business. What are the various points of contact at which the customer passes judgment on your enterprise? How many opportunities do you have to score points?

Think of your organization as dealing with the customer in a *cycle of service*, a repeatable sequence of events in which various people try to meet the customer's needs and expectations at each point. The cycle of service is a map of customer contact points in the organization. In a sense, it is your organization seen through your customer's eyes. The cycle begins at the first point of contact between the customer and your organization. It may be the instant at which the customer sees your advertisement, gets a call from one of your salespeople, or initiates a telephone or Web site inquiry. Or it may be any other event that begins the process of doing business. It ends—only temporarily—when the customer considers the service complete, and it begins anew when he or she decides to come back for more. (See Figure 3-1.)

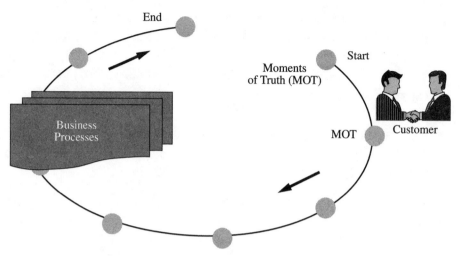

FIGURE 3-1   Cycle of service

To help you discover the critical moments of truth in your dealings with your customers, draw a diagram of a particular service cycle. Divide the cycle into the smallest possible increments or episodes that make any sense conceptually. Then identify the various moments of truth that occur in the cycle. Try to associate particular moments of truth with specific stages or steps of the customer's experience.

Since the service cycle is a tool to enable you to see service from the customer's point of view (rather than the organization's point of view), many "back room" events critical to your customer's overall satisfaction—things you do that the customer doesn't come in contact with— will not appear in a cycle of service diagram. It will be unique for your particular business. It may vary from one customer to another, from one version of your service to another, and from one situation to another. At any moment, each customer who is doing business with you is somewhere in his or her uniquely personal cycle. Of course, customers don't often consciously think of their experiences in terms of a cycle; they generally pay attention to whatever needs they have at the moment. But it pays for you to think about this cycle in specific stages because it is the very substance of your business. (Cycle of Service and Moment of Truth diagramming are dealt with in greater detail in Chapter 6.)

At a seminar with a group of health-care administrators, we asked the participants to diagram the cycle of service that ensues when a patient is wheeled off for, and eventually brought back from, a series of medical tests. After several minutes of discussion about the place of various orderlies, nurses, doctors, and lab technicians in the cycle, the task was completed. As they sat admiring their handiwork, one of the administrators said aloud, "My God! There's nobody in charge of this mess!" His insight proved to be a valuable one that we have since seen revalidated in other professional service organizations. His explanation went something like this:

> Our hospital is organized and managed by professional specialty—by functions like nursing, housekeeping, security, pharmacy, and so on. As a result, no single person or group is really accountable for the overall success and quality of the patient's experience. The orderlies are accountable for a part of the experience, the nurses for another, the lab technicians for another, and so on. There are a lot of people accountable for a part of a service cycle, but no one has personal accountability for an entire cycle of service.

When you are organized along functional lines rather than product or service cycle lines, no one is responsible for ensuring that each cycle of service goes off effectively. In the abstract, of course, the chief executive of the organization is accountable, and everyone who comes in contact with the customer—in this example, the patient—is responsible. But the simple fact remains that when no one is specifically accountable for the cycle of service, from beginning to end, the customer's experience with the organization is unmanaged. When the customer's experience—the moments of truth—goes unmanaged, mediocrity is assured.

FOUR FEATURES OF OUTSTANDING SERVICE ORGANIZATIONS

Four important characteristics differentiate outstanding service organizations from mediocre ones:

1. **Understanding the customer's moments of truth.** As discussed, a moment of truth is any point at which a customer comes into contact with any aspect of the organization and has a chance to form an impression of the quality of service provided. Customer approval is won or lost one moment of truth at a time.

2. **A well-conceived strategy for service.** A service strategy is the unifying idea that outstanding service organizations have discovered, invented, or evolved about what they do. It differentiates a company

from its competitors. This service concept, or service strategy, directs the attention of the people in the organization toward the real priorities of the customer. When this guiding concept is communicated to everyone in the organization, it finds its way into everything they do. It becomes a rallying cry, a kind of gospel, and the nucleus of the message to be transmitted to the customer.

3. **Customer-friendly systems.** The delivery systems are a means of distributing the organization's resources, based on service strategy and the package of services it intends to deliver. Successful service delivery systems become habitual and thus invisible. A delivery system that backs up the service people is truly designed for the convenience of the customer rather than for the convenience of the organization. The physical facilities, policies, procedures, methods, and communication processes all say to the customer, "This apparatus is here to meet your needs."

4. **Customer-oriented front-line people.** Without well-trained, well-managed, motivated people, good service cannot be delivered. Front-line people must be empowered to work on behalf of the customer through knowledge, policy, and culture. Managers of organizations that provide outstanding service help the people who deliver service keep their attention fastened on the needs of the customer. The effective front-line person is able to maintain an "otherworldly" focus of attention by tuning in to the customer's current situation, frame of mind, and need. This leads to a level of responsiveness, attentiveness, and willingness to help that marks the service as superior in the customer's mind and makes him or her want to tell others about it and come back for more.

These four factors are relatively simple in concept and easy to understand. Yet making them a reality is almost always a monumental task, especially in large organizations. Most of the remainder of this book deals with how to implement service management by actively managing these critical factors.

THE SERVICE TRIANGLE

The obvious questions at this point are: How should you approach the management of service? What can the leaders of a service enterprise do that will directly or indirectly maximize the quality of the customer's experience at the many moments of truth? Is there a framework for thinking about the task of managing for outstanding service? Just as the cycle-of-service model clarifies the customer's perspective, a company-oriented model helps managers think about what they need to do.

We think of the company and the customer as intimately engaged in a triangular sort of relationship, like the one shown in Figure 3-2. This *service triangle* represents the elements of service strategy, systems, and people that revolve around the customer in a creative interplay. The triangle model is radically different from the standard organization chart that is used to depict business operations. It represents a process rather than a structural approach, and it puts the customer squarely at the center of the business.

If you really are going to practice what you preach about developing a customer-driven organization, it makes sense to start with the customer as the focus for defining the business. Of course, the company exists to serve the customer. That is almost intrinsically understood. But beyond this, the

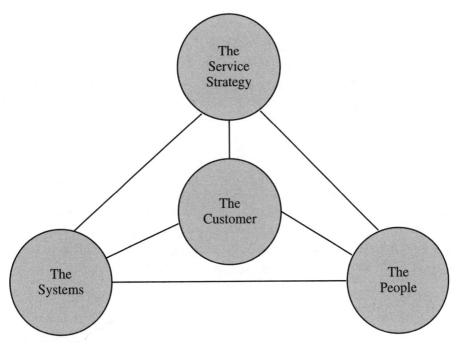

FIGURE 3-2   Service triangle
© *1984–2001 Karl Albrecht. Used with permission.*

organization exists to serve the needs of the people who are serving the customer. In other words, it is deliberately organized and managed for service.

Once you know what motivates the customer, you need to develop a workable model for service. That means establishing a basic business strategy that will differentiate your company from its competitors in your customer's experience. Formulating a nontrivial philosophy of service that can really make a difference is a challenge. Advertising slogans won't do it. The service strategy must mean something concrete and valuable to the customer, something he or she is willing to pay for.

Consider Target stores' service strategy. Boiled down to its essentials, the discount department store chain promises its customers: No-hassle merchandise returns; fast, accurate check out; assistance when you need it; and the merchandise you want when you want it. Target also guarantees clean restrooms, quick check and credit approval, shopper-friendly store layout, and friendly employees.[2]

Clearly, Target is armed with an understanding of its customer's buying motivations and has created a concept for service that positions the company advantageously in the marketplace. The service triangle can help you explore the interplay among the strategy, the people of your organization, and the systems that are available to them to get the job done. Each of the lines in the diagram represents an important dimension of impact. For example, the line connecting the customer and the service strategy represents the critical importance of building the service strategy around the core needs and motivations of the customer. This is no place for guesswork. Find out, if you don't really know, what goes on in your customer's mind when he or she thinks about your kind of service.

Conversely, the line that flows from the service strategy to the customer represents the process of communicating your strategy to your market. It is not nearly enough to give good service or that your service is unique in some way; the customer has to know it in order for it to do you any good.

The line connecting the customer and the people of the organization is the crucial point of contact, the interplay that accounts for most of the moments of truth. This interplay presents the greatest opportunity for gain or loss, and for creative effort. Also consider the line on the service triangle that connects the customer to the systems that presumably help deliver the service. These systems can include abstract procedural systems as well as physical elements. Many negative moments of truth in the business world arise because of system peculiarities and malfunctions.

When the customer's interests are treated as an afterthought in the design of service delivery systems, the situation is virtually programmed for mediocrity and dissatisfaction. Restaurant tables that are awkward or uncomfortable, cramped airline seats that jam people in like cattle, forms that don't make sense and are impossible to fill out, illogical or confusing building layouts, phone trees that dead-end, and administrative processes that burden the customer with tasks that could be handled by service employees all make it difficult for the people to provide service effectively.

The three outer lines of the service triangle tell stories as well. Consider the interplay between the people and the systems. How often have you seen highly motivated people prevented from giving the quality of service they really wanted to give because of nonsensical administrative procedures, illogical task assignments, repressive work rules, or poor physical facilities? In situations like these, a regression to mediocrity is assured. Front-line people are usually much better-prepared than their managers to find ways to improve the systems they use every day. The question is, Do their managers realize that fact, and are they willing to invite the employees to contribute what they know?

The line connecting the service strategy with the systems suggests that the design and deployment of the physical and administrative systems should follow logically from the definition of the service strategy. This seems obvious, but given the resistance to change found in most large organizations, it sometimes seems like a utopian idea. And, finally, there's the line between the service strategy and the people. That line suggests that the people who deliver the service need to have the benefit of a clearly defined philosophy from management. Without some sense of focus, clarity, and priority, it is difficult for them to keep their attention on service quality. Again, moments of truth tend to deteriorate and regress to mediocrity.

We will apply the service triangle in more depth in later chapters. At this point, let's begin thinking about the interplay of the key components of service and getting them to work in harmony. But first we want to urge you to consider a companywide approach to service.

WHY HAVE A CUSTOMER SERVICE DEPARTMENT?

If a company that's in business to provide a service has a department called the "customer service department," what are all the other departments supposed to be doing? Might it be that having a customer service department signals to the other people in the company that the customer is being properly looked after and that they need not concern themselves with the matter? Shouldn't the entire organization be one large customer service department, at least figuratively speaking? Think about some of the service organizations you have dealt with as a customer. How do the people treat you when you have a special need or peculiar problem? Do they take the initiative to help you solve it or at least steer you in the right direction? Or do they simply brush you off and mumble something about contacting customer service? This type of behavior at the moments of truth is all too common, and it quickly establishes a process of regression to mediocrity. The prevailing point of view is, "I have my job to do. It's somebody else's job to take care of this customer's problem."

This point deserves careful consideration. Although it is not always possible for a service employee to drop whatever he or she is doing and work the customer's problem through to completion, the perception of service quality at the moment of truth revolves around the customer's sense of having been helped and appreciated. A skillful employee can do this in many creative ways and in the normal flow of work.

This is the message the "Magic Kingdom" of Disney stresses. Disney is all about vacation time fantasy. The customer or "guest," as every customer is called, is transported into a magical fairy tale, where all things are wonderful and all things are possible. Walt Disney wanted every park employee or "cast member," as they are called, to understand the meaning of this experience for the customers. Disney drilled the message into every single one of them: "You are Disneyland."

Today, the company has determined that a typical guest at one of its theme parks will average 60 "contact opportunities"—points at which they come into contact with a cast member. Disney wants each of those opportunities to be a magic moment for every guest, so every cast member is encouraged to be proactively helpful. Every Disney cast member—whether custodian, engineer, or accountant—who sees a guest puzzling over a map or struggling to take a family photo, steps up to the plate and helps out.[3]

This point of view affirms that everyone in the organization who comes into contact with a customer, even accidentally, is potentially in a service role. The hospital administrator walking down the corridor can smile and say hello to the patient who is coming in or going out. The hotel maintenance person can greet the guest in the elevator and stop to give directions to the meeting rooms. The clerk in the airport gift shop can tell a passenger how to go about finding a lost item or how to page someone. In too many situations, at too many moments of truth, a "non-service" person turns a cold shoulder to a customer who needs help. This is the regression process in action. It doesn't take many small moments of truth, handled in mediocre ways, to create a standard of mediocrity. The challenge to managers is to make sure that this doesn't happen.

One of the most common symptoms of mediocrity in service is when the customer finds it necessary to run through an organizational maze to get his or her needs met. "That's not in this department" is an all too common answer. "You'll have to call Housekeeping (or Patient Records, or Maintenance, or Residential Services, and so forth)." If you are forcing your customer to learn your organization to have a problem solved, you may want to reevaluate your corporate conception of service.

Telephone companies are legendary for their customer runaround processes. When the old "Ma Bell" structure was in place, you could call up the company to have a telephone installed or service changed, and end up dealing with three or more departments. Quest, the twenty-first century version of U.S. West, demonstrates that the more things change the more they stay the same. If you call Quest with a question about your wireless family plan that ties each family member's cell phone to your land-line service, you talk to a customer service representative in one division (after waiting on hold, of course). But if you also have a question about your land-line service, you must call a rep in a different department and wait in a second telephone queue.

Financial institutions often operate like horse-drawn buggies. Many branch banks are so compartmentalized and regimented in an attempt to eliminate all risk that very few people can steer a customer through the maze on their own. Employees commonly know only one microscopic function of their organization and cannot offer customers a bit of help with any other.

These things do not occur out of malice. Service people don't get up in the morning, look in the mirror, and plan to abuse customers. What happens in so many of these situations is that nobody "owns" the responsibility for the solution to the customer's problem, and nobody sees the difference between carrying out job tasks and meeting customer needs. Service people can become so robotized that they greet any customer request with a standard response, even if the response is only marginally effective.

Furthermore, it helps to invite the "nonservice" people in the company to think of themselves as working in service roles. Administrative people, accountants, computer specialists, engineers, contracts people, and staff people of various kinds tend to think of themselves as somehow removed from the din of battle. All too often they look upon service people as the ones who deal with hoi polloi. They are sometimes tempted to think of themselves as "above" the level of service roles. A strong and determined chief executive can disabuse them of this elitist viewpoint and get them to think of service as a highly valued contribution.

BEING THERE: LEADING BY EXAMPLE

Will Rogers, America's cowboy philosopher and humorist, once opined that "people learn more from observation than they do from conversation." Senior managers of large companies and owner/operators of small companies can have a profound effect on the behavior of employees through the example they set. Peters and Waterman called it "management by wandering around." Jan Carlzon called it visible management. We call it "Being There."

Though once a rarity, more and more senior managers are aware of the importance of leading by very visible example:

- Early on, J. W. "Bill" Marriott, Jr., was a practitioner of Being There. His penchant for wandering corridors, hallways, and sub-basements inspecting and worrying after every detail—and for chatting with guests about possible improvement—is legendary in the organization. When a new hotel was being planned for the Walt Disney World complex, Marriott sat in on focus groups and met with meeting planners to find out what they wanted and needed for organizing top-quality corporate meetings. One comment he heard was that the ballroom space wasn't going to be large enough for big meetings. It didn't take long for Marriott to acquire adjacent property to provide the additional space.

- Erie "Chip" Chapman, III, president and CEO of U.S. Health Corporation from 1983 to 1995 and current president and CEO of Baptist Health System in Nashville, Tennessee, makes sure that he and his direct reports never lose touch with the Being There principle. One day each month Chapman and his team leave the power suits in the closet and don the uniforms of patient escorts, laundry workers, or maintenance people. They spend time in X-ray helping out the evening shift technicians, wheeling patients around the hospital, and assisting with intake interviews and folding sheets. They demonstrate through their actions the dignity of attending to the details—and the importance of learning from customers.

- At Stew Leonard's, the celebrated Norwalk, Connecticut, $100 million a year dairy store, practicing 360 degree Being There service is a family affair. Stew Leonard, Jr., and his father before him, wander the store shaking customers' hands and asking for suggestions. Twice a month, customers are invited to focus groups in the store's conference room—run by a member of management—often one of the Leonards.

One Friday afternoon disaster strikes: A computer failure shuts down the cash registers. Most customers wait (munching on free shrimp, courtesy of the management), but one woman leaves, drives 30 minutes to get home, then calls the store and complains to the manager that because of the computer crash, she now has no groceries for her husband's 60th birthday party, which happens to be that night. Within an hour, a car pulls up at her house and a Stew Leonard employee delivers her groceries—along with a birthday cake that says "Happy 60th, George. Sincerely, Stew." Guess what people talked about at that party?

Elitist attitudes and factional interests die hard in most organizations. Sometimes the accounting people act as if they think the organization exists so they can keep books on it. Some engineering people act as if the organization exists to support their intellectual hobbies. Some physicians act as if the hospital exists to cater to their overfed egos. It takes very strong management to get the people in these various camps to see themselves as supporting the people and processes that deliver the quality of experience the customer considers important.

ORGANIZATIONAL SCHIZOPHRENIA: CONFLICTING PRIORITIES

If managing the moments of truth is the essence of service management, then the essential process in managing the moments of truth is building a service-minded culture in the organization. If the moments of truth go unmanaged and service quality regresses to mediocrity, there is usually a concomitant poverty of spirit among the people in the company overall. A "don't-give-a-damn" attitude creeps into the nooks and crannies of the collective psyche. It becomes *de rigueur* to act as if one does not care about his or her job or about performance or achievement or about the satisfaction of the customer. Pride goes out the window, and the organization's collective attention turns inward to the mundane and the trivial. Unless leadership and inspiration are present, mediocrity tends to reinforce itself.

An even worse state of affairs, which exists in many large service organizations, is a sort of schizophrenic double standard. Top managers may talk about customer satisfaction, quality of service, and the like, and yet their day-to-day actions may be reinforcing something quite different—all too often, attention and obedience to themselves. This pattern of asking for A and rewarding B tends to create confusion, loss of motivation, and cynicism among front-line people.

Outstanding service requires focused energy. Slogans will not do it. Posters will not do it. Inspirational memos will not do it. It will happen when the managers of organizations step up to their responsibilities as leaders and articulate a concept of service which people can find believable, feasible, worthwhile, and rewarding. The organizational climate must be ready and the management commitment must be present for service management to take root and thrive.

SERVICE MANAGEMENT: OLD WINE IN NEW BOTTLES?

In briefing thousands of managers in a number of countries on the service management concept, and particularly in the United States, we have frequently had to field the question, "So what's new? This is just the same old 'customer satisfaction' stuff that we've known about for years. Isn't service management just putting old wine in new bottles?"

Maybe so, but let's take a closer look at the bottles. In the United States we have long paid lip service to customer satisfaction. We have been fond of saying, "The customer is always right," "The customer comes first," and all the rest. The last decade has seen a deluge of customer service books, seminars, and good intentions. Organizations wrestling with the issue have tried to get a firm hold on it by relying on approaches such as total quality and benchmarking, not to mention investing in that all-purpose panacea, technology. Still, most managers in most organizations leave the matter of customer satisfaction to the customer service department. They typically assume that someone is taking proper care of the customer, unless the number of complaints begins to get too high. Then, suddenly, it becomes time for corrective action.

We believe the service triangle offers a better alternative. It offers a clear-cut conceptual framework for thinking about the quality of service and how to manage moments of truth. It helps managers understand the design, development, and delivery of high-quality service

The next four chapters expand the key elements that comprise the service triangle—the customer, strategy, systems, and people—and discuss organizations that use these elements to deliver high-quality service. Chapter 4 examines organizations that have learned to focus on their customers and to understand their wants and needs. Chapter 5 describes the process of positioning the organization in the marketplace to find and articulate an effective service strategy. Chapter 6 explains how to design and build service systems with the convenience of the customer and employees in mind. Chapter 7 focuses on the service people on the front line and the crucial role they play in delivering customers' moments of truth.

THE CUSTOMER: KING OR PEASANT?

"To the customer, perception is all there is."

—Tom Peters

"THE CUSTOMER IS KING" is probably the most shopworn of all business slogans. It and dubious catchphrases like "The customer is always right" tout the claim that the company is paying attention to the needs and interests of its customers. However, the real test is not in slogans but in the actual experience of the customer. Too often, the customer gets treated more like a peasant than a king or queen.

The real test for today's organizations isn't in crafting catchy slogans or managing by motto, but in matching the right level and tenor of service to distinct customer "value clusters." As organizations again focus on becoming lean and competitive, the cost of a miscue—of applying limited service resources in the wrong way—becomes increasingly punishing.

This kind of value segmentation, referred to currently as CRM (customer relationship management) requires an intimate and multilayered knowledge of customer needs, wants, and expectations. Crawling inside your customers' minds, and developing more than an educated guess about what moments of truth help win their loyalty and what factors send them to the competition, is crucial to making the service triangle concept work. Only after a company has properly segmented its customers and viewed the world through their discerning eyes, can it figure out where to trade off "low-touch" options and "high-touch" care without jeopardizing customer loyalty or all-important word-of-mouth reputation. Indeed, if you're the kind of manager who just can't sleep well without a slogan guiding the way, "Know Thy Customer" is among the best you could choose.

CUSTOMER PERCEPTIONS: WHAT HAVE YOU DONE FOR ME LATELY?

First, we all know that the customer is not concerned with, and does not care about, the day-to-day problems inside the organization. Managers and employees can often forget this point, especially when they have to work with customers under less than ideal conditions. Scheduling difficulties, computer problems, inventory shortages, and labor disputes just don't register in the customer's mental scheme of things. The customer's only real concern in the situation is with getting his or her own very specific needs met.

In working with many organizations, we often find that managers only have the vaguest notions about what really counts in the minds of customers. Too often there's an abundance of opinion and a paucity of data. But developing a sophisticated, research-based knowledge of what makes customers tick—and then closing the gap between what they expect and what you provide—increasingly is what separates the service savvy from the service wannabes in the new millennium economy.

When we wrote the first edition of this book, there was little research available about the nature of customer expectations, which are the building blocks of all customer transactions. In the intervening years, service-quality researchers have done important new work on how customers form expectations. So much so that it is impossible to stroll through the business section of most bookstores without being overwhelmed by the number of works with the words "customer driven" in their titles.

We've learned that understanding customer demographics and tracking market trends is but one step on the road to customer intimacy.

Equally or perhaps even more important is *psychographic knowledge*, or gathering data on customer expectations, attitudes, preferences, beliefs, feelings, and social habits. The work of Texas A&M's Len Berry and colleagues Valarie Zeithaml and A. Parasuraman (mentioned in Chapter 2) laid the groundwork in the late 1980s.

Professor Berry puts the problem of these complex expectations in perspective:

> Consumer perceptions of service quality result from comparing expectations prior to receiving the service and actual experiences with the service. Quality evaluations derive from the service process as well as the service outcome.

In Berry's analysis, what consumers think they are going to receive, compared with what they perceive is being received, and the process they go through receiving it, determine their level of satisfaction. It is an all-or-nothing, three-factor formula based on the assumption that the level of our satisfaction with the entire process is the critical link to repeat business.

Consequently, service satisfaction is the result of a dynamic, not static, encounter. The consumer evaluates both process and outcome, and values both. Poor product can't be overcome by a good relationship with a customer, at least not for long. Nor will good product overcome poor treatment unless the situation is unique. A physical examination conducted by a smelly, grumpy, rude, and nasty physician is a bad physical, regardless of how technically competent the results are. When you are put off, even offended by the experience, you are not likely to want to repeat it, and you will not recommend it to others.

The mandate is clear: To create a distinctive level of customer service, management must understand, and on occasion shape, the customer's prepurchase expectations, influence the customer's evaluation of postpurchase quality, and ensure that the process of being served is not only painless and easy, but, when possible, enjoyable. We must manage not only what we do for the customer, but the way we do it—the totality of the customer's experience with the organization.

Complicating that task is the reality that service expectations are more variable than product expectations. Two people may hear the same promise: "Yes, ladies and gentlemen, Smedly Weight-Off Clinic guarantees easy, painless weight reduction in 10 days." Yet each walks through Smedly's door with very different expectations of what "easy" and "painless" and "guarantee" mean. Because a service is most frequently provided to or for one individual at a time, being able to respond to that variability is essential. The barber or hairdresser must be able to adjust to the customer's head because the "raw stock," so to speak, is controlled by the customer. "I'm sorry, sir, your head is not round enough for me to work on," won't do if the barber hopes to make a living.

A more extreme example is the physician who must balance a dozen variables to make a diagnosis and play out a dozen scenarios in prescribing a course of treatment. If every appendix was like every other or 95 percent was a tolerable surgery survival rate, medicine would be an easy, inexpensive, highly automated craft. It isn't. It requires discretion, extensive and intensive preparation, and skill.

Every service provider is expected—by the customer, anyway—to respond to the uniqueness of each special situation. Few may be expected or encouraged to respond to those uniquenesses 99.9 percent of the time with 100 percent accuracy, as a physician must, but the expectation is there, just the same.

CUSTOMER VALUE: DEFINING IT, DELIVERING IT, AND MEASURING IT

The following statement is not intended to insult the intelligence of the reader:

> ***If you intend to compete based on delivering outstanding customer value, then you'd better know what it is.***

Normally we wouldn't risk offending the experienced and well-educated people who read our books with simple statements like the one you just read. However, it has been our experience that many executives and managers can't pass the test that it implies. That is, they often believe they understand what the customer is trying to buy, but more often than not they are operating on the basis of their own internal assumptions and not on the basis of verifiable truth.

Customer value, that is, the fundamental benefit premise embedded in the customer's thinking process, is often much more subtle, complex, and layered than many executives and experts imagine. Many service providers fail to grasp the totality of this benefit premise, being imprisoned by the boundaries of their particular piece of it. For example, ask doctors, nurses, and other hospital workers what factors they believe patients consider important in their hospital stay. They may offer tried-and-true homilies such as skilled medical care, friendly and courteous staff, pleasant and comfortable surroundings, good food, and yaddita-yaddita.

Ask the patients, and they'll say things like "How do they treat my family and friends when they call, or try to visit me?" "Do they help me learn about my medical condition and take charge of my own continuing care when I'm out of here?" "Do they respect my right to make decisions about my own care?" And "How well do they coordinate with other care-givers who may be involved in my treatment?"

Patient research clearly discloses another critical value factor, which many medical people utterly fail to grasp or haven't the faintest idea how to deal with: *trust*. Or, more specifically, the absence of it. In general, most people do not trust hospitals, and for a very good reason: People can die there. Everybody has an Uncle Frank, or knows somebody, who went into the hospital and never came out. Hospitals are complex operations, working on a three-shift, round-the-clock basis, with constantly changing people and constantly shifting phases of care for each patient.

Conflicting advice or information from doctors and nurses, mis-placed medical records, medication errors, and more horrifying break-downs cause people to mistrust the hospital as a system. They know things can go wrong. Yet very few hospitals train their people in methods to build and preserve patient trust.

In an early application of service management in the hospital envi-ronment we discovered that individual patients displayed noticeably dif-ferent psychosocial "styles," that is, different configurations of emotion and attitude that affected their acceptance of treatment. Medical practi-tioners, however, tended to have an ingrained tendency to deal with all patients in relatively the same way. Even though the patients were sig-naling very different needs for information, emotional assurance, auton-omy, and participation in their care, they were all getting roughly the same "one size fits all" communication process. By developing a model of four primary patient styles, we were able to train hospital staff to rec-ognize these critical differences and capitalize on them in enhancing the patients' perceptions of value received on an individual basis.

One of the great unrecognized truths of service management is:

> *The longer you've been in a business, the less likely you are to really understand what your customers are trying to buy.*

This gives us a score of two reader insults in one chapter, but again we think we can back up this assertion as well.

A surprising number of firms, including ones that have been serving the same customers for many years, have never actually engaged in an explicit conversation with their customers about the definition of value. They believe they know what customer value is, at least in a general way, but they've never actually tried to confirm their understanding. And they've typically not tried to articulate it in simple, compelling language. "We know what our customers want," the executives confidently assert. "We've been giving it to them for years."

Not only do many service firms not do nearly enough customer value research, but most of the research they do tends to be distorted by their own preconceptions and wishful thinking. Good customer value research requires a healthy combination of objectivity, intellectual innocence, and willingness to hear things we don't want to hear.

Here is a case in point: One of the largest Wall Street brokerage firms commissioned a series of focus groups with their clients. The firm was trying to confirm or relearn the primary factors the clients considered important in their investing relationship with the firm. Using electronic keypad voting, the participants registered their opinions of the relative priority of the value factors they themselves had nominated during the workshop. Before the executives reviewed the results, we asked them to try to guess the value factors the clients had nominated and, having then seen the actual list, to try to guess the priorities customers had assigned to each.

The leading value factor, according to the clients, was one that none of the executives had thought to mention: portfolio performance. They were startled to realize that the clients, even though ultimately responsible for their own investing decisions, considered the overall performance of their portfolios a key element of their perception of the value they received from the firm. "After all," clients reasoned, "I have a professional broker who's supposed to be helping me with my investments. He calls me and tells me what to buy and sell, and when. Why have a broker if he doesn't help me grow my assets?"

In many cases, the executives and managers of a firm have imprisoned their concept of customer value in a kind of verbal cocoon created from their own private language of business. The customer often uses a more familiar and sometimes elegantly simple vocabulary of value. Here is another case in point: A firm that operated a megamall in the suburbs of Sydney, Australia, commissioned an investigation into the perceptions of value held by its clients, who were executives of retailing firms of various sizes. The firm's leaders wanted to get a better understanding of the thinking process by which these retailers decided where to locate their stores, when and under what circumstances to close them, and what they expected of mall managers.

Prior to the meeting with the retail executives, the executives of the center management firm tried to predict the key factors customers would name as important to them. They threw out a host of terms in the jargon of their own industry: accessibility, retail mix, shielding, cost assurance, and the like. When the conversation with the retail executives opened with the innocent question "What do you want from the center where you do business?" one of the executives answered the question very simply. "There's only one thing I want from you," he said. The team waited with bated breath and blank expressions for his reply. Then he said, simply, "Customers."

He went on. "I want customers outside the door of my shop. If you get 'em that far, I'll take it from there." All members of the client team were stunned by the sheer simplicity of his conception of value. Sure, he was willing to discuss assurances that his competitors wouldn't be in the same mall and that the mall would include "magnet" businesses to build traffic. But in the end, it really was as simple as he said it was: He wanted customers outside his door.

This is not to suggest that any particular set of executives of any particular service business is incompetent or incapable of understanding customer value. But we are reporting, simply, that many of them are *ignorant*, in the polite connotation of that term. They are the prisoners of their own expertise, knowledge, and experience. These kinds of customer-listening experiences should remind us constantly of the inevitable perceptual gap between those who serve and those who are served. By getting inside the minds and worldviews of those whose business we seek to earn, we can help them teach us what value is, as they see it.

According to George Bernard Shaw, we should throw out the golden rule because it's off base. Shaw said, "Do not do unto others as you would have them do unto you; their tastes may not be the same." This qualifies as the Platinum Rule:

Do unto others as others want to be done unto.[1]

Earlier, we discussed the importance of having a common vocabulary for thinking and talking about service. In the lexicon of value creation, we believe it is helpful to speak in terms of:

- **The customer value package.** The sum total of everything you deliver, both tangible and intangible, to the customer. This can include physical facilities or environments, physical deliverables, information, interaction with service workers, advice, empathy, sensory experiences, and a wide range of associated elements of value. The customer buys a total experience of value, not just a product or a service. An amusement park will have a very different value package from that of an insurance company; the value package offered by a university will be very different from that of a department store. Each has its unique structure, personality, and rules for engaging the customer. Each has its own criteria for assessing the value delivered. And each has its own possibilities for enriching the customer experience.

- **The value proposition.** The fundamental benefit premise offered to the customer, as the core concept of value underlying the value package; the essence of what he or she receives for the amount paid. Many executives confuse the value package with the value proposition: They try to sell a car rather than a total ownership and driving experience. Many try to sell insurance policies rather than the peace of mind associated with managing risk. When asked to express the mission of the enterprise, many executives can't get beyond the specifics of the value package to discern the value proposition behind it. The value proposition is the invisible truth that defines the appeal of the value package.

- **The customer value model.** A distillation of the value proposition into a relatively small number of measurable dimensions, or specific value factors. Each value factor is an attribute of the customer's total experience which affects his or her perception of value received. Typical value factors might be: the ambiance of a restaurant or a department store; access to inside information on some subject; the caring and considerate management of pain; a continuing relationship with one service provider who remembers the customer's needs; insightful advice from an expert; high-speed response to a request for information; willingness and capacity of a service employee to bend the rules in certain situations. Usually, about six to ten primary value factors are enough to define the core model. These critical criteria then become dimensions for measurement, improvement, and the design of the value package.[2]

It takes a bit of insightful thinking to get at the customer's core value proposition. It's not always obvious, and it's frequently not well articulated. John Gardner, a former U.S. Cabinet secretary and the founder of the activist group Common Cause, spent some time as a university president. "After a while, I figured out what the real [value proposition] was," he recounted. "Sex for the students, football for the alumni, and parking for the faculty. If those worked out all right, I didn't have many problems." There's a bit more to it than that, but he was probably on the right track.

THE CRITICAL DISTINCTION BETWEEN CUSTOMER LOYALTY AND CUSTOMER SATISFACTION

One important branch of the research done since the first edition of this book examines the difference between customer satisfaction and customer loyalty. Robert Peterson, a professor in the business school at the University of Texas at Austin, was intrigued that his research didn't show a stronger correlation between customers' stated satisfaction on survey instruments and their repurchase intention. In cross-industry satisfaction surveys he reviewed, Peterson found that 85 percent of customers claimed to be satisfied with service they received from an organization—rating it an average "three" on a five-point scale—but still showed a strong willingness to migrate to the competition, depending on a variety of factors.

One of Peterson's conclusions was that many organizations overlook the emotional components of service and that only by attempting to measure the extremes of customers' feelings on surveys (asking whether they love or hate your organization, for example) can you obtain a reliable gauge of their loyalty, or lack of it, in the face of competitive threats.[3] The theory holds—and common sense confirms—that customers with strong feelings about your organization, not those who place themselves in "satisfied" or "somewhat satisfied" survey categories, are your most predictable customers.

We refer to this nonlinear relationship between customer satisfaction and customer retention as "hockey stick" loyalty, portrayed by the hockey-stick-shaped curve shown in Figure 4-1. For instance, if your

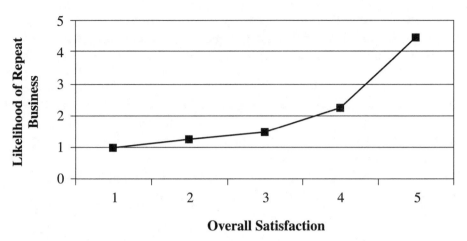

FIGURE 4-1   **Hockey stick loyalty**

organization improves its average ratings on a five-point customer satisfaction survey from one to two (unsatisfactory to poor), from two to
three (poor to satisfactory), or even from three to four (satisfactory to
good), you'll see only negligible or modest corresponding improvements in customer loyalty. But make the leap from four to nearly five on
that scale, from ratings of good to excellent, and you see dramatic spikes
in measures of expressed loyalty. Plot satisfaction against loyalty on a
graph, and your curve will look like a hockey stick. In other words,
someone who rates you a five or excellent, is, on average, two to six
times more loyal than someone who rates you a four. Those who rate
you from one to four will be "at risk" any time a competitor makes a better, or perhaps just different, offer, or simply for the novelty of trying
someone new.

In one case, a large U.S. phone company decided to examine the loyalty behavior and attitudes of customers who rated it "good," or an average of four on a five-point satisfaction scale. Management was alarmed
to find that more than 10 percent of customers who gave that positive rating had no intention of repurchasing products or services from the company, and another 50 percent of that group said they were undecided.
When the company did a similar analysis of "satisfactory" level responses, it found that 97 percent of customers so rating the company were at
risk of defecting.[4]

Customer loyalty has three defining characteristics: It's circumstantial. It's fragile. It's fleeting. Loyalty begins to fade as the level of service declines below expectations; customers want and expect service to be at a suitable level all the time. But loyal customers are more than just today's sale. They are tomorrow's and the next month's sale as well. An impressive body of research supports the notion that customer retention tactics should be the anchor of any organization's service strategy.

For one thing, the costs of acquiring new customers is often forbidding compared to the costs of retaining them, as so many of the pure play dot-coms learned the hard way. A study of more than 2000 online shoppers conducted jointly by Bain & Co. and Mainspring Communications Inc. looked at factors that lead to customer retention in the apparel, electronics, and groceries businesses. In the apparel industry, the study found that the average Web shopper wasn't profitable for the retailer until she or he had shopped at the site four times. This suggested that the retailer had to retain the customer for a year just to break even. Online grocers faced an even tougher challenge. They had to retain a customer for 18 months in order to break even.[5]

KNOWING MEANS MULTIFACETED LISTENING

Divining which moments of truth are critical to winning the loyalty of your best customers, and staying on top of customers' ever-shifting expectations, first requires mindfully and regularly listening to their needs and wants. Contrary to echoes that still reverberate from the quality movement, conformance to company specifications is not quality; conformance to customers' specifications is.

This level of listening doesn't mean periodically handing out snapshot surveys to appease management's fluctuating desire to "do some customer service around here." It requires documenting customer experiences and expectations in a multitude of ways and for a multitude of purposes. It means establishing a mix of qualitative and quantitative "listening posts" that ensures raw data are leavened by the real, often emotional voice of the customer.

Customer research should include fact *and* feeling, not just one or the other. Texas A&M's Berry encourages companies to build ongoing *service quality information systems* and not to simply conduct isolated studies. Conducting a study is analogous to taking a snapshot. Deeper insight and a sense for the pattern of change come from a continuing series of snapshots taken from many angles.

We place listening tactics in three categories, all crucial to developing a well-rounded understanding of customers' moments of truth:

1. **Scientific listening.** Scientific listening—what many might call traditional market or customer research—has at least three objectives. The first is to figure out whether your organization is doing the right things (those that have the greatest impact on customer retention). The second is to figure out whether the right things are being done well. The third is to figure out who among current, past, and potential customers agrees with and likes your direction. These activities take an ongoing, concerted effort, lest your organization be caught off guard by the hard turns to which customer expectations in every industry are prone today. Scientific listening can be both quantitative and qualitative, taking the form of comprehensive mail-in questionnaires, "tell us, rate us, help us" comment cards, usability testing, toll-free number hotlines, e-mail listening posts, focus groups, mystery shopping, and the like.

2. **Dramatic listening.** The goal of dramatic listening is to visibly demonstrate to your customers that you really are listening and not simply going through the motions. Dramatic listening, whether focused on improvements, complaints, or harvesting new ideas, leaves customers with the feeling of having been heard and confident that your company will honor the information received, and take action where warranted. That's why we say listening is a contact sport—listening without contact, or dramatic connection, is like looking without seeing. Given the rare experience of really being heard, customers long remember those organizations that listen well and will become loath to take their business elsewhere.

   Dramatic listening is best done on the front lines, over service counters and via call centers, where employees should be trained to listen not only for problems but also for those unexpected customer ideas that might spark profitable new services or fresh ways to cut costs. Given their day-in, day-out contact with customers, front-line workers become your best field researchers. The key to dramatic listening is openness and obvious acceptance of the customer's point of view, problem, or suggestion.

3. Motivational listening. Whether the data in question are about faulty parts per thousand or customer complaints successfully addressed, the most convincing information for the people in charge is information they gather for themselves. Many service-conscious executives or middle managers routinely spend time in the trenches, handling the phones, answering customer questions, or doing sales call ride-alongs to get a more visceral sense of customer needs and the daily challenges faced by their front-line staff. Others go under-cover to experience their organization's service from the customer's eyes. Experiencing things directly and personally can make an impact that hours of reading static customer satisfaction reports never can approach.

When Kenneth Macke was CEO of retailer Dayton Hudson Corporation (now known as Target Corporation), store managers became accustomed to his secret shopping tours. Macke would often show up incognito, browse sections of a store, and then stop at the service desk to scribble a note to the store staff, leaving his business card for startled employees. Things he was looking for: Are customers waiting too long? Are we in stock? Macke believed strategy and technological innovation that looked good on paper were useless if they didn't show up in the stores. Macke never left a "good" store without leaving a congratulatory handwritten note; "bad" stores received notes to the officers of the company. "The consumer is changing very rapidly," Macke told the Minneapolis *StarTribune*. "So I try to spend one day a week in our stores and competitors' stores so that I can see changes as they occur."

It's one thing to conduct listening campaigns after a product or service has been delivered, and quite another to listen and incorporate feedback as you design that product or service. Plenty of customer-focused companies have seen the benefits of incorporating the customer's voice into product design processes. Makers of computer hardware and software are only the latest examples, joined by browser companies, Web shopping sites, and other Internet-related enterprises. With product cycles dramatically shortened and speed-to-market increasingly a life-or-death performance factor, many of these companies now get their customer feedback in real time, via formal and ad hoc product usability testing. The thinking behind this kind of feedback is that: If you slap a new service or product on the Internet and it works, it's a product. If it doesn't, it's simply more market research. Some would argue that the vote-counting fiasco in Florida during the 2000 presidential election would never have happened had ballot designers done even a modicum of usability testing.

When Whirlpool Corp. conducted a survey of the oven-buying market in the 1990s, it found many respondents wanted a range with oven controls that were easier to clean. So Whirlpool engineers proposed using electronic touch pads, like those on a microwave, that can be easily cleaned with a sponge. However, the idea of push-button stove programming at that time was contrary to industry experience; earlier oven models with ordinary push buttons had been collecting dust in showrooms while consumers continued to choose those with conventional twist knobs. Whirlpool didn't throw in the towel, however. Engineers pushed forward with a touch-pad model, but decided to test user reaction every step of the way. Consumer volunteers played with computer simulations of the new controls while marketers showed prototypes to customers in malls. The result? A range with a simple touch pad that walked users from left to right on a control panel in an easy-to-follow progression of steps. It quickly became one of Whirlpool's hottest-selling models.

THE ROLE OF COMPLAINT HANDLING IN BUILDING LOYALTY

How deftly organizations handle customer complaints lodged at listening posts also determines how many of their paying customers will return to do business with them, and how many view the indifference or incompetence they've experienced there as a good reason for turning to the competition. The reality is that you can create all the toll-free call centers, automatic e-mail response systems, and frequently asked questions (FAQs) you want, but if customers don't get their problems adequately resolved upon first contact, their loyalty will drop like a lead balloon.

Pretending to assertively solicit customer feedback with one hand while backhanding customers with the other for having the gall to express their displeasure will quickly send customers on a hunt for a different company. Most customers, research shows, would rather switch than fight.

E-Satisfy.com has long documented the impact of effective complaint handling on customer loyalty, or customers' willingness to repurchase again from the same company after experiencing problems. E-Satisfy found in repeated studies across industries that customers who complain and are satisfied can be more loyal *than if they'd had no problem at all.* If their problems are resolved quickly—say on first contact with a toll-free line or with a front-line employee, rather than after multiple call-backs or visits—the customer's expressed loyalty grows substantially. Of those in e-Satisfy's research with major problems (over a $100 loss) who had complaints resolved quickly, 82 percent said they'd buy from the company again. Conversely, customers whose complaints were not resolved indicated only a 19 percent probability of doing business with the company again, and only 9 percent of noncomplainants—those who didn't bother to voice their dissatisfaction—were likely to repurchase from the offending company.

Another headline from their findings: A high percentage of customers experiencing problems prefer to suffer in silence. They don't bother to complain, but simply, quietly stop doing business with you, slipping underneath the radar to the competition. E-Satisfy.com's research finds that, on average, 1 percent to 5 percent of aggrieved customers complain to management or corporate headquarters; 45 percent complain to a front-line rep, agent, or branch office; and 50 percent of those who encounter a problem don't complain at all.[6]

Why do these noncomplainers vote with their feet rather than stay and try to work things out? Three reasons: 1) They think the organization doesn't care; 2) they have little hope that anything good will happen as a result of their complaining; 3) they fear either conflict or some future retaliation for daring to bring up a problem. These data suggest that rather than encouraging customers to keep problems to themselves, you're far better served by making it easy for them to find toll-free numbers, e-mail contacts, or similar means to lodge complaints. This, at a minimum, gives you a fighting chance of keeping or winning back their loyalty. In one of its early studies, e-Satisfy.com found that the existence of a toll-free number at corporate headquarters will, on average, double the number of complaints getting to corporate staff.[7]

Despite this, senior managers continue to equate a dearth of complaint activity with indications that customers "must be happy" with their organization's service quality. In that skewed vision, no news is good news. The general fear is that if they seek and receive customer complaints and no satisfactory corrective action results for the customer, organizations might be perceived in a worse light than had they not asked at all. It's also important that front-liners not be rebuked for bringing complaints or feedback to management, since they'll be less likely to do so in the future.

Theodore Levitt, retired Harvard University marketing professor, was among service quality researchers refuting the notion that it's better not to ask for complaints at all. "One of the surest signs of a bad or declining relationship with a customer is the absence of complaints," Levitt said. "Nobody is ever that satisfied, especially not over an extended period of time. The customer is either not being candid or not being contacted."

E-Satisfy.com also compared the costs of recruiting a new customer with the costs of retaining existing customers through effective complaint handling. An original study examined the advertising cost of winning new auto customers versus the expense of retaining an existing customer for a domestic auto company. The company had spent approximately $375 in advertising for each car sold, and it had a 50 percent base loyalty or customer retention rate, which meant the advertising cost *per new customer* was actually $750.

On the other hand, the "goodwill expense" in retaining an existing customer averaged $150. Therefore, e-Satisfy determined that it was five times as expensive to win a new customer than it was to keep a current one who had a problem. In later studies e-Satisfy found the real ratio of costs to win a new customer versus retaining a current one varies from 2 to 1 to 20 to 1 depending on industry, product type, and other variables.[8]

Even more important than inviting complaints, of course, is training those at your listening posts to effectively and graciously handle all kinds of customer problems. Understanding customers' emotional states when events veer from their anticipated course is essential to returning them to a state of satisfaction. This requires a combination of technical competence and an ability to set aside defensiveness or blame and focus on solving the problem at hand. It also requires solid guidance from management about how to effectively deal with anticipated problems.

High-touch hand-holding becomes far more important than high-tech efficiency when customers hit a stretch of white water and have the kind of problems FAQs or other self-service tools can't answer. They need people, not technology, to guide them through the rapids. The last thing they want, once they track down that human access point, is to wait in a 30-minute queue for a toll-free number, send e-mail that yields a hopelessly generic automated reply, or use a chat button that leads to a system shutdown instead of a helping hand.

Consider the problems experienced at Priceline.com, the well-known Web site that lets customers name their own price for plane tickets, hotel rooms, and more. Plenty of consumers enthusiastically climbed on that bandwagon without fully understanding all the convenience-for-savings tradeoffs, such as the limited number of direct flights available, late-night flights, being forced to take whatever brand was available, and not always being eligible for refunds. According to *Business Week*, when those e-customers had problems or expressed surprise at some of the travel conditions, it was often difficult to find someone to help. Those complaints triggered at least one state investigation. In the meantime, Priceline.com pledged to improve the human element in its customer service.[9]

Research from e-Satisfy.com also underscores that the customer is not always right; up to 40 percent of expressed dissatisfaction is caused by the customer's own mistakes or incorrect expectations. But the staff's objective in such cases isn't to assign blame or castigate stupidity. It's to clarify what happened, why, what you (or the customer) can do to resolve it this time, and what you can do to prevent it from happening again.[10]

CUSTOMER MOTIVATION AND THE CYCLE OF SERVICE

When a customer comes into contact with an organization, he or she sees the entire picture, not just one element. We've previously referred to this totality of experience and perception as the cycle of service. To use a commercial airline as an example, the cycle of service starts when the customer calls or goes online to book a reservation for a particular flight. It continues as the customer travels to the airport, checks luggage, boards the plane, eats a meal, lands at the destination, collects luggage, rents a car, and carries out business until it's time for the trip home. The process is then repeated in reverse, and the cycle is complete when both customer and luggage are safe at home.

At each different point in this cycle, customers come into contact with one specific part of the organization. Their perceptions can be altered or influenced by any rogue employee or poor design factor encountered along the way. From this standpoint we can see the customers have a certain paradigm or conceptual frame of reference in mind, while airline employees in varying departments or at different stops along the service continuum have their own individual agendas or paradigms. Each employee has a grip on only "one leg of the elephant," and is well versed in his or her own specific job duties. Unfortunately, all too often employees are only vaguely familiar with the responsibilities of other employees in the service cycle. Yet all of an airline's (or any organization's) efforts at marketing, advertising, and goodwill can be either greatly enhanced or be ruined by an appropriate or a rude response of a single employee. That makes proper selection and training of *all staff*—not just those with direct customer contact—of paramount importance to good service efforts. When the cycle of service is working at an optimum level, a customer's problem becomes the problem of any employee who comes in contact with the customer, not just of the customer service department.

Take Susan Poindexter, for instance, a customer service agent at Delta Airlines. One day while she was on duty at the Cincinnati airport, a woman traveling with two small children became ill during a stop in the city. The woman, who spoke little English, needed to go to the hospital immediately. It would have been easy for Poindexter to point to a cabstand or call a skycap or plead ignorance of the foreign language and hope that someone else would take charge. Poindexter instead accompanied the woman and her children to the hospital. When the woman was released, Poindexter took the travelers home with her and put them up overnight. The next day, she drove them back to the airport and got them boarded for home. That kind of initiative and caring is not mandated in any training manual.

THE SHIFTING NATURE OF CUSTOMER NEEDS

Today's fad may be tomorrow's antique. It's been proven time and again that a reliable, profitable line of business can quickly fade into obscurity if times change and customer needs or interests change. Few businesses existing today existed 50, 25, or even 10 years ago in anything like their present form. Many profitable businesses of yesteryear have found it necessary to change or die. We need only look at the stunning emergence and then rapid collapse of many dot-coms in 1999, 2000, and 2001 to see how quickly fortunes can change based not only on misreading customer needs but also by ignoring some age-old truths about how to run a successful business. In other words, the dot-commers found that growth and profit margins still mattered. Good business was still good business.

The history of organizations as adaptive entities is anything but impressive. It is all too common for a company to experience a radical change in the structure or direction of its industry and fail to mobilize its resources to cope with the change. This is often the result of ignorance or arrogance. Granted, it can be exceedingly difficult to redeploy the technology, resources, and attitudes of any mid- or large-size organization in any radical way.

Customer relationships today are fluid, not static. We can learn a great deal about adapting to changing customer needs by studying the history of organizations that have adapted poorly, as well as those that have adapted well. Let's look at churches for a moment. Churches as a group continue to have a real marketing problem, evidenced by the fact that attendance has steadily declined for a number of years. American churches used to provide spiritual guidance as well as serve as meeting places and centers of influence for people in small townships. In the past, churches were a principal source of social contact in rural communities. But people in today's "mobi-centric" society increasingly find this same kind of contact in jobs, social groups, nondenominational friendships, and neighborhoods. Although some churches have adjusted smartly to this trend, many have failed to adapt their "products" to the changing needs and environment of their "customers."

A company sometimes fails to meet customers' changing needs even when it is ideally positioned to lead the way. Many industries have fallen victim to the technological leapfrog effect that seems to characterize innovation in many fields. Both the hotel and railroad industries, to name just two, missed significant opportunities to expand and develop new customer service concepts in new industries. Both failed to see or failed to act on how the American middle class was changing—that it was growing and becoming more mobile.

The hotel industry has always thrived on catering to the needs of the upper and middle classes. However, as America's population expanded and our transportation options grew, we discovered that we needed (or preferred) inexpensive places to stay that could save us time and money. The American travel market was ripe for clean, inexpensive rooms located near airports and interstate highways. Presumably the hotel industry should have led the way in creating the motel industry as an extension of its own business. But, in fact, motels arose as almost a separate industry entirely. The Hiltons and Sheratons did not pioneer low-cost, convenient lodging. That innovation involved an almost completely new set of players.

The railroad industry was a real success story from its origins until the late 1940s. Train travel was popular, low-priced, and relatively efficient. Again, the railroad industry should have logically led the way in developing the new airline industry. Railroad executives were the transportation industry's leaders and experts. Their knowledge and "market sensing" should have contributed to and effectively developed the airplane as a new and improved option for travel. Who better to capitalize on the new passenger and freight-moving industry than the current leaders in the transportation field? Airlines emerged with aggressive leadership, and flying soon became more popular with travel and freight customers than rail travel. Railroad executives failed on two counts. First, they didn't anticipate the impact of the commercial airliner on their own business and as a result didn't contribute their expertise to this new form of transportation. Second, they failed to upgrade their technology, services, and equipment to match their customers' changing demands. This lack of innovation and inability to adapt contributed heavily to the decline in popularity and use of railroads.

Conversely, plenty of organizations have been able to adapt and survive by staying in constant touch with the market's ever-changing needs. Entire industries have adapted. For example, as demographics showed greater numbers of Americans moving into older age brackets, many businesses created special offerings (AARP memberships, Viagra, vacation specials, etc.) to the 50-and-up crowd. A classic example of "riding the customer listening curve" to stay a step ahead of the game is the Applebaum's Supermarket chain in the upper Midwest, now known as Rainbow Foods. In the 1950s executives there believed that frozen foods would soon capture the imagination of supermarket shoppers everywhere. Although U.S. consumers during that time had little freezer space, Arthur Applebaum nonetheless saw an opportunity for frozen orange juice and vegetables. What drove his conviction? As an on-the-floor, hands-on manager, Applebaum could often be found behind the counters asking customers what they wanted and needed. Listening carefully to their desires, he decided to swim against the tide of food industry trends, and he started building more frozen food space in his supermarkets. The move paid off handsomely and helped change the way people shop for groceries.

Although getting a firm grasp of slippery market trends can be a tall order, when it comes to *service delivery performance*, the good news is that you can score high marks simply by getting the fundamentals right. Research from Texas A&M's Berry, A. Parasuraman, and Valarie Zeithaml found that what customers often want most of all are the basics done well. Summarizing the 10 most important lessons gleaned from a decade of studying core principles of service quality, the trio wrote, "In all our customer research, we have yet to find evidence of extravagant customer expectations."

What their cross-industry studies did find were repeated demands from customers for organizations to be competent, keep their service promises, explain things adequately, be respectful, share the customer's sense of urgency, and be prepared. Friendliness and sincere apologies from a staff, the researchers found, can't compensate for unreliable service. But few of their findings suggest the inflated, unreasonably high expectation levels that many executives attribute to today's customers.[11]

THE ESSENCE OF "CUSTOMER-DRIVEN": BRIDGING THE GAP BETWEEN INTERNAL AND EXTERNAL PERCEPTIONS

There's often a great deal of assuming and guessing going on in organizations about customers' attitudes and habits, about what service attributes cement customer loyalty, and what makes customers susceptible to the competition's gravitational pull. It's not uncommon for senior managers to form their views of customers through long years of experience but with little actual data. In working with organizations across industries, we still find many executives have only the vaguest notions about what really counts in the minds of their customers. Here's a small, but telling, example, shared by a trainer in the hotel industry. She had been conducting a service-quality seminar of her own with the various managers and supervisors in her hotel. As the time approached for a coffee break, someone in the group asked, "What are the *moments of truth* involved in such a simple thing as a coffee break? What factors are important to a good break?" This led to a quick survey of the group to find out what elements they considered important to a quality coffee break.

During the break she conducted a little outside research. She asked the server who tended the coffee table what he thought made for a good coffee break. She also requested the opinions of the food and beverage manager and the manager of the hotel. The server, food and beverage manager, and hotel manager all agreed that the coffee should be of the highest quality, well brewed, and served in attractive china. It should be served from a polished, elegant coffee urn on a clean, attractively arranged table.

Curiously, no one in the trainer's workshop had mentioned any of these factors in the survey. Attendees wanted to get through the coffee line quickly without having to mill around in a mob scene trying to squeeze in to get a cup. They also wanted the coffee service area to be located close to the restrooms and telephones, a factor none of the planners had considered. It turned out that the trainer's "customers" (the seminar participants) thought of the coffee only as one part of a break that serves multiple needs. No one even mentioned the quality or flavor of the coffee, let alone the shine on the urn or china. "I wonder," mused our hotel trainer, "in what other areas we may be trying to appeal to our customers with things they don't really care about?"

It's risky to assume that we know what customers want and will pay for. Managers who have had little experience in gathering or analyzing psychographic information tend to give little thought to the process. Many of them rely on the "obvious facts" they know about their customers. But as we witnessed in the coffee break example, what we think is obvious may not even be true. To quote Sherlock Holmes, "There is nothing so deceptive as an obvious fact."

Other examples of companies that have misread or overlooked customer priorities—often due to an absence of data and excess of opinion—are legion. Such gaps between what customers really want and what companies give them aren't only costly in terms of misdirected capital investments, but also in terms of creating perceptions that what customers want can never compete with what management mandates.

Here are some other examples that highlight the importance of not only listening to customers, but making sure you ask the right questions:

- When staff at the University of Wisconsin Hospitals (UWH) in Madison surveyed patients who'd undergone heart bypass surgery, the patients' most frequent comment was that they were surprised, even frightened, to find themselves attached to a ventilator upon waking up—a high-impact moment of truth. "The feeling of panic patients expressed about that experience was tremendous," said David Gustafuson, professor of preventive medicine at the hospital.

  The hospital had never considered educating patients about what to expect in this part of their postsurgery experience. So in the next round of patient surveys, rather than asking only generic questions ("How did you like our doctors?") this question was added: "How well did we help you understand prior to surgery what it would be like when you woke up after surgery?"

UWH also got a few surprises when it surveyed 400 of its breast cancer patients. Among the patients' top requests were for rapid access to information about their conditions and to be able to communicate with other breast cancer survivors privately. As a result of the survey, UWH started sending 80 percent of its patients home with a computer that enables them to write letters to other breast cancer patients, access a library of breast cancer articles on the hard drive, and consult a list of 250 commonly asked questions.[12]

- While going over year-end budget requests, a new manager of a Chicago Marriott Hotel came across a $20,000 line item earmarked for upgrading the black-and-white TV sets to color in the bathrooms of rooms at the concierge level. At first glance it seemed like an important service improvement, but upon further rumination the manager had his suspicions. He began asking questions of his people, based in part on the assumption that they'd been listening closely to customers. First he asked the concierge-level staff and engineering employees how many requests they'd received for color sets in the bathrooms. "Actually, none," came the reply. "But we thought it would be a neat idea." Then the manager asked housekeeping staff what they were hearing from guests on the floor. What were guests asking for that we didn't already supply? The housekeepers cited, almost universally, irons and ironing boards. That's what the manager used the TV money for.

- Executives at a major bank had assumed that agreeable interest rates were the obvious key to winning the loyalty of major business loan customers ($500,000 and up). In fact, research found that the major factors causing the loss of these customers were related to the accessibility and responsiveness of the bank's personal relationship managers. It seems the client's CFOs were willing to forgive above market-average interest rates but not unreturned phone calls.

E-Satisfy's Goodman recommends that managers pick their battles in measuring customer service performance. He suggests that companies work to identify the five biggest "points of pain" for their customers—

areas that do the most damage to customer loyalty or retention—and concentrate resources on fixing those first.

FedEx is a believer in that philosophy, and in the past has used its Service Quality Indicators (SQI) index to focus first on fixing service problems with the greatest impact on customer retention. The SQI featured a series of categories, each weighted according to the degree of customer aggravation caused by a failure to perform as shown in Figure 4-2. The number of "average daily failure points" for each performance dimension is calculated by multiplying the number of daily occurrences for that component by its assigned weight.

IMAGE AS MANAGED PERCEPTION

Finally, we offer some thoughts about the service image. What are some of the factors that come to your mind when you hear the word "image"? These might include terms like goodwill, credibility, honesty, ethics, rep-

Item	Weight
Right day late service failures	1
Wrong day late service failures	5
Traces	1
Complaints reopened by customers	5
Missing PODs	1
Invoice adjustments requested	1
Missed pickups	**10**
Damaged packages	**10**
Lost packages	**10**
Overgoods	5
Abandoned calls	1
International SQI indicator	1

FIGURE 4-2   FedEx weighted service measures

utation, trust, a sense of permanence, consistency, quality, and integrity. These are some of the images a company can have. But what is an image? In service management language, an image is "a managed perception on the part of the customer of the way the company does business." How do we want our customers to perceive us? What kind of image do we want to earn by the way we conduct our affairs?

Understanding how a company's image is created is critical to the process of building one. The moments of truth concept reminds us that our image improves or deteriorates moment to moment and day by day as a result of the sum total of our customers' experiences with us. We manage the customer's perception—our image—by managing the moments of truth.

It is a curious fact that the three biggest service bargains in American society all come from institutions that have relatively negative service images. These are the telephone system, electric and gas service, and the mail system. Think about the cost of mailing a letter, for instance, in terms of the number of minutes you would need to work at your job in order to earn enough to pay for it. The equivalent cost is trivial. Consider your "labor cost" for a telephone call, even at long-distance rates. When it comes to your home heating bill, even with inflated prices, consider what you'd have to do on your own to gather and burn enough fuel to give yourself the same comfort level you get by turning the thermostat knob.

While it is fair to say that these three service organizations are not always brilliantly managed, they do provide valuable services for the prices we pay. Yet it is ironic that most customers are singularly unimpressed with these three institutions, which might still have image problems even if they always gave effective service, were represented by well-qualified front-line people, and had customer-friendly systems. The one aspect of the service triangle all of these organizations seem to neglect is the service strategy. They do not do an adequate job of communicating the perception of value to their customers. Most of them take a relatively passive role, based on the assumption that good service will earn them high marks. This assumption is clearly faulty. To improve their images, these institutions need to project a clearer, more believable message to the public. They need to do a better job of showing their customers what value they receive for the money they pay. In other words, these organizations need to develop service strategies that focus on customer awareness of their strong points.

5

FINDING AND DEFINING THE SERVICE STRATEGY

"There is nothing so frightening as ignorance in action."

—Wolfgang von Goethe

ANAGEMENT THEORIST PETER DRUCKER enjoys asking executives a disarmingly simple question: "What business are you in?" Finding a valid answer is especially critical for service organizations. It's a profoundly important question that really decodes to the fundamental definition of the value the enterprise creates. The answer evolves in the form of a service strategy, which is the organizing principle that guides the enterprise.

In this chapter we suggest answers to the most challenging questions facing every organization striving to make service quality a top priority:

1. What is a service strategy?
2. Why should we have a formal service strategy?

3. When is it necessary to rethink such a strategy?
4. What elements does it contain, and how are they arrived at?
5. What does it say?

Defining or revising the service strategy is often a challenging and creative task. In some cases good market research will clearly indicate a compelling way to position the organization in the customer's mind, a way that creates some clear differentiation from the competition. In other cases it might be necessary to wrestle with complex or conflicting questions and issues and to apply a great deal of executive judgment. In Chapter 6 we suggest some management-driven methods for developing a service strategy. Here we explore the thought processes behind an effective service strategy.

WHAT IS A SERVICE STRATEGY?

Many organizations do what they do because that's what they were doing last year, the year before, and the year before that. The great flywheel of habit keeps many enterprises on the same straight path long after it has become clear that they will face tough times if they don't learn to adapt. It takes a great deal of energy, determination, and intellectual courage to question the basic purposes and deliverables of your business. Yet this is exactly what more and more executives are forced to do as the structure of industry continues to shift, old markets dry up, and new markets develop.

ANATOMY OF A SERVICE STRATEGY

The definition of superior service is the foundation of a service strategy: the way you define what service quality is, why that quality is important to the customer, and what's at stake for the organization and its people. It's more than a slogan. Slogans can call attention to a service strategy, but the strategy is in the definition itself—the "image" of good service you want all employees of the organization to have in mind every time they face or think about the customer. Unless and until management is able to crystallize and communicate a single vision of service quality, the organization doesn't have a service strategy. And this vision must be communicated broadly—to everyone at every level and to the customer as well.

A word about "vision." The term is in danger of becoming trivialized and battered beyond usefulness, but it is still the best description of what we are trying to convey. A vision is an idea refined through experience and thinking. You don't get it from lying on a conference room floor chanting a mantra. It evolves and matures as your understanding of customers and your experience at delivering quality service increase. It's the model, the set of guiding principles, the concept. It isn't fuzzy. It is a clear, precise understanding of what your business is all about.

During a discussion we were leading on what a service strategy should and shouldn't do and say, an executive of the Dayton Hudson Department Store Company (now Target Corporation) quickly cut through the technical jargon for us. "In other words," he observed pointedly, "a service strategy is the 'bear any burden, pay any price promise we make to ourselves on behalf of our customer,' isn't it?" He "got it in one" as the English say, and much more succinctly than we had been able to. A service strategy is simply a statement of what you intend to do—must do, really—for the customer if you are to be successful in distinguishing yourself through service quality, whatever the business may be.

We would gladly give you a definitive formula for creating a service strategy if such a formula existed. Alas, it does not. But there is some guidance available. It is our observation that an effective service strategy has four characteristics. Specifically, an effective service strategy:

- Is a nontrivial statement of intent.
- Noticeably differentiates you from others.
- Has value in your customer's eyes.
- Is deliverable by your organization.

It is the fourth characteristic that distinguishes a marketing slogan and an advertising campaign from a service strategy. It's where most organizations go wrong. For example, when General Motors created Mr. Goodwrench as a symbol of excellence, the automotive community was taken somewhat by surprise. Not to be outdone, the denizens of a competitor's marketing department came up with a countermove. They decided that "No Unhappy Owners" would serve them well and initiated a marketing campaign with their idea. The first commercial was aired during halftime of a Sunday NFL game. The following Monday, owners were pulling into dealerships and declaring that they were unhappy owners. But since the whole idea was to one-up Mr. Goodwrench on the airwaves, service writers and managers in the dealerships weren't of a mind, nor had they been instructed, to do anything differently from the way they had before the advertisement was released. Rather than driving home a message of superior service, the poor treatment they received only alienated customers further.

A statement of service strategy functions first and foremost as an internal focus of effort. It is based on an understanding of a combination of organizational values, customer expectations of products and services, customer expectations of the process of doing business with the company, and an in-depth analysis of the strengths and weaknesses of the organization as it confronts the threats and opportunities in the current marketplace. That whole swirl of information and ideas must be distilled to a form that can be understood by employee and customer alike.

The ability to define and articulate a vision of service is becoming a critical skill in more and more industries. The caretaker executive, the action-oriented leader who likes to "ride to the sound of the guns," and the tradition-bound executive specialist all face a greater risk today of becoming obsolete or of making their organizations obsolete through inaction. More and more, the premium is on setting the strategic direction of a company in terms of a market-oriented service strategy.

Another way of defining service strategy is to describe it as "an organizing principle that empowers employees to channel their efforts toward benefit-oriented services that make a significant difference in the eyes of the customer." This principle should guide everyone from top management to line and staff employees. It should make a statement that says, "This is who we are, this is what we do, and this is what we believe in." It should define an organization's reason for being and provide unequivocal clarity of purpose.

Still another variation on the definition of a service strategy is this: a concept that describes the value to be offered. This point of view skews to the nature of the customer's experience. It revolves around the notion that value in the eyes of the customer is what truly counts, not value in the eyes of the company's R&D, sales, or advertising people.

If the concept of a service strategy is sufficiently definitive and benefit-oriented, it can serve powerfully as the basis of an advertising campaign, that is, as a public statement conveying to customers what the company hopes to be known and remembered for. It can also become a corporate statement emphasizing to every employee the importance of delivering high-quality customer service and an explanation of what that service looks like in practice.

WHY HAVE A SERVICE STRATEGY?

What good does it do to announce a service strategy? Is it a good investment of time to develop a carefully phrased statement of some sort? And what do you do with it once you have it?

First, an effective service strategy positions your service in the marketplace. It gives you a simplified way to present your message in a form that makes sense, has significance, and connects to customers' known buying needs or other motivational factors. The concept of positioning a service or a service organization in the marketplace, in the same sense as one positions a physical product, is rather new to the thinking of many executives. In Marketing 101 every business student learns about the concept of product positioning as an essential element in developing a market strategy. A Porsche occupies a different position in the market—that is, it appeals to a different set of values and preferences—from a Hyundai or Saturn. Porsche buyers may be similar to other car buyers in some ways, but when it comes to the choice of a car, they want a specific image and are willing to pay for image-enhancing features and performance.

It is possible to position a physical product distinctively even if it's quite similar to other products in its category. For example, in selling toothpaste we can present an appeal based on good health—"It prevents tooth decay"—or an appeal based on sex appeal—"It makes your teeth whiter, your smile brighter." Both of these positioning approaches target a specific type of customer or customer need. Similarly, we have options for positioning a service in terms of personal benefits—"Fly in comfort and style"—or utilitarian benefits—"We get you there on time."

Because organizations have not traditionally thought of service as a managed proposition or as a skillfully marketed proposition, the concept of positioning has not carried over easily into service advertising. It's easy to pick out those organizations that don't have a clear sense of their market positioning: Their advertisements don't say anything. When the marketing and advertising people don't know what the real battle cry is, they have no choice but to resort to puffy, low-content messages. For example, although many hotel chains invest heavily in full-page, four-color ads in airline magazines and business periodicals, many of their ads look vaguely alike. There may be a shot of a hotel lobby, a room, a pretty young desk clerk, or a "happy people" shot of seemingly powerful, expensively dressed people having dinner in the hotel's restaurant or a drink in the lounge. You could easily interchange photographs, captions, and corporate logos, and it would make little difference.

Many hotels also have trouble positioning their meeting and conference services, which can be very profitable. A typical commercial brochure advertising hotel meeting facilities has lavish photographs of the golf course, swimming pool, and restaurant, and maybe an occasional shot of an empty conference room. Catering people are often expert at putting customers up for the night and feeding them, but they often don't seem to have even the foggiest idea of what business people actually do during their meetings. At an executive retreat, for instance, the priority is on business, not golf. The senior management group may spend two or three full days locked in a conference room, wrestling with the strategic issues of the business. They like the idea of having recreational facilities available, but they choose the hotel largely on its ability to support their business activities. It would seem to make more sense for these facilities to promote the personalized support services that can make things go smoothly during a business meeting.

Banks also struggle in trying to figure out how to make themselves recognizable to customers. Their radio spots, TV, and print ads tend to be pathetically "vanilla" in content. Many resort to radio jingles in the hope of getting their names, at least, to sink into the subconscious of listeners. Yet after years of this kind of advertising, the man or woman on the street still thinks that banks are just banks and would have a hard time picking from a lineup those that stress service quality as a competitive lever and those that don't.

Only when your company has a clearly defined service strategy can advertising people use their most creative and effective techniques to communicate that message to the marketplace.

The second advantage of a clearly stated service strategy is that it provides a unifying direction for the organization. It lets managers at all levels know what the business is all about, what the key operational priorities are, and what they should be trying to accomplish. It tells them who they are, and maybe even more importantly, who they aren't. As

Michael E. Porter has said, "Strategy is making a tradeoff in competing. The essence of strategy is choosing what not to do."[1]

Third, it lets front-line employees know what management expects of them and what is important in the organization. It gives them a clear vision of what "service well delivered" looks like. Texas A&M marketing professor Leonard Berry says that, like actors on a stage, service providers need to understand the whole play—the setting, the context, and the point of what they're doing. They need to understand the big picture to understand the importance of their own roles and respond appropriately to customer cues. A distinct, well-communicated, and frequently modeled service strategy establishes the company belief that service to the customer is the most important driver of our company's success.

SORTING BUSINESS STRATEGIES INTO USEFUL PILES

There's no shortage of failed or weakened companies whose downfalls can be traced in part to core strategies that tried to be all things to all people. The work of two consultants highlights the importance of picking one competitive genre and striving to be the best at it, rather than trying to be an across-the-board world-beater. Writing in the Harvard Business Review, consultants Michael Treacy and Fred Wiersema contend that companies that have gained a leadership position in their industries have done so by narrowing their focus to one of three "value disciplines": Operational Excellence, Customer Intimacy, or Product Leadership. They found that it's the rare company that can excel in more than one of the three areas at the same time. "Companies that push the boundaries of one value discipline while meeting industrial standards in the other two gain such a lead that competitors find it hard to catch up," Treacy and Wiersema state.[2]

Companies choosing a strategic focus on Operational Excellence provide customers with reliable products or services at competitive prices, delivered with a minimum of difficulty or inconvenience. Those emphasizing Customer Intimacy segment and target markets precisely, tailoring service offerings to exactly match the demands of those markets thus enabling customers to feel unique and special. Those competing primarily on Product Leadership offer customers leading-edge products and services that make competitive products obsolete and distinguish the buyer as cutting edge.

.

Treacy and Wiersema's findings make particular sense when you think about companies that, say, try to focus simultaneously on six sigma product quality and instituting a world-class service recovery system. Such mixing of value strategies (trying to lead the market on two dissimilar fronts) is almost always doomed to failure. It's the rare company that can initiate and excel in more than one such discipline at a time.

If senior management hasn't decided where to focus the organization's attention, employees and customers will start to make up their own sense of meaning and create their own targets. Essentially, if you want to excite your people about the prospect of being number one, it helps if they know what they're going to be number one at.

WHEN SHOULD YOU RETHINK THE SERVICE STRATEGY?

Organizations usually rethink their basic service strategies for two reasons: (1) in order to anticipate changes in the market; or (2) in response to a crisis caused when they become dangerously out of touch with the market. Unfortunately, the latter case is much more common. The first situation usually occurs when the executives of a company systematically and regularly evaluate the company's relationship to its public. This typically takes the form of an annual executive retreat, a strategy session, or a planning review. Anticipating changes in the needs or motivations of customer segments is the key to realigning your service strategy. Effective service organizations constantly monitor the marketplace for signals that may foreshadow important changes in consumers' needs, preferences, or buying motivations. The time to rethink your service strategy is before these trends get into full swing, not after the fact when it's too late to slow the customer exodus to other companies, services, or products. The reality is that the longer you're in the service business, the greater the odds that you'll grow out of touch with your customers' needs. Believing you already know all you need to know about your market will land you in bankruptcy court faster than you can say "disappearing market share."

Consider recent developments in the retailing industry, for example. Two household names, J.C. Penney and Montgomery Ward, have struggled mightily and have been forced to close stores—and in Ward's case, shutter the business altogether—due in large part to slow reactions to changes in their markets, customer demographics, and buying preferences. Analysts say ineffectual marketing, dated merchandise, and poor store locations exposed the flanks of these two retailing icons to discounters like Target and Wal-Mart, "category killer" specialists, and even trendier retailers.

Systematic market research helps you sense shifts in consumer behavior; it's the invaluable corporate radar that tracks the forces shaping and reshaping your business. But you need more than market research to develop a sound service strategy. Strategic thinking, strength analysis, opportunity mapping, and survey tactics that measure service quality dimensions with the biggest impact on customer loyalty are other approaches that help mold strategy decisions.

The second, and unfortunately all too common, occasion for rethinking service strategy occurs when an organization is shocked into reacting to a crisis. A severe drop in sales or a significant loss in market share will have senior management calling all employees to battle stations. At this high-pressure point, however, it may not be easy to figure out how to remedy the situation.

In such cases contradictory data or conflicting management opinions may make it difficult to recognize the need to rethink service strategy. Executives may lose valuable months, or even years, debating about what to do. Without reliable market research information and a thorough service audit, executives may not realize they have lost touch with the real factors driving customer motivation and buying behavior. The difference between these two modes of adaptation first described is the difference between proactive and reactive executive styles. In the first example a company takes steps to rethink its service strategy before the marketplace changes. In the second example it reacts after the fact to a changing marketplace often with desperate attempts to keep customers from defecting to the competition. Unfortunately, the trends may be so strongly under way by the time the organization starts to adapt that it can take a painfully long time to win the customers back. Far too many organizations try to manage service from this defensive posture.

WHAT ARE THE ELEMENTS OF A POTENT SERVICE STRATEGY?

An effective service strategy brings three important concepts into play: market research, the business mission, and the driving values of the organization. By combining these three fundamentals, it's possible to evolve a meaningful approach to customer needs and expectations that will set you apart from the market clutter of seemingly generic or forgettable organizations:

- Ongoing market research and analysis should be the starting point for arriving at a good service strategy. Effective service companies tap into a variety of information sources to guide strategic service planning. They place a high value on continuous monitoring and investigation of their environments.

- Many organizations have an overarching vision statement and perhaps a mission statement as well. But to truly define service intentions, you also need a "service strategy statement." This statement must be measurable as well as understandable; only tangible standards of service quality make the vision real and applicable.

  You may understand clearly what it will take for customers to give you a "best in class" service rating, but that's of little use until everyone in the organization, from boardroom to shop floor, sees it as clearly as you do. The service strategy statement helps you align mission with the day-to-day actions of your employees. It might be derived from your organization's central strategy, or perhaps be unique to your own unit. The statement should identify your key customers (those whose retention is most critical to organizational health), identify your core contribution to those customers, and also describe what you want to be "famous" for in their eyes. It should be so unequivocal, easily understood, and easy to put into action that employees can always figure out what to do when faced with difficult customer service situations or decisions. As Horst Schulze, president and COO of Ritz-Carlton Hotels, put it, "Employees shouldn't be expected to deliver first-rate service if management can't first define it."

  Your service strategy statement also should be able to pass the "snicker test." In other words, it shouldn't cause employees to giggle, roll their eyes, or react immediately with skepticism about the organization's capacity to live up to it.

- The third fundamental element of an effective service strategy is a set of clearly stated and well-publicized corporate principles, which are the beliefs and values of your organization. Values help define a company's reason for being and help inform decision making as well. The more those corporate values overlap with employees' own values, the more committed those employees will be to doing whatever it takes to ensure positive customer experiences.

If any of these three elements is missing, top management should swiftly get them in place. Trying to develop a service strategy without a clear understanding of the realities of the marketplace, the real mission of the organization, or of underlying corporate values can be a frustrating and unproductive experience.

WHAT DOES A GOOD SERVICE STRATEGY SAY?

We'll try to answer the fifth and final question—"What does a good service strategy say?"—with a series of case vignettes that analyze the apparent strategies and niche positions of companies using service as a competitive lever. The companies offer a diverse range of products and services, but there are recurring themes throughout each operation. Each has a clearly defined idea of how it wants to imprint on and be perceived by distinct customer segments. In other words, there's nary an identity crisis in the group.

While the senior management teams of those organizations may have differing business philosophies and goals, they all agree that customer value is a vital component to their success:

- **LensCrafters.** By pairing independent optometrists with an on-site lens grinding lab and surrounding both with a comfortable showroom stocked with thousands of eyeglass frames, LensCrafters became an optical industry phenomenon in the 1980s. Glasses in an hour had not been considered an option in the chain optical business. The organization's market research showed that customers wanted a wider choice of frame styles than the average small optometrist could afford to stock, and those customers didn't want to wait a week or two for delivery. Another shrewd stroke of strategy was that the lab in each store was placed behind a glass wall, giving customers a confidence and comfort level by being able to watch lens grinding work in action. LensCrafters's original mission statement called for, among other things, creating "enthusiastically satisfied customers all the time."

- **Holiday Inn Hotels.** The Holiday Inn chain of hotels offers convenience at a moderate price for the business and middle-class traveler.

The hotels, now owned by Atlanta-based Bass Hotels & Resorts, are often located near the downtown or airport sections of most large to midsized cities. The hotel rooms are clean and comfortable. The properties provide built-in restaurants or are located close to various local eating establishments. While Holiday Inn may not rank among the four star hotels in the United States, its services make it an exceptional value for the traveler with no need or desire for upscale amenities.

- **Hyatt Hotels.** Like Holiday Inn, Hyatt Hotels offer comfortable surroundings for the business traveler. The difference between the two organizations is that Hyatt is definitely a luxury hotel, which prides itself on offering the best amenities to its guests. Its value proposition is providing a luxury environment for business travelers. The Hyatt Regency properties are all dramatic in their architecture and opulent in interior decor. They are also centrally located in most large cities. Hyatt management strives to offer its customers benefits designed to attract repeat business and establish brand loyalty. These services may not be offered by a hotel like the Holiday Inn, and the Hyatt hopes that the corporate customer will spend the extra money to receive the extra luxury service.

- **Dell Computer Systems.** One of the success stories of the 1990s, Dell Computer became a major player in the hypercompetitive personal computer industry by focusing on direct distribution to the business market and a desire to "out-service" the competition.

  Walk through Dell's corporate headquarters in Round Rock, Texas, and you'll see an omnipresent phrase adorning the walls and bulletin boards: "The Customer Experience: Own It." Yet unlike other computer sellers, Dell usually lives up to its slogans. The company separates itself from the competition through on-time and accurate order fulfillment, an efficient cost structure, an obsession with measuring service performance, and postsale support that is unrivaled in the market. Dell has also proven that great customer service doesn't always require live human help. By listening closely to customers, Dell determined that many welcome the chance to answer questions and fix problems on their own (and, by the way, at lower cost to the organization) through self-service options on Dell's Web site. The Web site now processes about half of all company transactions. The company was among the first to offer a natural language search engine on its site, and its Premier Pages concept set the industry standard in personalized online service by customizing support to customers' product type, system configuration, or industry.

- **Home Depot.** The nation's largest home improvement chain store focuses on do-it-yourselfers in search of materials, supplies, and the kind of how-to advice that's hard to put a price on. Home Depot established a clear identity not only with its orange warehouses, but also by hiring and training staff capable of giving practical advice that could be trusted by the novice fixers. The company places a premium on hiring people who are themselves savvy do-it-yourselfers. What they don't know they soon learn because employee training is continuous.

- **USAA Insurance.** San Antonio-based USAA was founded to serve a very specific type of insurance customer: officers in the U.S. Army whose transient lifestyles made them hard to insure as drivers. USAA, in other words, sought out a market most other insurers didn't want to touch. These days, the policyholders of USAA (which stands for the United Service Auto Association) are still drawn primarily from the ranks of active and retired military officers, but it's now a diversified financial services association. Again, departing from standard insurance industry practice, USAA opted to conduct most of its business through direct marketing, including mail, phone, and the Internet. USAA does little advertising and has few sales agents in the conventional sense, but relies instead on word of mouth for new business. Investments in electronic imaging technology, customer research, and employee training also contribute substantially to the organization's success.

- **Deluxe Corporation.** The philosophy of this St. Paul, Minnesota-based company is to provide errorfree checks at blinding speed and incomparable efficiency to its customers. Deluxe Corporation prints checks for banks and savings and loan institutions worldwide. The company is well aware of the fact that when banking customers open a new checking account, they want to receive their checks as quickly as possible. Deluxe developed high-speed printing techniques and spectacular accuracy in order to build its reputation among banking industry customers. The company's service strategy is built on extremely fast response and maximum convenience for bank customers.

SEPARATING HYGIENE FACTORS
FROM COMPETITIVE DISTINGUISHERS

There is a frequently misunderstood point about service strategy: Factors like cleanliness, attractive physical surroundings, and the flavor of food often do not qualify as elements of a service strategy. If the customer expects you to have a clean hospital, you get no bonus points for cleanliness; you only get demerits if it is not clean. In such a case, cleanliness is a minimum requirement to compete, not a strategy element. If all the other hospitals are dirty, then cleanliness might offer a competitive edge. But if the other hospitals are clean, yours had better be clean, too.

With some service strategies, such as those used by upscale hotels, factors like cleanliness and food quality are essential to success, but they are only "hygiene" factors. They are baseline elements that must be in place for the real service strategy to work. That strategy must provide an appeal beyond the customer's normal expectations, or their "givens."

Of course, not everyone wants to pay for up-scale services. Not everyone can. Markets for most services are segmented into at least three levels: price-oriented, value-oriented, and quality-oriented. A price-oriented buyer usually has limited disposable income and must use it wisely. He or she would dearly love to stay at a Ritz-Carlton property, but must instead settle for a Courtyard by Marriott. This is why the Marriott Corporation offers a complete line of choices.

The value-oriented buyer has more disposable income and more buying flexibility, but still prefers to make choices based on the trade-off between cost and value. This buyer might choose a top-of-the-line restaurant to celebrate an anniversary or other special occasion, but wouldn't go there just for an ordinary night out.

The quality-oriented buyer is a different breed. He or she occupies a socioeconomic niche that confers the freedom to choose from among the best hotels, restaurants, clothing, or vacations on the market. While not necessarily extravagant in personal tastes, this buyer wants top quality and has the money to get it.

This differentiation in buying preferences may show up in some unexpected places. For example, even though there is considerable opposition to and controversy surrounding outrageous medical care costs, some hospitals continue to do strong business by appealing to upscale customers. Specially equipped private rooms, extra services like DVD players, VCRs, computer access, and live-in accommodations for visiting relatives and friends all appeal to the more affluent patient who's ready and willing to pay for additional creature comforts.

On the following pages is the actual service statement of a well-known hotel chain. Note the attention to detail and key differentiators.

SLEEPWELL HOTEL

The Vision

SleepWell Hotel was created to meet the lodging needs of economy and quality minded frequent business travelers, as well as pleasure travelers looking for an affordable, safe and pleasant base of operations.

The Mission

We are committed to making SleepWell Hotel the premier hotel company in the moderate price lodging segment. We do this by providing clean, comfortable and functional rooms in a small, well-maintained and attractive hotel staffed by friendly, attentive and efficient people.

Philosophy and Beliefs

The key to our success is repeat business—guests who choose SleepWell Hotel time after time, stay after stay, because of room value and consistent quality of service and product.

We believe our guests make SleepWell Hotel their hotel of choice when:

1. They find our rooms to be clean, well-maintained and designed for work as well as rest.
2. They experience our staff as:
   - Friendly and Attentive,
   - Effective and Efficient,
   - Professional, and,
   - Easy to Do Business With.
3. They view the hotel in general as an attractive, well kept residence with a special "homey" feel.

OUR KEY DISTINCTION: CONSISTENCY AND CARE

We believe that two words distinguish us from every other moderate price hotel:

Consistency and Care

Consistency means that every time a guest returns to a SleepWell Hotel property, (s)he will experience the same high quality service in the same high quality residential setting.

We achieve consistency by:

1. Designing and building each SleepWell Hotel property to meet the same high standards of room design, common areas and amenity features.

2. Training SleepWell Hotel employees to perform guest sensitive operations such as reservation handling, check-in and check-out, message taking, and room maintenance and cleaning, uniformly and to the highest possible standards.

Care means that every guest will feel treated as an individual, and with respect.

Our guests feel cared for when we are:

1. **Friendly.**　SleepWell Hotel guests see us as friendly when we make eye contact with them, smile and call them by name when possible.

2. **Attentive.**　SleepWell Hotel guests see us as attentive when we give them our undivided attention, show we are listening and respond quickly to their requests.

    (When it isn't possible to give a guest undivided attention, making eye contact, acknowledging the guest's presence, and promising the guest attention soon, conveys the same message.)

3. **Effective and efficient.**　SleepWell Hotel employees are effective when we "Do the Right Things" and efficient when we "Do Things Right." Guests see us as effective and efficient when we respond to their requests quickly and competently.

4. **Professional.**　SleepWell Hotel guests see us as professional when we know our jobs well, can anticipate guest needs, and are willing to do the "little things" that say we appreciate the guest's business. Guests are impressed by our professionalism when we are knowl-

edgeable about the hotel (even areas we don't work in), the local area, and are ready to give directions and information when guests need them.

5. **"Easy to do business with."** SleepWell Hotel guests see us as easy-to-do-business-with when we:
   - Respond quickly to requests,
   - Are willing to help them though what they request may not be in our job description,
   - Accept responsibility for mistakes without blaming or reluctance,
   - See to it that problems are resolved—even if we can't do it personally, and,
   - In general, we use good judgment in responding to requests and problems.

DO CUSTOMERS ALWAYS KNOW WHAT THEY NEED?

Up to this point we've been talking almost exclusively about ways to fill expressed customer needs. In almost every serious discussion of the service management concept, there comes a point when someone becomes uncomfortable with our insistence on this obsession and challenges it. The objection usually goes something like this:

> Wait a minute! Sure, the customer has a role in shaping the design of our services, but there are lots of times when the consumer doesn't know what's possible. There are plenty of business successes built on products and services the consumer didn't have the slightest idea he or she "needed" until they became available.

Fair enough and true! There are plenty of examples of products and services inventing needs instead of the other way around. The telephone, automobile, credit card, and labor union are all examples of products and services for which there was no demand until they were invented. Throw in the airplane, representative democracy, the stock market, the written word, Post-It notes, the personal computer, and the World Wide Web for good measure, and we have the making of an interesting debate about the wellsprings of innovation.

Although we readily concede that it's possible to create something totally new for which there is no obvious and pressing demand in the marketplaces, it's a difficult and risky task. Innovation that is technology- or business-driven, as opposed to customer-driven, is doubly difficult to bring to life. Take something as seemingly logical and important as the automobile seatbelt. It makes sense and should be accepted by the consumer, but if the seatbelt were just another product and not a controversial life-and-death issue, and if the consumer were to simply accept or reject it on the face of its advertised features and benefits, it would have died off decades ago.

Creating a need and a demand where there is none—or worse yet, convincing consumers to do something they don't want to do and can't imagine they'll enjoy doing—takes three things: time, money, and more money. Discerning a need and filling it are far cheaper and easier, if not as entrepreneurially exciting, than betting your company on a conjecture.

6

BUILDING THE SERVICE DELIVERY SYSTEM

"You can take great people, highly trained and motivated, and put them in a lousy system and the system will win every time."

—Geary Rummler
CEO, Performance Design Lab

T HE SERVICE DELIVERY SYSTEM is all of the apparatus, physical and procedural, that people in an organization have at their disposal to deliver the customer value. This chapter describes a rationale for being good by design—an approach to designing the total service system in such a way as to maximize its effectiveness. For the next few pages we invite you to think "large"; to think in systems terms, as we explore the critical elements of service system analysis and design.

The components of a particular service system depend on the nature of the service and the organization. In a theme park, for example, much of the service delivery system consists of the physical facilities: the grounds, the attractions, the food service setup, the ticket sales operation, the cleanup operation, and all the other activities that make the park run. The delivery system also includes less visible activities such as food procurement, handling, and storage. Maintenance and repair of the facilities are also a crucial part of the service delivery system. Even though the customer never sees these and other key parts of the system, they are essential to the delivery of total value.

The key success factor, where the service system is concerned, is that it be perceived by users as customer-friendly. Service delivery systems that are low on the friendliness scale tend, by their very design, to subordinate convenience and ease of access for the customer in favor of the convenience of the people who work within the system. A customer-friendly system, on the other hand, is one whose basic design makes things easy for the customer.

The design of an effective service delivery system actualizes the service priorities spelled out by the service strategy. It is a customer-friendly system because it starts and ends with customer needs, expectations, and buying motivations. What do "friendly" and "unfriendly" systems look like? Walk into the typical federal, state, or city government office and you will probably experience a system designed for the convenience of the people in the system, not for the customer. Incomprehensible signage, long waiting lines, multipage paper forms requiring microscopic writing skills to fill them out, and a customer movement pattern resembling a Marine Corps exercise course are the hallmarks of customer-hostile systems.

On the other hand, in a customer-focused system, at say, a Walt Disney World or a Pearle Vision Optical store, signage is generally large, colorful, and easy to read and comprehend. Waiting and queuing are minimal and carefully managed, and there are always people available to courteously help the customer.

THE SERVICE PACKAGE

One of the most helpful concepts in service management is the notion of the *service package*. This term, which originated in Scandinavia, is widely used there in discussing service systems and evaluating service levels. It may also be called the *customer value package*; in this book, we use both terms to mean the same thing. Service management experts vary in the definitions they offer, but most agree on something like this:

The service package (or customer value package) is the sum total of the goods, services, and experiences offered to the customer.

It may help to think of the service strategy, the service package, and the service system as interrelated in the following way:

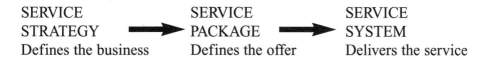

SERVICE	SERVICE	SERVICE
STRATEGY	PACKAGE	SYSTEM
Defines the business	Defines the offer	Delivers the service

The service package concept provides a framework for thinking systematically about the delivery system. Your service package follows logically from your service strategy. It constitutes the basic value you deliver. Your service system—from design to measurement—follows from the definition of this service or customer value package.

There is no mystery to this service package idea. In most organizations there is already an existing set of goods, services, and experiences. With rare exceptions, value packages usually start small and evolve over the years. When they need reinventing, it helps to go back to first principles and think through the entire design in light of the original service strategy.

While each enterprise will have its own unique and distinctive customer value package (i.e., the set of tangibles and intangibles it delivers to its customers), it is possible to identify certain generic dimensions of customer value, which can serve as a common framework and common language in designing, building, diagnosing, and fixing service delivery systems.

We can think of the customer value package as having seven more or less generic dimensions or aspects, as depicted in Figure 6-1. Each business will have its uniquely different version of each of the components. However, all customer value packages have certain common aspects, as detailed in Karl Albrecht's book, *The Only Thing That Matters: Bringing the Power of the Customer Into the Center of Your Business*.[1] Let's see how these seven components go together to form the infrastructure for delivery of customer value.

1. **Environmental.** The physical setting in which the customer experiences the product. It could be a hospital room, a bank lobby, an airplane cabin, a barber chair, a department store, the sidewalk in front

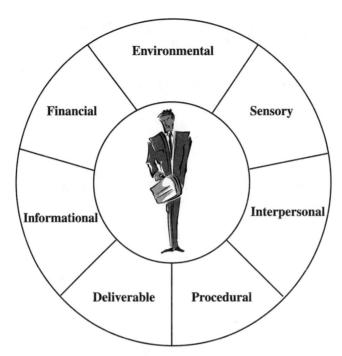

FIGURE 6-1   **Customer value package**

of an automatic teller machine, a fitness center, or any of a limitless number of possibilities. In the case of service at a distance, the environment may be the customer's own premises, possibly augmented by the telephone or online connection through which he or she makes contact with the business.

2. **Sensory.** The direct sensory experiences, if any, that the customer has. They may include sights, sounds, flavors, physical sensations, pain or discomfort, emotional reactions, aesthetic features of an item of merchandise, and the ambience of the customer environment.

3. **Interpersonal.** The interaction the customer has with employees or, in some cases, with other customers, as part of the total experience. This dimension includes friendliness, courtesy, helpfulness, physical appearance, and apparent competence at handling important tasks.

4. **Procedural.** The procedures you ask the customer to go through in doing business with you. They may include waiting, explaining his or her needs, filling out forms, providing information, going to var-

ious locations, and being subjected to physical manipulation or treatments.

5. **Deliverable.** Anything the customer physically takes custody of during the service experience, even if only temporarily. It would certainly include an item of merchandise purchased, but it could also include the tray of food served by an airline or a hospital. It might not always be a product in the conventional commercial sense, but the customer receives it nevertheless. Other examples are checkbooks, rented videotapes, menus, travel documents, and life jackets.

6. **Informational.** The aspects of the customer experience that involve getting the information needed to function as a customer. This includes simple things like whether the signage in a facility enables the customer to figure out where to go, whether he or she can decipher the invoice or account statement, and whether he or she can understand the insurance policy. It can include critical factors such as whether anyone has adequately explained the use of some item of equipment or whether the customer knows what to expect of a critical medical procedure.

7. **Financial.** What the customer pays for the total experience. In most cases it's obvious: It's the price. In others, it may be less obvious. For example, an insurance company may pay the medical bills, but the customer is still aware of the price.

Every enterprise should subject its customer value package to continual and critical scrutiny, with the objective of constantly improving it. Using the seven components just described, company leaders can conduct a "value audit" of the customer interface to see how well it works. It is also important to get the direct input of customers in this audit, in order to discover defects or opportunities not obvious to the leaders themselves. As a practice exercise, prior to auditing your own customer value package, consider the case of an automobile dealership. What features of each value delivery component require attention?

- **Environmental.** The display lot, the showroom, the sales floor, the reception area—what do they convey? Is the place clean, attractive, professional-looking, inviting? Does it make the prospective customer feel welcome and comfortable?

- **Sensory.** Does the place feel like a good place to do business? Does the prospective customer have positive sensory experiences? What does it feel like to sit inside the car? How does it feel to drive it? How does it sound on the road? Is it appealing to the eye?
- **Interpersonal.** Are the people friendly, courteous, and considerate? Do they attack the person who just wants to browse, or do they respect his or her dignity? During a sales conversation, do they build trust and confidence on the part of the customer, or do they make the customer feel uncomfortable by applying pressure tactics?
- **Procedural.** Is the firm easy to do business with? Are employees flexible, or do they insist that the customer follow their procedures? Do they minimize the customer's paperwork?
- **Deliverable.** The car itself: Is it what the customer actually ordered? Does everything work? Is everything clean? Are the financial documents in order and comprehensible? Is the fuel tank full? Is there an extra set of keys?
- **Informational.** Are the vehicle documents all in order? Does the customer fully understand the terms of the purchase? The warranty? The procedures for correcting defects? The maintenance schedule? Does someone take the customer for a ride in the car and make sure he or she understands all the controls?
- **Financial.** Does the customer feel the price is fair? Does he or she fully understand the financial arrangements, including extra charges, insurance, and finance charges? Does the customer feel he or she received real value for the money?

Here are some examples of other customer value packages to consider in training yourself to analyze things from the perspective of the customer's experience:

- Getting a loan from a bank
- Spending a day at Disneyland
- Sending a package by overnight delivery
- Spending a weekend at a hotel
- Attending classes at a university
- Shopping in a bookstore
- Having surgery in a hospital

- Renting a tuxedo for a wedding
- Taking a vacation on a cruise ship
- Applying for a permit at a city department

Once you feel fairly familiar with the thinking process behind the customer value model, begin to apply it to your own business. What does your interface look like, feel like, and act like to your customers? Can you say with confidence that the design of your value package fully reflects the customer value model that's the basis for your business? Or did it just grow and evolve, reflecting the convenience of the organization more than the convenience of the customer?

Richard Normann of the Service Management Group in Paris likes to distinguish between *core services*—the big benefits the consumer is looking for—and *peripheral services*—the little things, or added bonuses, that go along with the big benefits. A similar distinction, used in Scandinavia, is between the primary service package and the secondary service package. In contemporary terms, we could also call them the primary and secondary value packages. The primary value package is the centerpiece of your service offering. It is your basic reason for being in business. Without the primary package, your business enterprise would make no sense. It needs to reflect the overriding logic of your service strategy, and it needs to offer a natural, compatible set of goods, services, and experiences that go together in the customer's mind to form an impression of high value.

Your secondary value package needs to support, complement, and add value to your primary service package. It should not be a hodgepodge of "extras," thrown in with no forethought. All these secondary service features should provide "leverage," that is, help build up the value of the total package in the customer's eyes. Understanding the potentially synergistic relationship between the primary value package and the secondary value package can point the way to some creative and effective approaches to the design of service.

In a primary-care hospital, for example, the core service to the patient-customer consists of medical treatments, nursing care, medications, information, and lodging. Secondary, or peripheral services, include the comfort and convenience elements such as the telephone and TV, the visitor convenience provisions, the gift shop, the pharmacy, and all the rest.

In a hotel the core value package includes a clean, properly equipped room. The secondary value package includes extra services such as wake-up calls, automatically receiving morning coffee and newspaper, laundry or shoe-shining service, and transportation to and from the airport.

The distinction between primary elements of service and secondary elements can often be crucial. When two or more companies are competing in roughly the same market for the business of the same customer and they are offering the same basic services, the only way any of these companies can gain a competitive edge is by offering a differentiating form of added value.

Once a core service has done its job (met the primary need), the peripherals of the service package tend to emerge as key factors in the customer's decision. In many situations the only possible difference between competitors lies with these peripherals. Often the basic products and services offered by company A and company B are virtually indistinguishable from one another in the eyes of the consumer. The customer responds to the peripheral features to judge the relative value of the competitive offerings, which tend to create the differences in "personality," or style of service. The strongest company in the marketplace may turn out to be the one that offers the best-designed package of peripherals.

EXPECTATIONS: CUSTOMERS AND COMPETITORS KEEP RAISING THE BAR

Customer needs and expectations have an unsettling way of not staying satisfied for long. Fads come and go, trends rise and fall, and new ways of living and doing business emerge. As people get older and the population undergoes noticeable demographic shifts, it becomes necessary to rethink products, services, and whole markets. Psychologist and gerontologist Ken Dychtwald has skillfully profiled the changing needs of the collectively aging U.S. population. Decrements in visual acuity, hand-eye coordination, strength, and stamina of customers are rapidly playing a role in the perception of customer-friendly design.[2]

As people become familiar with products and services they once considered new or novel, their expectations tend to change. F. Stewart DeBruicker and Gregory L. Summe refer to "the customer experience factor."[3] Their analysis suggests that the more experience customers have with a product or service, the more discerning they become about their own needs and the variety of ways available for meeting those needs. They add that customers are not all alike and that their needs and motivations change as their experience with a product or service increases. Consider two distinct types of customer: the inexperienced generalist, who is naive about your particular product or service, and the experienced specialist and sophisticated buyer, who is quite familiar with your product or service.

One of the most significant phenomena we've encountered since the publication of the first edition is the importance of the "contrast effect" on customer satisfaction. Call it the "FedEx Factor." Until Federal Express Corporation made guaranteed, next-day shipment of small parcels and letters an everyday, taken-for-granted occurrence, customers never really knew how important speed of delivery could be. But the FedEx next-day delivery standard has become the bar by which all others—postal service, United Parcel Service, Airborne Express, DHL, and the like—are judged.

As importantly, FedEx speed, Disney courtesy, and Ritz-Carlton class have set standards that influence customer satisfaction outside their industries. The attitude is: If FedEx, American Express, United Parcel Service, and the General Electric Answer Center can answer their phones in two rings or less, why can't my bank or my HMO or my auto dealership or my local dry cleaner? World-class performance in one venue can effect expectations in all venues.

To make things tougher, service peripherals can quickly evolve into core expectations. Call it "peripheral migration." When American Airlines invented the first frequent flyer program in 1981, it was a revolutionary—and classic—value-adding service peripheral. Today, frequent flyer programs have become a core expectation, one that has made airlines worldwide its unwilling hostages. Airlines, quite literally, owe their customers billions of dollars of free flights and can only hope that a large percentage will go unclaimed. This has occurred despite the fact that frequent flyer mileage accumulation has proven to be a modest to weak driver of customer loyalty.

SYSTEM INTELLIGENCE: ESCAPING COLLECTIVE STUPIDITY

In his book *Brain Power, Learn to Develop Your Thinking Skills*, Karl Albrecht immodestly advanced "Albrecht's Law of Collective Stupidity":[4]

> *Intelligent people, when assembled into an organization,*
> *will tend toward collective stupidity.*

We can think of our business systems as more or less "intelligent," to the extent that they not only serve the purposes for which we designed them, but to the extent that they can adapt to demands we didn't anticipate when we set them up. A service delivery system can display at least five primary dimensions of intelligence, as follows:

- **Performance intelligence.** This is the extent to which the elements of the total system—the people, processes, procedures, policies, information, and physical resources—work together to create the intended value, without wasted time or resources and without unintended side consequences. This is the core value level of intelligence. In a hospital, it means that the patient leaves alive and on the way to recovery from his or her disorder and from the treatment applied to correct it. In an airline, it means that the passenger arrives on time, in good condition, and in good spirits—with his or her luggage intact.

- **Corrective intelligence.** This is the extent to which the system has the built-in capacity to fix its mistakes and make amends for its malfunctions. The highest form of this intelligence is, of course, prevention or at least early detection and correction. Its lowest form is the situation in which the customer has to serve in the role of quality assurance, or in which external forces have to come into play to force the system to do what it was supposed to do.

- **Exception intelligence.** This is the extent to which the system can adapt to unfamiliar or nonstandard demands. Its ability to meet special needs of the customer, operate under unusual circumstances, work around obstacles such as missing or faulty information, and substitute one form of value for another creates a kind of second-order intelligence of adaptation.

- **Recovery intelligence.** This is the capacity of the system to make things right for the customer when it has malfunctioned so severely as to destroy his or her perception of value, and to create a disastrous experience which will almost certainly result in the loss of the customer's future business. This issue—and opportunity—of recovery is such a significant element of service management that we devote a major part of the discussion later in this chapter to making it into an art form.

- **Extra-value intelligence.** This is the capacity of the system to add value for the customer in ad hoc, unusual, and unprogrammed ways. It may depend on the ingenuity of individual service employees, special strategies for dealing with particular customer situations or needs, or a general policy of going to great lengths to create value. It can even extend to new inventions and innovative ways to create value.

These five intelligences, or dimensions of system capability, can go together quite powerfully to make the delivery of customer value not only reliable, but also efficient, economical, personalized, individualized, and even unique.

Consider how these five system intelligences are expressed in a system such as the Disneyland theme park. *Performance intelligence* comes from thoughtful and careful design of the physical systems; attention to a multitude of aesthetic factors; careful selection and rigorous training of cast members; well-designed work standards and protocols; and positive, attentive supervision. The rides don't break down, Mickey Mouse shows up for work, the food is plentiful and tasty, the parade starts on time, and all the rest of the processes work the way they're supposed to work.

Corrective intelligence comes from high levels of knowledge and positive attitudes on the part of cast members and supervisors, powerful policies that dictate making things right for the guest at almost any cost, and a generally proactive attitude toward quality.

Exception intelligence is virtually a Disney trademark. It is built into the value system, the policies, the educational process, and the management practices. Employees have the authority within broad limits to take action in unusual situations and to react to unusual requests as cooperatively as possible.

Recovery intelligence is also a matter of pride, carried by cast members and supervisors alike. Everyone in the park understands that if a guest has an unusually bad experience at the hands of the system, it is a moral obligation of those involved to make things right. This can involve remarkable levels of commitment, time, resources, and even money.

Extra-value intelligence is also an art form in the Disney parks. Dennis Snow, formerly director of external programs at Disney University in Orlando, loves to recount the ways in which cast members surprise their guests. On one occasion, a guest asked a cast member where he could get some ice. The cast member, who was strenuously engaged in helping other cast members move a large parade float into its storage place, had to direct the guest toward one of the kiosks nearby. Although he was not able to accompany the guest the short distance to the kiosk, he pulled out his walkie-talkie and signaled the cast member who was stationed at the kiosk.

"There's a guest headed your way," he said, "wearing a blue shirt. He needs a cup of ice. Could you get it for him?" As the guest arrived at the kiosk, the cast member there was holding out a cup full of ice for him. "Here's your ice, sir," he beamed. The guest, thunderstruck, didn't realize, of course, that he'd been part of a spontaneously choreographed service experience.

We can think of the five system intelligences as supporting and enhancing the value created by the service delivery system, as illustrated in Figure 6-2.

DESIGNING, DIAGNOSING, AND FIXING SERVICE SYSTEMS

Traditionally, analysis and planning (in the strategic sense) have held little appeal to people in charge of service systems. Many, if not most, of

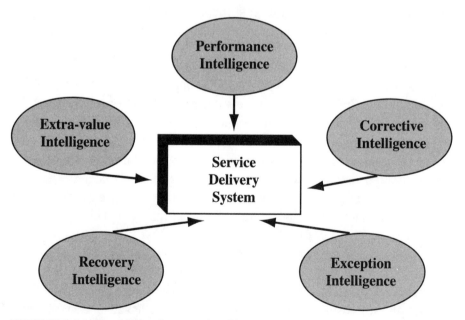

FIGURE 6-2   Five kinds of system intelligence

the service systems we typically encounter on a day-to-day basis seem intractable, unmoving, and unmovable.

For most of the twentieth century, "service" had been an afterthought in most industries. Managers treated it alternately as a marketing gimmick or a necessary evil and costly by-product of the manufacture and delivery of "real products." Service was seldom seen as a major strategic thrust and certainly not as a business proposition unto itself.

In the mind of the aspiring industrialist of the early twentieth century, service was inseparably associated with *servility*—with maids, butlers, bellhops, coachmen, and undertakers. It was hardly the sort of thing a would-be Rockefeller, Morgan, Turner, or Gates would think of as a source of profit. It was held that the only awareness a true captain of industry should have of the quality of service was being on the receiving end.

Oddly enough, and to their dismay, many retail e-commerce startups of the 1990s had that same mindset and suffered the consequences. The commercial landscape is littered with the bones of e-tailers who couldn't figure out effective service elements for their e-solutions.

Within the context of that image of service, it is small wonder that most contemporary service systems are so bad. It isn't so much that anybody purposely built them to deliver mediocre service. It is that they have been intellectually abandoned and allowed to "evolve" on their own. This is a case of simple historical neglect. When you allow an organizational system to evolve on its own, you can be fairly sure it will evolve in the direction of self-convenience, becoming introverted rather than outwardly focused. G. Lynn Shostack, president of New York-based Joyce International, former senior vice president of New York's Bankers Trust Company, and an expert on service delivery, agrees with this perception of service quality. In a *Harvard Business Review* article she comments:

> Examples of poor service are widespread; in survey after survey, services top the list in terms of consumer dissatisfaction. Ideas like H & R Block's approach to tax preparation, the McDonald's formula for fast-food service, and Walt Disney's concept of entertainment are so few and far between that they seem to be the product of genius—a brilliant flash that can never be duplicated.[5]

It is a striking feature of the well-planned and well-executed service system that the service itself seems simple and uncomplicated. The system works so well and the service is produced so effortlessly that the system is nearly invisible. For example, if you have ever visited a large, modern theme park, you have probably marveled at the cleanliness of the grounds and the beauty and bounty of the flowers and shrubs. You may have said something like, "My, my. I wish our yard (city/company) could be as spotless and well groomed as this. How do they do it? They must have really exceptional people doing the work." Not so. In fact, Disney, Universal Studio Theme Parks, Busch Gardens, and most of the other well-known theme parks do most of what they do with minimum-wage employees, the same teenagers we can't even get to pick up their socks at home. How do they do it? There is nothing magic or superhuman about it. For example, think about the flowers, shrubs, and trees you found so attractive at Walt Disney World. Disney, like most theme parks, has a large, well-trained horticultural staff that spends many hours tending the flora. As a guest, you never see these people at work because you aren't supposed to. They do most of their work at night when the park is closed to the public.

Cleanliness involves similar sleight of hand: It's going on right in front of you all the time, but you hardly notice it. A swarm of youngsters is constantly floating through assigned areas of the park, picking up papers and mopping up spills. In the best-known of the theme parks, the Disney properties, there are special vacuum-powered trash transport tubes located all about the grounds. As a guest, you will never see an employee rolling away a giant cart bearing a smelly mass of accumulated trash. In addition, there is a sort of industrywide behavioral norm at work. Everyone who works in a theme park, from the president of the corporation to the newest hot dog vendor, is expected to pick up trash wherever it is spotted. Out of sight, out of mind. They keep it out of sight, and it never crosses your mind that somebody has to get rid of all that trash.

The point is that although the best theme parks are almost always shiny clean, odor free, and pretty to see, it is planning, forethought, and follow-through that keeps them that way, not superhuman effort. Conversely, examples abound of systems that serve the organization first: hospital admission systems focused on payment rather than pain; car repair operations concerned with cost responsibility and warranty fine print rather than repair; bank loan systems that make the customer feel like a crook or a deadbeat rather than a financial partner; government bureaus preoccupied with forms at the expense of function; and IT departments concerned with machinery and methods rather than timely information.

In order to make a service system truly customer-friendly, we must design it or reinvent it in a comprehensive way. Richard Normann, who was closely associated with the SAS turnaround story, makes this observation on the successful service system as a model from which others can learn:

> In practice, it is difficult in a service operation to distinguish clearly between the service, the process of providing the service, and the system for delivering it.... [The key to designing a successful service] is, briefly: the ability to think in wholes. The integration of structure and process is indispensable to the creation of effective service systems.[6]

DESIGNING FOR VALUE: THE SERVICE BLUEPRINT

It becomes more and more evident that services can and must be systematically designed if they are to be reliably delivered. While that may raise the specter of assembly-line-like, engineered work with no room for individual style and personality, that need not be the case. The purpose of designing services in a systematic fashion is just the opposite of dehumanization. The goal of systematic design is to minimize the forms, procedures, and folderol that stand between the service and the customer. At the same time, the service designer must always be concerned that the consumer receives the service he or she expects from the organization and at a cost the organization can manage profitably.

Some service systems, or at least their procedures, are fairly simple. That doesn't necessarily mean that they are effective, efficient, or intelligent. But it does make them fairly easy to describe and explain to the employees who have to make them work. But you don't have to go very far up the scale of complexity before you get to a state of affairs in which there are serious opportunities for collective dumbness to set in. A department store, a hotel, a hospital, or even a small mail-order firm can easily involve a wide enough range of complex activities and skills that its performance can suffer for lack of an intelligent design.

Some companies attack the problem of designing service systems with considerable energy, talent, and perseverance. Some use the latest techniques of modeling, paper testing, costing, and even prototyping. Typically, however, these admirable techniques are beyond the feasible level of investment, level of expertise, and possibly the level of interest on the part of the executives and managers who run most businesses. In practice, it is helpful to have a few basic systems tools and diagramming methods for designing service processes and for evaluating their effectiveness in operation. In this discussion we offer several representative systems tools, which are reasonably simple to use and which have the advantage of being readily understood by all participants on a management team or service quality task force.

One of the most useful of these tools is the *service blueprint*, which is a method for describing how the various participants in a service process collaborate to create the intended value. While some quality practitioners like to develop process blueprints that are extremely detailed and complex, there is also great value in using a simplified diagramming technique, such as the "playscript" method, which portrays the participants in a service process—including the customer—as actors in a coordinated sequence of events.

The following simplified version of the service blueprint, developed by Karl Albrecht,[7] is a flow diagram that depicts the customer's experience in the cycle of service, side by side with the respective actions of the various departments that are involved in delivering the service. It shows the time line of the various actions taken by the customer and the contributing departments as well as how they feed into one another. This tool applies best when you're dealing with quality issues involving several departments, all of which have to cooperate successfully to achieve a quality outcome. The value of the service blueprint is that it makes all the backroom processes customer-focused, and it shows exactly how they intertwine to make the cycle of service come out the way it does.

Figure 6-3 shows a typical service blueprint for a room service order in a hotel. Note that the boxes under the "customer" column are the moments of truth the customer experiences and that they make up a complete cycle of service.

Service blueprinting, whether you use simplified models or very detailed ones, helps in isolating points in the process where a current service is weak or prone to failure. This makes it possible to install checkpoints, safeguards, and failsafe procedures that reinforce performance intelligence as described previously.

Once we have scrutinized the blueprint for completeness and we have assessed and compensated for the main vulnerabilities, some simple service costing and profitability analysis can begin. In the case of an existing service, the process is fairly straightforward. Stopwatch studies can develop standard times and deviation envelopes for the processes on

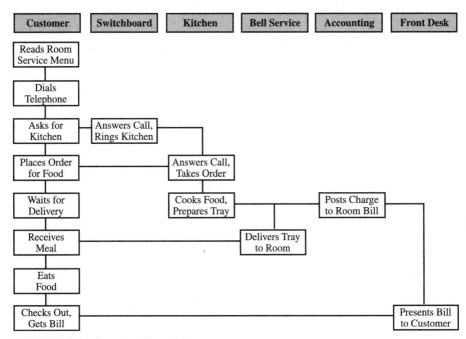

FIGURE 6-3   Service blueprint

the blueprint. It is possible to play "what if" games using the blueprint. Asking hypothetical questions about changes to the service and calculating the effects on profitability allow for creative design ideas and keep the unworkable ones out of the service system.

MOTIA: THE MOMENT OF TRUTH IMPACT ASSESSMENT

Ron Zemke, along with Performance Research Associates colleague Dr. Chip Bell, use the concepts of cycles of service and moments of truth to create an experience engineering approach they refer to as the Moment of Truth Impact Assessment or MOTIA. The cycle of service and moment of truth impact assessment are ways of looking at a specific customer service from the customer's point of view, capturing the most important events, or moments of truth, in that service experience, and dividing those moments into their component parts. The data for this analysis come from a variety of sources: customer interviews, surveys, and observations; employee experiences with customers; knowledge of the service process; and customer complaints and compliments.

The assembly of these data into a coherent map of the customer's experience with the cycle of service follows the course of the customer's contact with the organization, beginning with his or her perception of a need and terminating when the customer perceives that his or her need has been met. This cycle of service is reported from the customer's viewpoint and not the organization's; hence, the cycle does not end until the customer perceives it has having ended.

In any cycle of service, there are different types of customer/organization contact. Sometimes the contact is intense, while at other times it is casual; sometimes it is repetitive and institutionalized; it may also be intermittent or occasional. As a full cycle unfolds, the customer may come in contact with a variety of people and with different pieces of the organization. To the customer, each encounter with the company is part of a single cycle, beginning with a particular need and ending with fulfillment—good, bad, or somewhere in between. In the customer's mind, the cycle is a single "event," although that same customer may well discern small encounters or subevents within the overall event.

To unbundle the cycle of service into its moments of truth, and to further unpack these moments of truth into their component pieces, is a formidable but essential task if one is to discover what one does well—and keep doing it—and what one needs to fix, if that's the case. Each moment of truth along the cycle is a point where the customer has an opportunity to make a judgment about the organization's quality of service. Because each moment of truth in the cycle is a discrete encounter, the customer has a set of discrete expectations for each encounter. A complete map must include these specific expectations as well as the things customers say they encounter that detract from or enhance their experience of that moment of truth.

Figure 6-4 shows a cycle of service for the repair of a residential telephone. The first moment of truth, from the customer's point of view, is the discovery that the phone is not working, followed immediately by the moment of truth, "I figure out how to call the phone company." In all, there are 14 moments of truth in the "repair" cycle—from the customer's point of view.*

---

*The discerning reader will notice that this cycle of service is a little dated. In the new millennium the second step in the phone repair process is to figure out what phone company is responsible for fixing your phone—no easy chore.

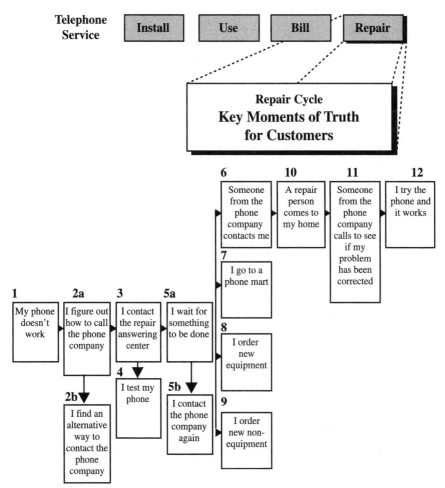

FIGURE 6-4   Sample cycle of service

Once the key moments of truth in the customer's cycle of service are captured and agreed upon, they are then broken into component parts. These component parts are mapped into three categories:

1. **Standard expectations.** These are the minimal expectations customers have for a given moment of truth. They vary from specific actions that customers believe will be taken to the way customers will feel about some part of the experience.

2. **Experience detractors.** These are the customer experiences that have made the specific moment of truth under consideration a

disappointing or annoying experience. Some of these may be actions, inactions, and simply reactions to events and things in the environment.

3. **Experience enhancers.** These are specific experiences at the given moment of truth under consideration that led to an exceptionally good experience from the customer's point of view.

There are also *potential enhancers*, which are things that could lead a customer to make a very positive judgment about the organization's service at the specific moment of truth in question. (See Figure 6-5).

Figure 6-5 focuses on one moment of truth—number 3, from Figure 6-4: "I contact the repair answering center." This moment of truth is explod-

I Contact the Repair Answering Center		
Experience Detractors	**Standard Expectations**	**Experience Enhancers**
• I can't understand the operator's words. • I had to call more than once. • I had to listen to a recording that made me feel unwelcome. • While I am on hold, I get silence, which makes me wonder if I am disconnected. • The operator sounded like he was following a form or routine questions. • I thought the operator rushed me. • I got Mirandized. "Are you sure that there may be a ..." • The operator told me to go to the phone mart to have my phone tested. • I was not able to walk into an office and talk to someone personally.	• I will only have to call one number. • I will call a local number. • I will be treated fairly. • The operator will speak clearly. • The phone will not be busy. • The operator will answer within a reasonable time. • The operator will be a real person. • The operator will speak pleasantly. • The operator will listen to my problems in a manner that lets me know he understands my problems. • The operator will seem competent, helpful, and understanding. • The operator will promise me a solution within a reasonable time.	• The operator had a melodious, well-modulated voice. • The operator communicated a sense of urgency. • The operator really understood my problem, had heard it before, and knew just what to do. • The operator apologized sincerely. • The operator asked me about medical emergencies or other special situations that might warrant sooner-than-normal repair. • The operator made some comment that let me know that he was aware of my area (i.e., sounded like a neighbor). • The operator offered to have work done at my convenience.

FIGURE 6-5   Sample moment of truth impact assessment

ed into the three component categories described above. Notice that the component descriptions are written in a manner that makes them memorable rather than painstakingly literal. For instance, under detractors is the bulleted point, "I got Mirandized."[8] That is shorthand for a description given by a customer, "I felt like I was being given a Miranda warning when they were telling me what my payment obligations would be if the problem I was reporting was in my phone and not in their wiring." That specific comment was chosen to represent a class of detractors—being robotic and officious in informing the customer of a potential fiduciary obligation.

Another important thing about these bulleted points is that they are representative of classes of behavior customer contact people are expected to be competent in or to avoid, but they are not rigidly inclusive. They are, for the most part, illustrative, but not exhaustive. They are more behavioral than descriptive, and they are written from the customer's point of view. They do, however, give a comprehensive overview of the competencies and lack thereof that are most important and memorable to the customer seeking repair service.

Whether you choose to use Shostack's method, Albrecht's blueprint, Zemke's MOTIA, or some other system, there are several additional benefits to the process of diagramming the service delivery system.

- Decisions about staff procurement, allocation, and development become clearer when you can see, right there in front of you, the kinds and number of people needed to operate and manage the service system.
- Considerations about where automation might save money and where personalized human contact is a must can be pinpointed using the blueprint as a discussion focus.
- Competitive services can be studied and analyzed by diagramming them and comparing blueprints.
- Used as the focus of productivity improvement discussions, service blueprints can make employee participation much easier to develop. Employee involvement is a critical issue in decentralizing complex service decisions and in engineering a way to avoid the design problems that characterize new service introductions.

Perhaps the most important benefit of applying rigorous analysis to the development and management of services and service systems is what Normann refers to as "the ability to think in terms of wholes and of the integration of structure and process." Tools and techniques like the service blueprint free us to move in that direction. The ability to conceptualize a service in a rational and manageable fashion is critical to solving the next level of problem beyond transportability, which is the problem of keeping a successful service organization on the path of continuous growth and innovation.

THE RECOVERY IMPERATIVE

The blind spot in many service delivery systems is that they fail to anticipate that something may go wrong. In production management, allowance is made for breakage, spoilage, duds, and units that simply don't meet the specs. Some bad products can be discovered in quality control before they ever reach a customer. For products that fail in the field, there are repair facilities and service technicians.

Service systems, on the other hand, are too often managed as though anything other than perfection is inconceivable. Few businesses handle the redress of service errors in a preplanned, systematic fashion.

Even if the company never flubs its lines, there will be times when needs and expectations fail to mesh to everyone's satisfaction. In such cases, it's crucial to address customer problems and service delivery glitches as quickly and as completely as possible. When the unexpected but inevitable occurs, the customer-centric are ready, willing, and able to swing into action. They work as hard when things go wrong as they do to make things go right the first time out.

The word for this kind of system intelligence, as previously described, is "recovery." It arose in the previously mentioned British Airways, and was based on that newly privatized airline's initial efforts to understand customer expectations after years of operating as a government-run entity: "It had never occurred to us in any concrete way. *Recovery* was the term we coined to describe a very frequently repeated concern: If something goes wrong, as it often does, will anybody make a special effort to set it right? Will someone go out of his or her way to make amends to the customer? Does anybody make an effort to offset the negative effects of a screw-up? Does anyone even know where, when or how to deliver a simple apology?"

The word is a good one. It connotes an effort to return things to a normal state, to make whole again. Most organizations have the traditional service department—a group of people who are charged with fixing what breaks. That is a reactive and very minimal kind of recovery. More than damage control, a good recovery system is a positive, managed effort to attack a problem so thoroughly and wholeheartedly that there will be no possibility the customer might walk away discouraged, disappointed, or wishing he or she had never gotten involved with the company in the first place.

Is this kind of effort worth it? Data compiled by e-Satisfy are compelling. Its National Consumer Survey, conducted for the U.S. Office of Consumer Affairs, found that resolving problems quickly and efficiently had a positive impact on customer retention. Consumers who had problems, complained, and had their problems satisfactorily resolved were more likely to be "brand loyal" than consumers who didn't have problems, and significantly more loyal than customers who experienced problems but failed to register a complaint. Even in instances when the complaint was not resolved in their favor, nearly half the customers who made the effort and were listened to indicated that they would give the offending company another try. Working to normalize relations with an unhappy customer is one of the highest-value activities a service organization can undertake.[9]

Building an effective service recovery system begins with two things: knowing the customer's expectations and understanding what the service breakdown looks and feels like from the customer's viewpoint. There are two distinct levels to the latter: annoyance and feelings of victimization. Annoyance is the minor feelings of irritation we get when the service experience falls slightly short of what we expected. Feelings of victimization create a more serious breakdown and engender a major feeling of anger, frustration, or pain. Recovery takes a different form depending on whether the customer feels annoyed or victimized. The difference between the two is easy to see from specific examples:

- When your flight is 1 hour late, you are annoyed. When being 1 hour late causes you to miss the last connection to your destination and you have to sleep in the airport overnight, you feel victimized.
- When one of your two phones is out of service, you are annoyed. When your only phone is out of service and you have a heart condition, you feel victimized.
- When your car breaks down and you have to ride to work with a neighbor, you're annoyed. When you are a traveling salesperson and

the car breaks down because the repair shop, for the third time, failed to fix a problem and now you're going to miss several previously scheduled calls on very short notice, you feel victimized.

Central to the difference between annoyance and victimization is the way the customer feels about the breakdown. When the customer is left dependent rather than merely inconvenienced, and truly angry rather than mildly irritated, you are dealing with a victim. Any service breakdown will require the deliverer to jump through a few hoops to get the customer back to neutral. More hoops are required to correct a case of victimization than an annoyance.

Research by Ron Zemke (recounted in his book, *Knock your Socks Off Service Recovery*[10]) found that a sequence of as many as five elements is involved in effective recovery. The first two are imperative in dealing with annoyed customers; all five are required for working with customers who feel victimized.

- **Apology.** Recovery absolutely demands some acknowledgment of error immediately following a breakdown in service. If the flight from Sydney to Canberra is more than an hour late taking off, yet the flight attendant makes the standard speech and the pilot comes on the intercom to announce the altitude with no mention of the lateness, you begin to wonder whether the airline is so accustomed to being late that its people treat it as normal.

  An apology is more powerful when delivered in the first person. A corporate "we're sorry" lacks the sincerity and authenticity that comes when a person takes responsibility and acknowledges on behalf of the organization that the customer was mistreated.

- **Urgent restitution.** Because both the outcome and the process of service delivery must be managed, a sense of urgency is important even when things go as planned. It has new, more critical meaning when applied to recovery. Sometimes an expression of gallant intent is sufficient, but the customer must perceive that the deliverer is doing the best job possible to get things back into balance without delay. There are points for good intentions and customer-driven effort. Part of the power of this ingredient is the demonstration that the deliverer has the customer's interests at heart.

  If the customer is annoyed, an apology and urgent restitution, done well, are likely to return things to normal. If the customer has been victimized, recovery is more complex, and the following three ingredients must be added to the recipe.

- **Empathy.** Expressing compassion may be the mother lode of all service gold. Victimized customers are likely to insist that before you attempt to redress their views or feelings you first demonstrate that you understand them. Empathy is the expression of "I know how you must feel. I care about you. I can relate to your misfortune. I can identify with what has happened." In its highest form, the customer feels affirmed and cared about.

   Sincere expressions of empathy are quite different from expressions of sympathy. Sympathy occurs when one shares another's pain. Empathy is showing compassion for the person in pain without feeling that pain personally—it's a shoulder to cry on, a source of strength. There are great risks with sympathy because the helper joins the help rather than the other way around. Those who resort to sympathy are themselves "one down" and prove the axiom that misery loves company. Where sympathy is helping people feel better about being weak, empathy is the kind of understanding that helps them feel strong again.

   For example a Hawaiian woman who spoke limited English was en route to Roanoke, Virginia, recently to visit her daughter. After 6000 miles, 18 hours, and 4 stops, she got to Charlotte, North Carolina, only to learn that the Roanoke airport was closed due to snow and ice. On her last leg of the journey and now only 1 hour from her destination, she was informed she would have to stay the night in Charlotte. The gate attendant made all the arrangements, called her daughter for her, then sat with her for a while, asking the woman questions about Hawaii and her daughter. As tears welled up in the woman's eyes, the gate attendant spontaneously embraced her and said, "You've come so far, I know you really want to see her." The woman smiled through her tears and said, "I'm glad you are my friend."

   The apology tells the victimized customer that it matters that there was a breakdown; empathy adds that it matters that a person was hurt in the process. An axiom is, "When service fails, first treat the person, then the problem."

- **Symbolic atonement.**The fourth ingredient in the recovery recipe is some symbol of atonement. At its most basic level, it is a gesture that clearly says, "We want to make it up to you." Atonement is not a pound of flesh. The symbol or gesture is the key. It's the "It's on us. No charge. Here's a coupon" type of demonstration.

For instance, a man walks into a crowded fast-food restaurant for a sandwich, small fries, and a soft drink to take back to his office. When he placed the order, he was told it would take about 3 minutes for the sandwich. It was noon, lines were long, and some delay was acceptable. But as the minutes stretched to nearly 10, he grew increasingly impatient. Eventually the order was ready and the service recipient came eyeball to eyeball with the provider. Before he could vent his anger, the cashier was already in tune with his feelings. "I'm very sorry," she offered. "I know you were in a hurry. I gave you a large order of fries because you had to wait. I hope you'll come back again." Apology, urgent restitution, empathy, symbolic atonement—right out of the recovery textbook. That kind of performance is no accident. The system was designed and the employees trained for the eventuality of a breakdown.

- **Follow-up.** This last ingredient—follow up—not only provides a sense of closure, but it also serves to affirm the authenticity of the recovery response and provides a means of feedback. Properly managed, follow-up also can be a tool to promote the self-esteem of the service deliverer. The front-line person who takes a beating when things go wrong can walk away feeling good as a result of follow-up. "We may have messed up, but things are okay now."

Chip Bell relates a recovery experience he'd observed at a hotel's front desk. A traveler had been attempting to check in only to be told that the hotel was overbooked and no room was available for him.

"I'm sorry," the desk manager explained. "We're overbooked, and even though you have a reservation, I'm afraid we don't have a room for you this evening. I know this isn't acceptable, and we apologize for it. What I've done is taken the liberty of making a reservation for you at a hotel near here. Just take this card to the front desk at the Parker House. They're expecting you. I know you're upset. I would be too in your place. But I hope you'll find the accommodations there as acceptable as they are here. And here's $10. This should cover the cab ride over there, plus the tip."

Hardly mollified, the guest had taken the note and cash and walked away muttering to himself. Chip, however, had stuck around, so he saw an already good example of recovery extended to include follow-up. As the disgruntled traveler walked out to the cab-stand, the desk manager turned to an associate and said, "He doesn't look like he's very happy with us yet. Give him about 15 minutes to get over there, get registered, and up to his room. Then call him up and ask him if the accommodations are acceptable. While you're at it, invite him to come back tomorrow morning and have breakfast, as our guest, on our concierge level. Tell him we'll leave an envelope in his name with the concierge with a note for the hostess at the restaurant."

Complaints and problems can be an asset when they are handled well. E-Satisfy's data clearly support a well-designed, conscientious recovery effort. They also suggest, however, that a poor or grudging recovery effort may be worse than no effort at all. In the words of the study's authors, "Some companies handle complaints so poorly that they would be better off not soliciting complaints." In these cases, they note, doubly dissatisfied customers indicate less inclination to patronize a business again than those who suffered the first breakdown in silence.

A FINAL ADMONITION: REMEMBER THE CUSTOMER

A final note: We began the discussion of service design, or service engineering as we sometimes call it, by pointing out that most service systems don't—service, that is. The basic problem—and the reason we believe in the value of the kinds of tools we have just discussed—is that the organizations we want to serve others tend strongly toward serving themselves.

In designing service systems, we need to remember above all else that our logic is not necessarily the same as the customer's logic. As we have seen, the customer has a special perceptual frame of reference that is unique to his or her specific needs in a specific situation. Passing through the cycle of service, the customer sees the service in terms of a total experience, not as an isolated activity or set of activities. People cannot see a service system as caring and concerned if its design leads employees to focus only on the performance of "tasks" and not on the value provided to the customer.

Losing sight of the customer's logic can lead your organization to become introverted. Employees who don't understand the services they deliver in holistic terms easily get caught up in methods and procedures and lose sight of the effect their organizational apparatus has on the customer. Insisting that your customers should follow complicated procedures they don't understand, insisting that the customers should learn to speak your language, and playing departmental pinball with the customers are all sure signs that your people have lost the customer focus.

The ability to understand the customer's needs and wants, to determine the nature of the service package, and to audit the current strategy can be summed up in a simple phrase, "Always be learning." The best service strategy is the one that is constantly being questioned, challenged, refined, and improved.

Creating services that meet customer needs, designing systems and procedures that assist rather than insist, and engineering customer-contact jobs that allow the employee to work in advocacy rather than opposition to the customer's interests is the real management challenge for service systems.

THE CARE AND FEEDING OF SERVICE EMPLOYEES

"The way your employees feel is ultimately the way your customers will feel."

—Karl Albrecht and Ron Zemke

ET'S REVIEW THE PLATITUDES: "People are our most important resource." "The front-line people are really the ones who make us or break us." "Those in the trenches are the organization's true heroes." Slogans like these are so commonplace that one might assume that the companies that recite them must live by them, at least most of the time. On the contrary, it's quite common to find a sharp disparity between the people-first slogans found in company literature or advertising campaigns and the hard realities of the customer contact front line.

In the unconscious view of many managers, front-line people are the least important ones in the organization. Front-line jobs typically draw the lowest pay, get the least training and development, have the lowest potential for growth and advancement, and have the most turnover. If the front-line people do count, you certainly couldn't prove it by examining the reward systems in most organizations.

THE LAST FOUR FEET

Any rational view of managing the moments of truth tells us that it is crucially important to mobilize the best energies of the people who are continually forming and re-forming the customer interface. Richard Israel, who is an expert on the training and development of retail sales people, offers a useful perspective on moments of truth. He says, "In any kind of retail or service business, the factor that has the biggest effect on sales is 'the last four feet.'"

Working with a major furniture retail chain, Israel found that much of the enormous advertising investment evaporated at the moment when a customer walked into the store and encountered a nonsupportive psychological environment. "The whole purpose of advertising," says Israel, "is to get the customer to come in the front door. After that point, advertising can't do anything more for you. It's up to the people in the store to take over at the last four feet." Yet in his view all too often the sales or service person loses the opportunity by failing to deal skillfully with the customer's real needs and concerns.

Because retail sales people in particular typically receive little formal training compared to people in other occupations, a large majority of them have to learn the techniques of selling more or less by accident. If they survive in the job long enough, they will learn the merchandise, prices, and other particulars of the sale. But rarely do they have a chance to learn the special social skills and personal philosophies that make for effective selling. Many retail companies might invest less money in advertising and more in developing the critical front-line skills and still be ahead in terms of total sales and profits. Fewer than 1 in 50 dot-coms train the people who interact with their customers. One study suggests that the average U.S. company spends under $7 a year on the formal training of front-line, customer contact employees.

Whatever we can say about retail people, we can usually say just as well about front-line people in other lines of business. It is no exaggeration to say that in the majority of organizations, the care and feeding of front-line people could be vastly improved.

CRITICAL INCIDENTS CAN MAKE YOU OR BREAK YOU

The customer in a busy, crowded restaurant says as the server approaches, "I'm in kind of a hurry," to which the server snaps, "You'll just have to be patient, *sir*. I'm working as fast as I can. As you can see, there are a lot of other people ahead of you." They end up in a silent, cold, perfunctory transaction, with no warmth, no humor, and no tip. Here is a critical incident—a moment of truth gone sour. The customer's next sentence, had the server not interrupted him, was going to be, "What could I order that would take only a few minutes to get?" Intending no criticism, the customer was simply trying to communicate his particular needs. He ended up thinking, "I wish I had gone somewhere else. I sure will next time."

Neither person in this episode was necessarily right or wrong, but nevertheless the situation went off track. Ultimately, however, the service establishment loses, because the customer may never come back. Moments of truth like these can have a big effect on business.

If we think back to the concept of the cycle of service, we can try to relate the customer's conception of what's happening to the service person's conception. Such conceptions may be vastly different, and indeed they are *likely* to be different, because each of them has his or her own distinct focus of attention, need system, and set of priorities.

Some moments of truth are more telling than others, more critical to the customer's decision as to whether to keep his or her business with you. The moment when a customer first sets foot inside the hotel; when the service manager at the repair shop presents the bill; when the physician's receptionist first greets the patient-customer—these are all leverage points. If handled well, if *managed*, they can strengthen the image of the service establishment in the customer's mind. If handled clumsily, as they often are when they go *unmanaged*, they can create apprehension, animosity, and negative expectations.

Again thinking about the cycle of service, we can diagram the customer's chain of experiences from the very beginning to its nominal completion, and we can identify the moments of truth at each stage. The most telling of the moments of truth are the "critical incidents"—those moments of truth that have a significant valence or high impact on customer impressions. It makes good sense to manage all the moments of truth, and it makes even more sense to single out the most critical of them for special attention.

THE IMPORTANCE OF CUSTOMER-ORIENTED FRONT-LINE PEOPLE

It seems obvious that for an organization to thrive, the front-line people need to operate with a consistently high level of concern about, and attention to, the needs and expectations of the customers. Obvious or not, one doesn't have to look very far to find abundant examples of a lack of customer orientation in a variety of businesses. If service people are unfriendly, unhelpful, uncooperative, or uninterested in the customer's needs, the customer tends to project that same attitude onto the organization as a whole. Paraphrasing Jan Carlzon's words: "To the customer, *you* are XYZ Company."

A case in point: A man walks into the men's clothing department of a large department store, possibly looking for a particular item or maybe just to browse. Within 10 seconds of his entry into the department, a salesman descends on him like a wolf guarding its territory. "Hi, there. How are you today? Is there anything I can help you with?" The aggressive eye contact, the well-practiced singsong delivery, the self-assured manner all say to the customer, "*I'm* the one who's in control here."

Perhaps some men like to be approached this way, but the majority seem to find this overly familiar, dominating approach offensive. In the majority of cases like this, the last 4 feet blow the sale. Unless the customer really needs a particular item or happens to spot something of interest, he is likely to brush off the salesperson politely and hurry on.

Now consider the following alternative: A man wanders into the clothing department and looks around tentatively at the bewildering array of suits and sport jackets. There are different racks with different styles, sizes, and prices. The salesman approaches him tentatively, maintains a social distance of about 10 feet, and asks, "Would you like me to point out your size, sir?" The customer replies, "Yes, please." The salesman asks his size and shows him to the racks containing suits that fit him. This represents astute judgment on the part of the salesman. He realizes that many men don't shop for suits very often and that the typical man walking into a suit department doesn't know where to begin looking at the choices. The salesman has done something helpful without being perceived as aggressive. He has created a comfort situation for the customer, and he has paved the way for possible further interaction, advice, a try on, and possibly a sale.

Many psychologists and sociologists contend that these miniature episodes between human beings, going on thousands of times every day, recapitulate our basic interactions as animal creatures. The study of *prox-emics*, which deals with nonverbal communication, spatial context, and body language, has much to say about human interaction in commercial contact situations.

Left to their own devices, poorly trained or untrained front-line people usually have no choice but to cobble together whatever methods they can to help them sell; they build their own idiosyncratic, often superstitious, repertoire of selling skills and philosophies. Unfortunately, many of the things they try don't work very well, and there is no one to provide performance feedback or help them learn. Better training and better orientation to the selling situation can help salespeople produce much higher volumes than simply leaving them with an "I-can-sell-anybody-anything" attitude.

It should go without saying that service people need to have a certain level of maturity and social skills to do an effective job. Yet it is remarkably common to find downright toxic people placed in front-line contact jobs, even crucially important jobs. One situation that occurs disturbingly often deserves recognition as a bona fide syndrome of poor service quality: the "battle-axe receptionist" syndrome. A customer walks into the front lobby of the building, wanting to know where to go or whom to visit. The person who handles this moment of truth is Gravel Gerty. She treats visitors like pests.

Gerty has been with the company for more than 20 years and has worked for just about every manager in the place at some time or other. They have been passing her around from department to department, and somebody finally had a bright idea: "Let's put her out in the reception lobby. That way she won't bother any of the *employees*." She doesn't bother anybody inside the building, but she plays havoc with the impressions outsiders—paying customers—have of the company.

To make matters worse, they may have combined the job of receptionist with the job of switchboard operator. Gerty does both—poorly. She knows, of course, that she is considered excess baggage by the various people in charge, and is hostile about it. Instead of confronting her with her poor performance and providing developmental opportunities for her, the managers have been shuffling Gerty around the organization for years. They don't realize it, but they have put her in exactly the position where she can do the most damage.

There are far too many people in service jobs who have no business being there. Because of the prevailing impression among managers that anybody can do a typical customer contact job, selection and training tend to receive little emphasis. Low-paying jobs such as switchboard operator, receptionist, and counter worker don't usually require great technical expertise or product knowledge. Consequently, it is common practice to place minimum-wage, minimally qualified people in these positions, which all too often are critical-incident positions.

Quite a few people who lack the temperament, maturity, social skills, and tolerance for frequent human contact make up the characteristic profile of a skilled service person. Often people of this kind fall prey to the personal pressures of the day-to-day contact situation and become toxic toward customers. *Contact fatigue* is a recognizable syndrome experienced by front-line people who either can't handle extensive human contact or get too much of it under some circumstances. In the latter case, managers need to make sure that front-line workers are scheduled for sufficient periods away from customers. Without such "off stage" time, the result often can be a form of masked hostility that shows up in *robotization* of the job ("Thank-you-have-a-nice-day—NEXT!") or in petty forms of one-upping directed at the customer.

For example, the overstressed, robotized, misplaced restaurant server may bring the customer a Mexican dish with melted cheese and then "forget" to tell the customer the plate is fresh out of the oven and too hot to touch. A shop clerk may deliberately withhold a bit of useful information that would be helpful to the customer in making a buying decision. One cannot prove that the service rendered is necessarily bad, but it lacks the element of willingness to do something for the customer as another human being.

On the other hand, consider the following episode described by consultant Jay Hall. Hall found himself standing out in the parking lot of a hotel one afternoon, along with many of the other guests, watching the fire department put out a small grease fire that had broken out in the building. Somehow in the melee, the catering staff had managed to set up coffee service on a table in the parking lot. The guests were standing around enjoying coffee, waiting to find out what would happen next. In keeping with the rather light-hearted attitude prevailing in the situation, Hall wisecracked as he came to the coffee pot, "What? No cream?" The young man serving the coffee looked startled and said, "Just a minute!" Right away, he dashed back into the smoke-filled kitchen and came out 2 minutes later with a pitcher of cream. "Now that," says Hall, "is what I call a service attitude."

Of course, that isn't the kind of thing you can specifically teach someone to do in a service business, but you can create the conditions so that your employees are ready, willing, and able to go those extra 4 feet.

BUILDING THE SERVICE CULTURE

The concept of corporate culture is widely discussed these days, and rightly so. Of all the things we can say about the management of service, the most important is this: Unless the shared values, norms, beliefs, and ideologies of the organization—the organization's culture—are clearly and consciously focused on serving the customer, there is virtually no chance that the organization will be able to deliver a consistent quality of service and develop a sustained reputation for service.

Clear performance standards are important. A sensitive and efficient feedback system is important. A clearly defined service package, a good delivery system, proper training, and good management are also important. However, unless the culture of the organization supports and rewards attention to customer needs, service will get no more than lip service over the long run.

Carve that in stone. Knit it into a sampler. However you do it, you must make sure that you carry with you, every working hour, the notion that your job and your part of the organization exist because of and for the customer. If you don't believe that and act on it, others in the organization won't either.

It is easy to believe in the importance of service to the customer and the impact of the culture, and yet not believe that *your* role in the game "counts." If you are the president of the company, it is easy to tell yourself, "But I am at the helm. I hardly ever see a customer anymore. I only see bankers, managers, and stockholders." A staff person can with equal ease rationalize that "I am just a cog in the middle of the machine. I just run the numbers [buy merchandise, conduct training, cut the payroll]. I never see a customer. I have no part in the customer service thing." And it is equally easy for the clerks, call center service reps, salespeople, and field repair people to find a way to say, "Who, me? I don't have any influence over how this outfit treats customers. I just follow the rules right here in the rule book." *Satisfaction of customer needs is either everyone's business, or it might as well be no one's business.* That's the way business will be transacted. The "feel" of who is in charge of the customer's needs is very much a belief that rests in the culture of the organization. That's the way it works at Dell Computer, that's the way they think at Disney, and that's the way they do business at American Express. As a result, that's the way it is: If your organization's culture doesn't show that serving the customer is the most important thing you can offer the customer, it isn't.

Vijay Sathe, management professor at the Peter F. Drucker Graduate School of Management, Claremont Graduate University in Claremont, California, has studied the effects of culture on such organizational processes as communication, cooperation, commitment to goals, decision making, and implementation. He cautions that a strong—in his words "thick"—corporate culture, the kind Disney, AmEx, Dell, REI, and Federal Express are touted to have, is a double-edged sword:

> It is an asset because shared beliefs ease and economize communications, and shared values generate higher levels of cooperation and commitment than is otherwise possible. This is highly efficient.... Culture is a liability when the shared beliefs and values are not in keeping with the needs of the organization, its members, and other constituencies.[1]

One of the strongest service cultures we know of pervades American Express Corp., the New York-based financial services giant that's also the world's number one travel agency. In the mid-1980s, then CEO Lou Gerstner, Jr., delivered this message to AmEx's front-line troops, reflecting a belief system that still holds sway in the organization today:

> Superior service to our global customers is neither a simple slogan to be periodically recited nor an ancient tradition to be abstractly venerated: It is our daily mandate which we must execute flawlessly all over the world. Moreover, because our consumer franchise depends so heavily on unexcelled customer service, our company's internal value system must emphasize the primacy of our dealings with clients above all other business priorities. In my mind, and I believe in the minds of our customers, second-class treatment from American Express equates to intolerable treatment. So perfection—or something very close to perfection—is the only acceptable daily standard for our customer service in American Express.

This message was delivered at one of the company's Great Performers Award luncheons. The Great Performers are those people in American Express who have distinguished themselves by exceptional service to the customer anywhere in the world in the past year. Each year since 1982 several hundred employees have been nominated in each

AmEx region, and regional winners become eligible for the company-wide recognition program and a trip to New York City for the Grand Award Winners recognition dinner.

What does it take to be a great performer at American Express? Some of the AmEx stories are almost unbelievable. In January 1995, an earthquake leveled much of the Osaka/Kobe area of south central Japan. Eight members of the Osaka office of American Express—an office reduced to rubble in the quake—immediately set up shop in temporary quarters in Osaka and Tokyo, and worked an exhausting day and night schedule of providing emergency service to customers. They arranged for evacuations; emergency replacements for lost travel documents, passports, and visas; and made emergency cash advances. They did all this despite the fact the each member of the AmEx team had suffered a loss of personal property or damage to a home. Some even suffered physical injuries.

The exploits of other great performers may be less dramatic, but they leave no less of an impression on grateful customers. AmEx employee Nancy Boccardo of Langhorn, Pennsylvania, for instance, received a call from a customer whose car broke down en route to the airport with a client. Boccardo left her office, picked up the customer and his client, and drove them the remaining 40 miles in time to catch the client's flight. She then arranged to have the customer's car taken to a garage for repairs and drove him back to the office.

Abraham Punnoose and Chetan Goswamy of American Express's Bombay, India, office received a call from a customer who had lost all his travel documents, cash, and credit cards and for the last 30 hours had been held incommunicado in immigration at the Bombay airport. Punnoose convinced the general counsel in New Dehli to go to the airport and issue a replacement passport. In the meantime, Goswamy made new travel arrangements for the customer and personally delivered emergency funds and new airline tickets to him at the airport.

As touching as these stories are for their purely human interest, they are also intriguing as examples of living corporate legends—war stories that illustrate and prove publicly that an organization does value and reward customer service. As Claremont's Sathe puts it, such examples help everyone in the organization interpret and understand the values and beliefs of the organization. When the pivotal value of the culture is service and the stories and legends of the organization revolve around that value, so do most other aspects of that corporate culture.

A final note on American Express: If we take management's words and the hero stories in isolation, they can make the organization sound too good to be true. It sounds like a heaven on earth, an "everybody-is-so-nice" sort of company. American Express is anything but that. We know people who have a bag full of stories about how tough the internal dealings are at AmEx and how fierce the competition is for advancement to ever suggest that the company is a charity in disguise. But those who run American Express day to day understand that at the top of the list of the organization's considerable assets are the people in the trenches who operate its worldwide offices and communications network. In a sense the test of any organization is the culture that top management creates and maintains.

EVERYBODY IS SERVING SOMEBODY

It's not too much of a stretch to say that everyone in a service organization has a service role, even those who never see the customers. This applies to administrative people including supervisors, middle managers, and even executives. Olle Stiwenius of Scandinavian Airlines asked, "What is the purpose of the organization?" And he answered his own question in this way, "*Support*. The organization exists to support the people who serve the customer. It has no other meaning, no other purpose."

It's one thing to get the front-line people into a customer-oriented mode. It's quite another to sell that gospel to people in noncontact roles. It often happens that inside people, those who never deal with the customer, become preoccupied with inside concerns. They may spend so much time and effort dealing with information, procedures, forms, and reports that they become completely introverted in their point of view. "It's somebody else's job to take care of the customer. My job is to make sure these reports get in on time."

When inside people lose the sense of being connected to the customer, regardless of how distant the connection may be, they become bureaucrats. They can no longer see how the results they produce help the company meet the wants and needs of the market. It telegraphs a profound misconception when a person says, "I don't have anything to do with the customers."

The simple message to all the people in an organization should be this:

> *If you're not serving the customer,*
> *you'd better be serving someone who is.*

This is an important realization, and it qualifies as a bona fide principle of service management.

We can classify the people in an organization into only three categories, according to this point of view. The first category includes the *primary service people*, those who have direct, *planned* contact with the customer. The second category includes the *secondary service people*, who usually serve the customer unseen, but who do have *incidental* contact with customers. And the third category includes everybody else; these are the *service-support people*. In a hospital, for example, a primary service person might be the attendant who brings a tray of food to a patient. The secondary service person in this instance would be the person who prepares the food for the patient. A typical service-support person might be the supervisor of the food service unit.

The last statement borders on heresy in the minds of traditionally minded, authoritarian managers. Is management itself a service? The service management viewpoint declares that it is. In a customer-driven culture, management becomes a special form of service, subject to evaluation of its role and its effectiveness, just like other services. Peter Drucker, the elder statesman of management thinkers, once remarked, "Most of what we call management consists of making it difficult for people to get their work done."

This internal service philosophy, expressed in terms of the interplay of services in an organization, remains a foreign concept to many businesses. The idea that everybody in an organization has a "customer" still strikes many American managers as novel, and some as blasphemous. It points the way to a new model for excellence in terms of the total organization. A service-oriented organization can truly "turn on" when everybody, or almost everybody, can focus on knowing whom to serve, learning what the important needs are, and finding effective ways to meet those needs.

MOTIVATION AND COMMITMENT ARE FRAGILE

It is obvious to the most casual observer that business organizations vary remarkably in the overall spirit that exists among their employees. In some organizations there is a high energy level, a sense of accomplishment, and even a sense of excitement on the part of the front-line people. In others there is a prevailing lassitude, a burned-out sense of detachment and indifference.

The service orientation is something most managers dearly love to see in employees, and they recognize it when they see it. But most of them haven't the faintest idea what causes it. Many managers who take pride in their problem-solving skills feel bewildered when presented with evidence of mediocrity or toxic performance at the front-line level. Many of them have little or no idea what to do or where to begin to solve this problem.

The lamentations are familiar: "What's wrong with people these days?" "Don't they realize that the customer is paying their salaries?" "You just can't find good people any more." But really there is nothing wrong with people. It's just that people tend to react to their environments. Motivation and commitment are fragile and circumstantial. As we have previously observed, when the moments of truth go unmanaged, the service level regresses to average, which in a competitive environment means mediocre. To have a high standard of service, it is necessary to create and maintain a *motivating environment* in which service people can find personal reasons for committing their energies to the benefit of the customer.

Many managers consider the psychological factors involved in employee motivation an unfathomable mystery, but we have known as much as we need to know about motivation since the time of Alexander the Great. The human being is a wanting animal. People commit their energies to the extent that what they do brings them what they want. What they want may be psychological—a feeling, a status, or an experience. Or it may be material—money may be sufficient for some. In any case the job of management is to engineer a motivating environment.

J. Willard Marriott, Jr., chief executive of Marriott Hotels, suspects that treating people supportively is antithetical to the attitudes of many managers. "Let's admit it," he says. "In a lot of companies there is a hostile attitude. There are people who like to fire people. Some managers may not know it, but they have created a fear-oriented climate. They may call it 'productivity-oriented,' but if their people are afraid of them and tattle on one another, it's no good." How does Marriott see his role as chief executive? He doesn't hesitate or hedge: "My job," he says, "is to motivate them, teach them, help them, and care about them."

How can we tell when we have a motivating environment? How do we evaluate the psychological setting at the grass roots of the organization? There are four important variables, all of which we can measure through employee surveys, which give a fairly reliable picture of the psychological state of affairs.

- **Quality of work life.** Quality of work life, as reported by people from their own individual points of view. This includes factors like job satisfaction, job security, pay and benefits, opportunities for advancement, competent supervision, harmonious surroundings, and justice and fair play. A high level of perceived quality of work life will not necessarily guarantee high motivation, but a low level will almost certainly demotivate people.

- **Morale.** High morale is usually a necessary indication, but not always a sufficient one, for high commitment. It is possible for service people to have low morale for any number of reasons and still do their jobs with a high level of commitment and creativity. Conversely, it is possible for them to have high morale and yet not give their best energies to the job. But in general the link between morale and commitment is fairly clear.

- **Energy level.** This is measured largely in terms of a sense of individual wellness and psychological well-being. Energy level, as the term is used here, implies the opposite of *burnout*. Service people in various stages of burnout typically have low personal energy and find it difficult to get excited about any new venture.

- **Optimism.** A general sense of *optimism*—a belief that there are new possibilities, new ways to do things, new levels to achieve— often goes together with morale and energy level, but not always.

If the leaders of the organization hope to foster high levels of motivation and commitment on the part of customer contact people, the first task is to evaluate the present motivational environment. If the environment needs repair, the second task is to repair it. Until the environment is reasonably ready, there can be little hope of lasting improvement in the service results.

BRASS BANDS AND ARMBANDS DON'T WORK

It is tempting for some executives to resort to corny theatrical measures in the hope of getting the front-line employees turned on. Such measures are usually a substitute for the more expensive and more challenging process of reengineering the motivational environment. A fairly typical approach is for executives to hold a top-management retreat, unveil the new corporate service campaign, invent a catchy slogan, and send all the middle managers out into the countryside as evangelists of the new gospel. Typical elements of this theatrical approach include making videotapes of the chief executive expressing his commitment to customer service, putting up posters, passing out lapel buttons, posting service proclamations to the corporate intranet, and selecting the service employee of the month.

Unfortunately, without an infrastructure in place to carry out a concrete program, the show-biz approach typically fades away in a few months. In more extreme cases it falls flat in the face of employee cynicism. Some executives talk and act as if they believe employees never think about what's going on in the organization and that they never discuss things with one another. Many senior employees have lived through one "flavor of the month" after another, and have long since given up expecting top management to follow through on any major campaign or program.

The employees in one large organization developed a simple catchphrase to express their attitude toward years of unfulfilled management campaigns—"BOHICA." It's translation is: "Bend over—here it comes again!" In the face of this kind of cynicism on the part of mature working adults, it's no wonder that many executives approach the idea of an organizationwide campaign with apprehension.

Note please that we are not saying managers be grave, stone-faced, and humorless—the embodiment of the captains-of-industry portraits that still hang in far too many boardrooms. Quite the contrary. Skilled executives have often been great cheerleaders. Bill Marriott says, for example, "If you don't generate excitement, you don't generate much." Herb Kelleher, chairman of Southwest Airlines, can be practically evangelical in the way he pumps up his employees and promotes having a good time on the job. Showing enthusiasm and excitement about the mission of the organization is one thing, but partaking in a shallow, cynical, superficial "whip-up-the-troops" campaign is quite another. Your employees are as quick to spot a con job as are your customers. Like golf, baseball, and tennis, it's the follow-through that makes the difference.

An even more grave mistake than launching an unsupported theatrical campaign inside the organization is launching a collateral advertising campaign in the marketplace. It makes little sense to brag to customers about committed employees and quality service before the message is true. Many executives are remarkably naive about the length of time needed to make a major change in the organization's culture. An advertising campaign promising exceptional service launched by a company that delivers a mediocre level of service can easily backfire with double effect. Before the campaign customers simply consider the service mediocre and don't think much about it. Along comes an advertising campaign promising excellence, and suddenly the customers perceive the grotesque disparity between the promise and the reality. It would have been better not to advertise at all in such a case. Better yet would be to make real improvements in the service level and then advertise them.

What we call the "brass-bands-and-armbands" approach usually doesn't work without the presence of three critical components:

1. A clear, concrete message that conveys a particular service strategy which front-line people can begin to act upon.
2. Significant *modeling* by managers, that is, demonstrating by their behavior that they intend to enforce and reward service-oriented actions taken on behalf of the customer.
3. An energetic follow-through process, in which management takes action to provide the necessary training and resources and to align the systems and procedures of the organization to support the new service philosophy.

SMILE TRAINING DOESN'T DO IT EITHER

Another common approach that many managers take in their search for better front-line performance is trying to teach employees to "have better attitudes." This has its own peculiar pitfalls. Attitudes seem to be very important, but they are also very hard to pin down. The concept of an attitude becomes especially elusive when one tries to isolate it to a teachable definition. We can give plenty of examples of "good attitude" and "bad attitude," but can one teach a person to have a good attitude? We want front-line people to be customer-oriented, and we know this attitude when we see it, but we don't know how to describe it except by example. People who specialize in corporate training often wrestle with the question of attitudes. How can we teach a person to be friendly, for example?

The attitude-training approach usually involves training programs that focus on specific social techniques, such as eye contact, smiling, tone of voice, standards of dress, and the like. Many employees refer to this kind of training as "smile training" or "charm school." To make matters worse, the training might have been inflicted on them by a hypocritical manager whose own attitude about people could not be viewed as a model.

Certainly, front-line people need to know how to handle irate customers. They also need to know how much abuse you expect them to tolerate, how to calm a fevered brow—even the brow of bona fide customer from hell—and how far to go in righting a wrong. They may even need to learn some psychological self-protection skills, but *not*, we contend, how to smile and be civil.

Frequently organizations can thwart the will to serve by introducing contradictory systems. At one major airline senior management gets service "religion" with clockwork predictability. Every few months the chief executive officer gets up to his elbows in customer complaint letters, so he orders up a new batch of customer service training. Each time he finds a new vendor or a new in-house manager who is willing to take yet another crack at improving customer relations. Out goes the directive again: "Send your people to the customer service program!" The complaints trail off for the rest of the quarter, but the second week of the next quarter is when the audit people go out into the field to run stopwatch rallies on the front-line people.

"They are moving the lines too slowly," announces the operations auditor after a few hours of timing the ticket agents. And of course the station manager, the boss of the ticket agents, feels the heat and responds with, "Knock off the small talk with customers. Get 'em moving!" Then the chief's in-basket starts filling up with complaints again, and the cycle is ready to start all over.

Front-line training can play an important part in improving service orientation, but only if the people who receive the training see it as worthwhile and helpful. Too often, experienced employees find the proposition of smile training or attitude training insulting. Some of them may desperately need to improve their social skills, but if they don't think they do, then training will probably not help, especially when nothing else in the system changes. With training, it's not the case that if a little is good, a lot is better. Relevance counts as much as, if not more than, hours logged in the classroom or at the computer.

HOW TO USE TRAINING AND DEVELOPMENT EFFECTIVELY

Properly used, training and development can have huge payoffs in service performance. According to one renowned study, employees who receive formal job training reach "standard" performance levels faster (72 percent faster), generate less waste (70 percent less), and are better at customer troubleshooting (130 percent better) than employees who learn their jobs through the time-honored but highly inefficient "watch Jill for a few hours, and then we'll turn you loose on customers" approach.

Corporate training methods have now evolved to a fairly sophisticated level, and training programs typically involve more than employees sitting around listening to lectures. Techniques of job task analysis, competency modeling, computer-based job simulation, and training needs assessment can produce well-designed training programs targeted at the specific learning needs of the organization, often shortening the time from "start to solo" for new service hires. With the advent of online training and performance support, customer contact people can access more troubleshooting and product knowledge information when and where they need it, not tied to a training department's rigid class schedule.

The key to making training pay off is knowing what we want the trainees to be able to do when they have finished the program. An effective training process starts with a performance analysis. We must analyze the various jobs to be done in serving the customer well and then spell out the knowledge, attitudes, and skills required of the person doing the job. Indeed, the concept of training, among experts in the United States and a number of other counties, is evolving toward the premise of performance improvement and performance assurance.

To make a difference in customers' perceptions of your organization, front-line service training also has to be about more than the generic service principles found in your organization's policy manual. To be effective, your training should be tailored to the specifics of your own business and your own customers and their unique problems, priorities, and demands. It should reflect the complexity of the world your people must perform in day in and day out. It should immerse them in customers' most common queries and complaints and the best ways you've found of handling them.

Training should also strike the right balance between teaching technical skills and people skills. A service rep who quickly fixes a customer problem or competently installs a product—but in a sloppy or rude manner or after missing a scheduled appointment—can often do more harm than good for repeat business.

The point takes on particular importance with the emergence and growth of the Internet, e-mail, and live text chat as customer support tools. The tendency is to try to win customers over with the sheer speed and efficiency of the technology, often giving short shrift to social or interpersonal skills still required of service reps working at computer keyboards. As John Goodman, head of e-Satisfy.com, remarks, "At the end of the day, E-customer contact is still a human activity." In a March 2000 study done in conjunction with the International Customer Service Association (ICSA), e-Satisfy.com found that, "While new and emerging technologies will continue to enhance the efficiency of E-customer service, the real improvements to both customer satisfaction, loyalty and cost-effectiveness will come from improving the human disciplines, such as use of effective hiring profiles, training, and management practices that address new multi-channel contact environments."[2]

Once we know what it takes to do a particular service job well, we can figure out the most cost-effective way to help people learn those capabilities. Here we have a wide variety of options. If the job knowledge and tasks are fairly simple, then on-the-job training may be all that is needed. But travel with care, since customers have little tolerance for new hires in the throes of on-the-job training. More demanding jobs may require special, classroom-based training programs designed just for the needs of those positions, along with effective coaching and targeted performance review.

It's also important to recognize that different people may have different learning needs. A seasoned service employee coming from another organization or industry will probably not benefit from an A-B-C type of training program designed for entry-level people just coming into the workforce from college or high school.

There is also a place in a good training plan for a certain amount of personal enrichment training. This is a method that Scandinavian Airlines used especially well. Personal enrichment training deals with matters such as self-esteem, confidence, values clarification, interpersonal skills, stress management, and goal setting. The theory behind this kind of training is that helping people review their personal effectiveness and rekindle their energies will automatically pay off on the job. The belief is that persons who feel better about themselves and who have a clearer perspective on life goals, personal skills, and rewards, will have more creative energy to put into the job.

Personal enrichment training is usually a more promising avenue than trying to teach people to have a "good attitude," which is the usual approach in smile training. Rather than focus on attitude, the training dwells on personal skills. This avoids the intellectual trap of trying to define attitudes for people in sterile behavioral terms. This is not to say that we should try to outlaw the discussion of attitudes in training, merely that we should focus on more concrete factors. We can approach the matter of attitude on the job by encouraging employees to strive for measurable results that show up in terms of customer feedback. If we get high marks on customers' report cards, we can conclude that the service

---

JOB AIDS: WHEN TRAINING ISN'T THE ANSWER

Despite its many benefits, training isn't always the right solution to service quality problems. The Sierra Pacific Power Co. in Reno, Nevada, opted instead for simple job aids—in-the-field reference guides—in its quest to improve the service skills of front-line workers.

Customer feedback had indicated that many of the utility's field personnel—meter readers, linemen, and others who regularly came in contact with customers—were ill prepared to answer customer questions about company operations that didn't pertain directly to their specialties, such as questions about payment plans, tree trimming, or emergency services. Even more problematic was that most of the field workers didn't know to whom at Sierra to refer these customers for answers.

When the problem was brought before the company's Customer Focus Training Committee—charged with identifying ways to improve external and internal customer service via training initiatives—the decision was not to call for more training but to develop a job aid—a trifold, laminated reference card that field workers could carry in shirt pockets to use as a resource guide in assisting customers. The card lists the most common functions inquired about by Sierra customers and matching phone numbers to call for answers. When customers have questions, the field personnel refer to their reference cards and then write down the appropriate phone number on "Happy to Serve You" cards also carried with them, handing the card over to customers.

people have the right attitudes. The contribution of training is to help them figure out the right tactics and actions to take in dealing with the customer.

SELECTION: FINDING PEOPLE WHO ARE WILLING AND ABLE TO SERVE

Another important part of the formula for success in service is filling service jobs with people who can do them effectively. Aside from levels of job knowledge and skill, which can vary considerably, there are several key factors that make for success and effectiveness in dealing with customers.

For one thing, a service person needs to have at least an adequate level of maturity and *self-esteem*. It is very difficult for a person to be genuine and cordial toward a customer if that person is moody, depressed, or angry about his or her life and circumstances. Second, the service person needs to have a fairly high degree of *social skill*. He or she needs to be reasonably articulate, aware of the normal rules for social interaction, and able to say and do what is necessary to establish rapport with a customer and maintain it. And third, he or she needs to have a fairly high level of *tolerance for contact*. This means that they can engage in many successive episodes of short interaction without becoming psychologically overloaded or overstressed. Contact overload is a recognizable syndrome in front-line work, and some people are more susceptible to it than others. The effective service person needs to be able to withstand many contact episodes without becoming robotic, detached, or unempathetic.

All three of these requirements add up to what some psychologists call "emotional labor." In emotional labor jobs, the self is the instrument of action. The service person must deliberately involve his or her feelings in the situation. He or she may not particularly feel like being cordial and becoming a 1-minute friend to the next customer who approaches, but that is indeed what front-line work requires. Unfortunately, all three of these key characteristics are subjective and difficult to measure. Pencil-and-paper tests are out in many cases, at least in American industries, because of the possibility of discrimination and because they are very difficult to validate. But there are some ways of improving your hiring odds beyond appraising snazzy résumés and gauging applicants' practiced one-on-one interviewing skills. Plenty of organizations claim success using behavior-based role-playing in interviews, for instance. Some read from a transcript of an actual conversation in which a customer has a specific need to resolve. They then have the candidate pose questions as if he or she were the service rep and the interviewer were the customer. The idea is to look for open-ended, probing questions that yield the maximum amount of information rather than simple yes or no questions. Other organizations make "angry customer" tapes and role-play with job candidates. The candidate listens to the irate customer, with the interviewer reading lines from a transcript and having the candidate respond aloud.

Some organizations even engage potential job applicants in role-playing exercises over the phone *before* inviting them into face-to-face interviews, screening out candidates who do poorly. The phone screening saves both the interviewer and the candidate valuable work or travel time.

Disney has been known to begin its front-line hiring process by showing all interested candidates a video *before* they even fill out an application. The video describes the "fit" necessary between employer and employee for someone to be hired and stay in the job. Disney claims that the video itself culls between 10 and 15 percent of prospective workers who decide they're not interested in Disney after all, saving the company time and recruiting costs.

It's important that any selection system screen for psychological hardiness and the ability to work under pressure. It takes a special person to deal with the craziness of intense, daily customer contact. In this context, previous summer jobs at a local retailer or a fast-food chain that were thought to be mindless suddenly become important performance indicators. Retail experience in particular can be a good litmus test; no matter how good a candidate is, he or she will have been forced to deal regularly with unhappy customers.

Selecting for flexible and nimble thinking also is important. Part of the hiring regimen of one software company we know is to ask customer service job candidates for an example of how they bent or broke a rule to help get a job done. In essence, the organization looks for people who have said somewhere in the past, "This is a dumb rule. It does not help me take care of customers. It gets in the way. I am going to break it, bend it, or find a way around it, and figure out later if I need forgiveness."

Personnel selection, placement, and turnover also present special difficulties in service industries, largely because of economics. With few exceptions, front-line jobs are typically low paying positions that have relatively little career potential. Turnover rates of more than 100 percent are commonplace in these jobs in many companies. Because of the structure of such industries and because of prevailing customs about pay and advancement, a service job is not generally a highly prized position.

However, the work of two Harvard University researchers showed how vital good selection and employee retention strategies are, not only to customer satisfaction but to reducing the high-recruitment and new-employee training costs associated with high turnover. Leonard Schlesinger and James L. Heskett found, for example, that at Marriott Corp. a 10 percent decrease in employee turnover was directly related to a 1 to 3 percent decrease in lost customers and a more than $50 million increase in revenues.[3]

THE IMPORTANCE OF PERFORMANCE
MEASUREMENT, COACHING, AND FEEDBACK

A customer-oriented front line is definitely what we want. However, it is often a challenge to form a clear image in the collective organizational mind about what it means to be customer-oriented. In some cases it is possible to develop standards for service performance fairly easily. In other cases it may be quite a challenge.

We need to communicate the service strategy to front-line people from the outset, so that they know what we want them to concentrate on. Then we need to continually let them know how they're doing. The weakest link in many organizations is the lack of a "closed-loop" feedback process that gives corrective coaching to the people delivering service on a day-to-day basis. In many cases, if not most, front-line workers are forced to guess about how well they're fulfilling the service strategy. A study by Development Dimensions International found managers' feedback and coaching skills to be sorely lacking. Overall satisfaction with coaching and feedback was rated 3.5 on a scale of 1 to 5 in a survey study of 1149 people. Effectiveness of the performance appraisal process in general was given an alarming 2.9 on the same scale.[4]

The need to provide performance measurement and feedback to service people may be likened to the need for effective market research in order to set service strategy. If we don't know what evaluation factors customers have on their report cards—what performance factors are most critical to ensuring their repeat business—we don't know what actions on the part of the service people will get high grades. Consequently, we don't know what to tell them about the effectiveness of their contributions.

In a large West Coast city, for example, managers wanted to improve the service performance in the area of permits and licenses. City executives directed subordinate managers and organization development staff to "find ways to make that function 'customer-oriented.' The people coming in to apply for licenses and permits are *citizens* and *taxpayers*. We're not doing somebody a favor when we provide a permit to build an addition to a house, we're doing a service. We must treat them like customers, not like naughty children."

When a staff task force went to work on the problem, it ran headlong into an immediate dilemma: how to define "customer-oriented service." Just about everyone could offer some for instances and some horror stories they would like to keep from happening again, but the question turned out to be more complicated than it appeared. Was smiling at the permit applicants proof of customer orientation? Was speed in processing applications the primary factor? Was personal treatment more important than speed and efficiency?

The task force knew it first had to determine what report card citizen-customers were using to rate the service. What expectations and needs did they have? Without such a model, how could managers hope to instruct front-line people in better service? How could they hope to train new people in good service behavior, if the task force itself couldn't define it? This led to customer research that identified the key needs and expectations of the permit applicants and formulated a set of service standards for people involved in the permit process. Then the city could begin to measure performance by periodically repeating the market research in miniature, along with customer surveys and spot interviews.

Regular measurement and feedback, properly applied, tend to make an organization a *cybernetic* entity, one that responds adaptively to its environment. The front-line employees are more aware of what works and what doesn't, and they have a better sense of their own effectiveness. Management also has a better picture of what's happening overall, and can use the measurement information to see how well the service strategy is working.

$$8$$

DULL MOMENTS AND SHINING MOMENTS

"It's kind of fun to do the impossible."

—*Walt Disney*

W E HUMANS HAVE A LONG history of learning from stories. Ancient hunters returning victorious to the home cave may have paused to celebrate their victory with some woolly mammoth hors d'oeuvres, but then they assembled the tribe to tell the story of how they tracked, chased, and finally brought down the beast. Those stories made the hunt memorable and passed along hard-won knowledge about how to pursue and kill prey to those still learning the art of the hunt. But more than hunting skills were passed along; early humans also learned to love good stories well told. We still do. We love stories and parables. We love hearing them. We love telling them. And we learn from them.[1]

Clearly, we can learn a great deal about customer focus by dissecting the elements of the service triangle and analyzing the interplay among people, systems, and strategy. But tales from the customer service trenches instruct on a more emotional level. These real-life moments of truth don't just put a human face on the theory; they teach, inform, entertain, warm, and warn. Good stories strike a common chord within us, and they nudge our view of the world just enough so that we learn and remember something new.

The following stories come from a variety of sources: Some are "found" stories—stories we discovered in newspapers, magazines, and newsletters; some are memorable incidents from our own lives and those of our friends, family, and co-workers; and some have been sent to us by the people on the giving or receiving end of the moment of truth in question. What these stories have in common is that they are instructive, thought provoking, and, in some cases, even inspiring.

We have divided them into "dull moments"—mishandled moments of truth—and "shining moments"—moments of truth when human creativity and commitment resulted in a memorable experience for a customer.

We start with the dull. Each of these tales illustrates in some way a failure of one or more of the three critical elements of the service triangle: The organization's service strategy was faulty or nonexistent, its front-line people failed to come through for the customer, or its service system got in the way with nonsensical procedures, rules, or policies. As you read the following stories, keep the service triangle in mind and make your own diagnosis. Which component or combination of components of the service triangle went wrong?

At the other end of the spectrum, the stories of shining moments demonstrate how customer interactions can be positive and memorable when the elements of the service triangle work together. As you read these stories, identify the key component you believe made the difference.

THE DEVASTATINGLY DULL

Dull Moment #1: Learning—the Hard Way—to Say "Sorry"
An uneventful Northwest Airlines flight from Orlando, Florida, to Minneapolis, Minnesota, normally a $3\frac{1}{2}$ hour flight, was beginning its descent when it suddenly began to circle instead. The captain announced that a thunderstorm over the Twin Cities would delay landing for a few minutes. Soon he informed passengers that the plane didn't have enough fuel to continue circling, so the flight would be diverted to Fargo, North Dakota.

After landing in Fargo, another announcement came from the flight deck: Since the pilot expected to take off as soon as the plane was refueled, passengers would not be allowed to leave the plane. As the minutes ticked past, passengers *were* allowed to leave their seats, and the line lengthened outside the one functioning bathroom in coach. After an hour, passenger grumbling began in earnest. Flight attendants insisted that they'd run out of soft drinks—and hard ones. And, although the airport terminal was less than 100 yards away, the staff did not replenish the supply.

At hour two, the volume of passenger complaints increased, although civility prevailed. At hour three, the captain's insistence that he wouldn't allow anyone off the plane because he expected to be cleared for take off to Minneapolis "momentarily" was met with groans and unprintable epithets. A flight attendant was the first to snap. Red-faced and furious, she began to berate a complaining passenger: "You don't know what a thunderstorm can do to a plane—tear it from the sky, rip it apart. We've got to wait here." She was talking about a thunderstorm that had passed 3 hours earlier.

Finally, 4 hours after landing in Fargo, the plane took off for Minneapolis. After a 40-minute flight, it landed safely, but taxied to the far reaches of the airport and pulled to a dead stop in a deserted corner of the tarmac. Now what? The plane had lost its arrival gate hours earlier, and had to wait for one to open up. After an hour, the pilot announced that a passenger had a medical emergency and immediately taxied to a gate.

As frazzled and furious passengers made their escape from the 727, there was nary a Northwest employee in sight—no flight attendant, no pilot, no gate agent. No offers to reroute those with missed connections. No offer of frequent flyer miles or even a free drink coupon. Passengers were left only with the firm resolve to write scathing letters of complaint to Northwest Airlines—and to avoid it in the future whenever possible.

A few years later, Northwest passengers subjected to similar treatment didn't acquiesce so easily. During the now notorious snowstorm debacle at Detroit Metro Airport in January 1999, dozens of Northwest planes sat on the tarmac—some for more than 8 hours—stranding passengers in planes without food, water, or, in some cases, functioning lavatories. The incident resulted in a class-action lawsuit filed on behalf of more than 7000 passengers against Northwest, which was charged with unlawful detainment and other less egregious customer service infractions. The airline settled the suit for $7.1 million in January 2001.[2]

Dull Moment #2: Perils of Policy

Mark Zweig of Nattick, Massachusetts, stopped at a local store to make some last minute purchases for his Fourth of July party. Though the store had recently changed hands and he'd experienced some service slip ups, he continued to shop there because it was close to his home.

No more.

Zweig handed the clerk a credit card for his $18 worth of purchases and was curtly told, "Can't take it." When asked why, the clerk told him there was a $25 minimum purchase required for credit card use. Zweig said he'd been coming there for years and had never encountered this problem. "You have to understand," the clerk said, "we pay three-and-a-half percent on credit card purchases. It's an inconvenience for us."

Zweig asked if he was going to be turned away for want of $7 and "inconvenience" on the part of the "convenience" store. The clerk shrugged and said, "That's the policy." When Zweig said he would not be back, the clerk's response was, "The door swings both ways."[3]

Dull Moment #3: The Role of Guilt

One of Karl Albrecht's former staff members related a peculiar "service" episode in a hotel. She and her husband had just checked into the hotel in the midafternoon. They hadn't brought in their suitcases, since they were just driving through and would only be staying one night. They had hung up their clothes for the next day in the closet, and they both were in the small anteroom just off the main sleeping room.

They heard a key turn in the door lock, the door opened, and in walked the assistant manager of the hotel, accompanied by a young lady from the front desk staff. "Judging from their conversation," the staff member recounted, "they thought the room was unoccupied, and they'd decided to use it for a little 'recreational' break. When we came out into the room and let them know it was occupied, they were caught completely off guard. They didn't know what to say."

Obviously embarrassed, the two employees left. Not particularly dismayed, but certainly amused, the staff member thought little more of the incident. However, at checkout time, she noticed that the room charge had been canceled and that breakfast was complimentary. "Maybe," she said, "guilt plays some kind of a part in customer service."

Dull Moment #4: Mission Impossible

Judy Fishman, publisher of *Dental Lab Management Today*, was on a mission: She wrote to over 100 toy manufacturers in hopes of locating a particular stuffed dog her son had loved—and lost. A number of empathetic companies responded, two offering replacement dogs and several others with calls or notes. The one that had an exact replica of the dog sent a note requesting a check for $7.75.

"I immediately sent a check," Fishman related. "And then I waited. And waited. And finally left on vacation. Upon my return I found a letter from the company with my check attached. The customer service rep wrote to say she was sorry, but she had quoted me the wrong price. If I still wanted to purchase the item, I was to please send a check for $17.

"I called and asked the rep if she would mail the dog before she received my replacement check. She said no and that it was their policy not to send anything out until the check has been received.

"I said I understood, but that I really wanted it as soon as possible. Would they take a credit card?

"'We don't take credit cards,' she said.

"'Is there anything I can do to speed delivery?' I asked.

"'No,' she said. When they received my check they would send the dog.

"So I waited once more. Another 2 weeks went by. Still no dog. I called to ask a rep what happened to my order. She told me the company, according to policy, was waiting for my check to clear. I told her that in comparison to reactions from other toy manufacturers, her company's policies made it hard for me to do business with her.

"She replied that they weren't like other companies.

"That was painfully obvious."[4]

Dull Moment #5: The Age Limit for PB&J Sandwiches

A customer looked over the menu in a restaurant and saw very few choices that seemed appealing. Suddenly she spotted an interesting option: a peanut butter and jelly sandwich. "Now that sounds like just the thing," she beamed. "I haven't had a good peanut butter and jelly sandwich in ages. That and a glass of milk will hit the spot." When she asked the waitress for the sandwich, she received a chilly reply: "Sorry. That's in the children's section on the menu. You can't order that."

The customer asked, "I don't understand. Why does a person have to be a child to order that particular sandwich? That's really what I would like to have." When the waitress firmly refused to place the order, the customer asked to speak to the restaurant manager. He offered the same story. "I'm sorry, ma'am. We don't serve children's orders to adults." Angry and incredulous, she decided to have lunch somewhere else.

Dull Moment #6: Trust-Busting System

When Ken Summers, a Colorado Springs consultant, checked into a hospital for neck surgery, he was told that he had to answer an extensive list of questions about his health and personal and insurance data. He was then presented with a plastic card he was told would automatically call up his records throughout his stay at the hospital. "I was told I'd never have to give the data again," Summers said.

But as he went through pre-op tests and checks, every lab, every technician, every doctor, every nurse asked him to answer the same set of questions. "I tried to give them the card, but they didn't know what it was," he said. It was clear to him that the hospital's systems were set up for administrative convenience rather than the customer's.

"I was sitting in a room filled with cold metal objects when the seventh nurse of the day walked in and asked why I was there. By the time I was taken into surgery, my dissatisfaction had reached this point: I noticed there were two clocks in the operating room: One said five minutes to noon, one said five after noon. All I could think was, which one will they use for my time of death?"[5]

Dull Moment #7: Poor Training Shows

Dennis Huber of Alto, Michigan, was on his way to pick up his wife when he decided to stop at a Mobil service station. He filled up his gas tank, went inside, and gave the clerk his Visa card. The computer prepared a transaction slip, and then the clerk told Huber he also needed his phone number or license number. Huber told him he didn't need that information and that he preferred not to provide it.

The clerk became visibly agitated and insisted that Huber give him the information because it was "company policy." Huber explained that neither his contract with Visa nor any law required him to provide that information. The clerk again refused to let Huber sign the charge slip.

After several minutes, Huber told the clerk he would have to leave for the airport, whether or not he let him sign the slip. The clerk replied,

"You'd better not try to leave." Huber could only infer that the clerk planned to physically prevent him from leaving. At that point the clerk called the police and told them that a customer was refusing to give him a phone number or license number.

Since Huber didn't have time to wait for the police to arrive and straighten the clerk out, he suggested that if the clerk had to have his license number he could easily step out the door and see the license plate. "This seemed like a revelation to him, and he did so, and finally allowed me to leave," said Huber.

Huber's take on the incident? "I felt he was not only poorly trained but was somewhat unstable. Imagine the headline: 'Customer Assaulted by Clerk for Refusing to Divulge License Number.' Imagine me ever setting foot in that station again."[6]

Dull Moment #8: Bad Systems Win Every Time

Kathy Ridge, a Charlotte, North Carolina, consultant, went to the grocery story one evening to pick up a deli tray. The night clerk informed her that the woman who made them up had left for the evening. "I didn't know that making deli trays was such a specialized skill," was her first response.

Ridge decided to improvise by building her own. She asked the clerk to thin-slice a half pound of ham. He did, wrapping the slices in waxed butcher paper, writing the price on the package, and putting it on the deli counter. She repeated the process with turkey, roast beef, Swiss cheese, American, and Colby. She selected more than $20 worth of food.

As the neatly wrapped packages piled up on the counter, she noticed a stack of large empty plastic trays on a back table. Sudden inspiration: "How much for one of those with a plastic lid?"

"Lady," came the response, "you can't buy a tray unless you buy a *tray.*"

"Excuse me?"

"*You can't buy a tray unless you buy a TRAY.*"

Ridge first surmised she was dealing with a front-line person in desperate need of a personality transplant. But she soon realized the real issue: The store's inventory control system was based on counting the trays. It wasn't that the clerk didn't *want* to help her. He just couldn't figure out how to do it.[7]

SHINING MOMENTS ON PARADE

And now, in dramatic contrast, here are some shining moments. These are stories that illustrate what is possible when the people and the systems come together to give their best to customers.

Shining Moment #1: Making Any Wish Come True

Birthday wishes do come true, especially if you're wishing for them at the Italianni's restaurant in Plymouth, Minnesota, and your server is Deb Gordon. When a guest celebrating his birthday at the restaurant wished for a special dessert—an item not on Italianni's regular dessert tray, but from another eating establishment—Deb didn't flinch.

"We try to work by the GRAND philosophy here, which means, 'Guests' requests are never denied,' " Deb said. "When my customer said he wished he could get a Peanut Buster Parfait from Dairy Queen for his birthday dessert, I wanted to make sure he got his wish."

Deb told her manager about the request, and arrangements were made to get to the nearest Dairy Queen to get the specified dessert. A short 15 minutes later, Deb presented the Peanut Buster Parfait to her stunned birthday guest.

"It was fun to see the look on his face," she says. "It made the dinner very special for him."[8]

Shining Moment #2: Rip-Roaring Recovery

It was a foggy night in San Ramon, California, and Jim Clepper was having trouble locating his hotel. Just as he was about to give up, he came upon a sign that read, "Marriott Construction Gate."

Through a computer glitch at Marriott Hotels and Resorts' reservation center, Clepper had been booked at a Marriott that wasn't slated to open for another 6 months.

Although a bit agitated, Clepper wasn't overly perturbed about the incident; he found a room in a nearby town and went about his business. But his travel agent suggested he write a note of complaint to the hotel chairman, J. W. Marriott. He did, and the result made Clepper a Marriott fan for life.

Marriott sent him a personal letter of apology along with a voucher for a free night's stay. "I thought that was the end of it," said Clepper. But soon after, Marriott's reservations department also wrote to apologize. "Then I thought it was over for sure."

Not so. The matter came to the attention of a marketing director at the new Marriott in San Ramon, who told the general manager about it. The two decided to have some fun with it. Clepper would be brought back for a better experience when the hotel was finally open.

The welcome mat rolled out for him included free first-class air travel from Houston to Oakland. At Oakland International Airport, a helicopter picked up Clepper and his wife and flew them to the hotel's front door, where all the employees stood at attention to greet him like a visiting potentate.[9]

Shining Moment #3: Beyond the Call of Duty

A GE customer called the GE Answer Center asking for one of GE's famed *Microwave Guide and Cookbooks*. There was nothing unusual about that except that customer Nelta Rea wanted a version first published in the early 1980s, a version that has been updated several times since then. Fortunately, Rea was connected with GE center rep Marsha White.

"I tried to interest her in one of our new cookbooks, but she really had her heart set on that old one and the recipes in it," White said. "When she described the book's cover, I realized it was one I had in my own cookbook collection. She offered to buy it from me, but I told her that every cookbook deserves to be used, and I'd be glad to send it to her free, since she would use it."

Rea was so impressed with Marsha and the GE Answer Center that she sent a letter to CEO Jack Welch. In describing the incident, she wrote:

"Now, I think that's beyond the call of duty. We built a new home and have all GE appliances in it. I know you have a lot of good employees, but in my book Marsha White and [her supervisor] Tina Hammons are GREAT!"[10]

Shining Moment #4: Exceeding Expectations

L.L. Bean's reputation for service recovery has reached almost mythical proportions. To Karen Larson, a management consultant in Maple Grove, Minnesota, the company's penchant for exceeding expectations is rooted firmly in reality.

Larson sent back to L.L. Bean a shirt she had purchased that had worn out after many years of hard use. The shirt had frayed at the cuffs in an unusual way, and Larson thought the company might be interested in that kind of product information from a customer. "I made it clear in my letter that I was not looking for any sort of compensation from them," she said.

Not long afterward, Larson received a phone call from an L.L. Bean customer service rep who told her that the company would like to replace the shirt but that it no longer carried it in the color she had originally purchased. "Although I made it clear I wasn't expecting a replacement, it seemed important to her," Larson said. So Larson gave the rep her color preference and size information. The rep then told her that the shirt was on sale for half price, so L.L. Bean would be sending *two* shirts to her at no cost.

"Just when I was thinking the company had managed to exceed my already high expectations," Larson said, "they did one more thing: A few days after I got the shirts in the mail, I received a check to cover the postage cost I had incurred when mailing the original shirt."[11]

Shining Moment #5: Manny to the Rescue

Kristin Tillotson's century-old upright Steinway piano had to be moved from an icy sidewalk to the second floor of an old duplex with a narrow, U-shaped staircase and narrower-still doorway. The two movers hired to muscle the 900-pound load into its new home measured, mumbled, and shook their heads. Finally one of them said, "Call Manny."

So Tillotson, a staff writer at the *Minneapolis Star Tribune*, called Manny's Piano Moving Inc. of Ham Lake, Minnesota. Tillotson's moment of truth with Roland (Manny) Schwartz was so memorable that she wrote a column about it. We'll let her tell the rest of the story:

"There sat my piano, chilling on the curb. Fifteen minutes later, another truck pulled up. A wiry, silver-haired man and a couple more guys got out.... He strode up the steps, got out his tape measure and assessed the scene.

'We're gonna get her up there,' he said in a pass-the-salt tone....

"Then Manny went to work, giving terse orders to his team as they pinched flesh and performed involuntary plies to keep the piano intact.... As the others suspended the giant instrument of torture precariously on its end over a step, Manny stuck his head underneath to check the width. A slip of someone's wrist and he'd be one-dimensional.

"'OK, stop, it's not worth your life!' I yelled.

"He ignored me....

"... 'How much extra do I owe you?' I asked, my eyes on the piano now standing in my living room—safe, sound and still in tune, 45 minutes and three extra lifters since it had landed on my doorstep.

"Manny straightened, wiped his hands on his jeans and picked up his gloves.

"'Nothing,' he said, looking no more strained than if he'd just taken a sip of coffee. 'Well, just this—don't go moving to a new place in the next six months.'"[12]

Shining Moment #6: Pets—and the People Who Love to Feed Them
Lori Smith, a customer service rep at Hill's Pet Nutrition Inc., the Topeka, Kansas, manufacturer of Science Diet and other specialty pet foods, received a call on a toll-free line from a distressed pet owner in Texas. The woman's 12-year-old cocker spaniel was not expected to live through the night due to a severe heart condition. Just before leaving the university veterinary center with her dog, the owner had received one of Hill's special dietary foods to feed her ailing pet if it did survive the night—a hope the vet had cautioned against.

When morning came, the cocker spaniel had indeed survived, and the owner called Hill's to discuss the use of the special food. Hill's is obsessed with the well-being of dogs and cats. In fact, the company was founded to further the work of a veterinarian, Mark Morris, Sr., who pioneered the treatment of ailing pets through diet. The company's customer care program is called the BUDDY system in honor of the German shepherd who was one of the world's first seeing-eye dogs. In 1943, Buddy had developed kidney failure, and Dr. Morris had successfully treated him by changing the nutrient levels in his food.

It seems the Texas vet had given the sick cocker spaniel a reformulated Hill's pet food that hadn't actually been put into distribution yet. Now, the owner couldn't locate more of it. Believing the dog might survive longer than a day or two, Lori went into action. She calculated the feeding requirements for the dog and began a search for more of the reformulated food. After a number of dead-end phone calls and nearly an hour's effort, she finally found someone in the company who could supply the new formula if the dog continued to defy the odds.

By the end of the day, Lori and her new-found confederate had rounded up two cases of the reformulated product and had shipped it overnight to Texas, at no expense to the customer, of course.[13]

Shining Moment #7: Body—and Service—by Roger's

Lindsay Willis is one of those super-charged, fast-talking, fast-thinking people who is always in a hurry. She's a premiere customer service researcher, avid golfer, and, if truth be told, a little bit of a hot-rodder. So it wasn't surprising when she reported that her new gold Mercedes had been in an accident. What was surprising was the service she experienced at Roger's Body Shop.

Roger's wowed Willis from minute one. Her researcher's eye cataloged the experience: The establishment was clean—almost spotless— she noted; the estimator went to work no more than 3 minutes after she walked through the front door; assessing the extent of the damage to her rear bumper took less than 15 minutes; and, while the estimator looked over her car, he called a rental agency to line up a rental car while hers was being worked on. "I didn't want to put you in an Escort for the week it's going to take to repair your car," he told her, and continued to call around in search of a car closer to her obvious personal preferences.

But that was just the overture. A day later, Willis received a card in the mail, reminding her when she was to bring her car in for the repairs and that the repair would take a week but that the rental car would be ready when she came in. The repair did take 5 days, just as promised. During that time, she received two calls updating her on the status of the work.

When she returned to pick up her car, she noted that not only had the repair been done perfectly, but her car had been washed and vacuumed, and the floor mats had been cleaned. A week after she picked up the car, she received this follow-up call: "Hi. This is Marv from Roger's Auto Body. We just want to know if everything was great with your car and with our repair process. (It was.) If anything comes up, feel free to call me personally, and we'll take care of it immediately."

Automobile dealers, used car salespeople, and auto repair shops are always at the bottom of the pile in customer satisfaction surveys and esteem. But as Lindsay Willis's experience proves, that certainly isn't part of the natural order of the universe; it's just the way some run their businesses.[14]

Shining Moment #8: Online and Personal

While trying on clothes at Lands' End recently, business writer Sarah Fister got great advice from a sales rep on styles that flatter her figure.

"Avoid wearing double-breasted jackets, tailored collars, and sleeves above the elbow," she said.

"At least I assume she was a she," wrote Fister. "In fact, I never saw her or heard her voice. And I didn't actually try on the clothes." The advice came to Fister through the "Your Personal Model" feature, one of several customer service tools offered on Lands' End's Web site (www.landsend.com). "I simply typed in my weight, height, dimensions, and coloring and, voilà, a somewhat accurate model of me appeared on my screen. I got to dress her up, ask for style advice, try on sample outfits, and, in theory, see what the clothes looked like on me before I bought them.

"And when I couldn't find the style of pants I was looking for, I contacted a rep named Jean H. via the Lands' End Live link (an online chat window). I told her what I was looking for, and she promptly took control of my Web browser, displayed two options on my screen, and informed me of the available sizes and colors. This was all done without ever speaking live to anyone...."[15]

9

QUALITY AND PRODUCTIVITY: THE MEASUREMENT AND ACTION IMPERATIVES

"Quality really is just doing what you said you were going to do. That's the most important part of the quality revolution, I think. Management has learned that they actually can do something about it by defining the requirements—finding out what the customer wants, describing that, and then meeting that exactly."

—Philip Crosby
Quality Guru

LTHOUGH THERE ARE MANY ISSUES to address in the management of service delivery, quality and productivity are at the core of most of them. Whether service is your primary product or only a part of it, delivery must be effective, efficient, and dependable if it is to have value to the customer. The service must be predictable and uniform; the customer has to be able to depend on what it will look like in delivery, how long it will take to deliver, and what it will cost. A Big Mac is a Big Mac is a Big Mac. It is the same, dependable Big Mac whether it is cooked, wrapped, and sold in San Francisco or St. Moritz, Switzerland. How you feel about the Big Mac is irrelevant. The McDonald's system ensures that wherever you are in the world, when you order a Big Mac, you will be getting exactly what you anticipated; your expectations will be met. That doesn't mean that McDonald's Corporation is a 100 percent unwavering, "any-color-you-want-as-long-as-it's-black" production line. There are local market variations and adaptations, like the availability of wine in France and of vinegar as a condiment option in Canada and England. The folks at McDonald's world headquarters in Oak Brook, Illinois, don't flinch when they are accused of industrializing the hamburger. Quite rightly they take pride in a Big Mac always being a Big Mac.

Though McDonald's Corporation is an obvious example, it isn't alone in its quest for uniformity and quality in services, nor is it alone in achieving that goal. Caterpillar Tractor and FedEx also make the delivery of service a quality affair, regardless of where in the world that service is delivered. One of the most historically chronicled service deliverers is Rolls Royce. The following account, while undoubtedly apocryphal, has the feel of the obsession for quality that pervades Rolls Royce and the service reputation it enjoys:

> A member of the English peerage, the Earl of Anywhere, is vacationing in the Swiss Alps. On a winding road just outside the village of Zernez, his Rolls coughs to a stop. The Earl and his chauffeur walk into the village, whereupon the chauffeur calls London to report that not only is the master's Rolls stopped dead in its tracks on a lonely mountain road, but it also appears to have a blown head gasket. The driver is instructed to return to the car and set out several flares; help is on the way. Within the hour a helicopter bearing two technicians sets down in a nearby field. With a minimum of discussion the men in spotless white coveralls set about their task. In less than 90 minutes his lordship's Rolls is again purring like the proverbial English tabby.
>
> Several months go by, and the chauffeur realizes that he has yet to be billed for the work on the Rolls. Thinking the cost of the helicopter alone will break his maintenance budget, he doesn't press the matter. Finally, after 8 months and no invoice for the service, he phones the factory service center. A cordial voice on the other end of the line listens to the tale and asks the chauffeur to hold while he checks his

records. "No," the service manager replies when he returns, "there is no record of such an emergency service call." After a short silence he adds, "But of course why would there be? A Rolls Royce never breaks down in the field."

While stories like this enshrine exemplary service providers, they also do a disservice. They inadvertently convey the notion that there is something mystical, or at least something superhuman, about the delivery of quality service. Such stories of service heroics suggest that the delivery of service, unlike the production of widgets, cannot be a predictable, controlled, and dependable process. The myth of service quality as an issue beyond management control is so pervasive that when good service is standard issue for an organization, we go to great lengths to discount it rather than to learn from it. Take the myth of Disney service magic.

It is absolutely true that Walt Disney both invented the theme park industry and set the standards of acceptable customer service by which we judge the hundreds of theme parks around the world. All the same, it is not true—as some people have wrongly implied—that only Disney knows how to meet those standards. Indeed, it is remarkable to see time and time again how well parks like Universal Studios, Busch Gardens, King's Island, and Carowinds have recreated a Disneylike service environment while still maintaining their own unique entertainment identities. It is a fact, of course, that the management teams of many of these other successful parks are usually peppered with Disney graduates. This tells us two things: (1) the Disney people do a great job of training managers; and (2) the act of creating a high-quality service environment is a transportable event.

IMPROVING SERVICES THROUGH INDUSTRIALIZATION

As mentioned earlier, some service management experts have made disparaging comments about the "industrial" approach to service on the part of exemplars such as McDonald's Corporation, Wal-Mart, and Midas Mufflers. While it is true that a McDonald's isn't a Windows on the World, a Wal-Mart store isn't a Tiffany's, and the neighborhood Midas shop isn't staffed by a Rolls Royce pit crew, no one save these few critics is suggesting that they should be. It is a touch of hypocrisy that allows such critics to both decry and devour industrialized fast food from different sides of the same mouth.

Harvard's Theodore Levitt, a vocal defender of industrialized approaches to service, is steadfast in his belief that improvement in quality and productivity in the service sector is hampered by the erroneous belief that improvement in service is limited by our ability to change the skills and attitudes of the people who perform the service:

> This humanistic conception of service diverts us from seeking alternatives to the use of people, especially to large, organized groups of people. It does not allow us to reach out for new solutions and new definitions. It obstructs us from redesigning the tasks themselves; from creating new tools, processes, and organizations; and, perhaps, even from eliminating the conditions that created the problems.

Levitt's point is not that all services should be automated, or that the people providing them should be turned into mindless semiautomatons. Far from it! His point is that when it comes to service, we haven't begun to take advantage of the improvement possibilities of automation. To Levitt, the fact that the McDonald's approach achieves "the carefully controlled execution of each outlet's central function—the rapid delivery of a uniform, high-quality mix of prepared foods in an environment of obvious cleanliness, order, and cheerful courtesy," on a nationwide basis— makes McDonald's a wonder to behold and a marvel worth our study, if not our emulation. It's a fact that McDonald's has become a runaway commercial success as the result of a system that emphasizes the substitution of equipment for people wherever possible as well as the setting of explicit performance standards and methods for people to observe. All this simply suggests that we have barely begun to understand what possibilities there are for improving both the productivity and the quality of service.

Levitt is also quick to point out that fast food is not the only service domain where industrialization has been beneficial. The mutual fund is a way of getting people to invest in the stock market without the expense of multiple sales calls and transactions. Expertise is concentrated in the fund managers, thus sparing customers and salespeople the need to duplicate that same expertise. The bank credit card—Mastercard, Visa, and so forth—is a simple way of extending loans to reliable bank customers without the expense of rechecking their creditworthiness every time they need to have credit. And finally, let's consider the humble supermarket. The substitution of self-service for clerk service has helped contain food prices, speed up the food shopping process, and increase food shopping options for consumers. It didn't exist until it was invented by and patented by Memphis, Tennessee, entrepreneur Clarence Sanders in 1916. Of course, today, the act of pushing a shopping cart along a carefully planned and laid out system of aisleways seems the only "natural way" to shop for food. It seems so logical, natural, and common sensical that we don't really "see" this marvelous, effective, and efficient service production system. It is virtually transparent. When industrialization of service works well and helps us as consumers, it seems eminently reasonable and sensible. It is only when we are contemplating the industrialization of our own line of work or our own business that it seems threatening and risky.

Service can be industrialized in three ways: (1) by using hard technologies as a substitute for personal contact and human effort (the e-commerce ploy); (2) by improving work methods in a systematic manner (referred to as the use of soft technology); and (3) by combining those two methods. In other words, industrialization simply means that you automate where you can; you systematize and standardize where you can't; and you stop thinking that some services are exempt from this formula. It's the balance of the three options that counts.

The soft technology solution, which Levitt describes as "the substitution of organized preplanned systems for individual service operatives," is the solution followed by McDonald's, KFC, Domino's Pizza, and Jiffy Lube oil change centers. It is instructive to think for a moment of all the places where the soft technology approach works so well that we simply take it for granted today. The supermarket has been with us since the early 1900s when Saunders invented what became the Piggly Wiggly chain. The open stack library was a soft technology service innovation. The Christmas Club, the mutual fund, the restaurant salad bar, the packaged travel tour, and the fitness club, are all soft technology service innovations we take so much for granted that their basic design is invisible to us.

The hard technologies are the service innovations we notice the most. The ubiquitous ATMs (automated teller machines) and airline e-ticket machines are obvious examples. Less obvious are the airport X-ray machine that has replaced the labor-intensive luggage hand search, the automatic car wash that has replaced hours of handwork, and lots of coin-operated devices including everything from food dispensers to highway toll collectors, which are labor-replacing hard technologies. In health care, automation has improved both quality and efficiency. The electrocardiogram has replaced the physician's sometimes fallible ear, the CAT scan is superior to X rays for soft tissue examination, and automated lab equipment has taken much of the error out of the lab technician's hands. The video camcorder has replaced the old home-movie outfit and cut out the expense of the film processing lab. In the home there are more mechanical service providers—washers, dryers, vacuum cleaners, environmental sensors—providing more amenities than most of us could ever afford if we had to hire individuals to perform the same services.

In the realm of mixed systems, good examples are the Midas Muffler shops owned by the Whitman Corporation and Jiffy Lube oil change stores owned by Pennzoil-Quaker State. These limited service outlets move the consumer in and out in a flash by using special tools designed for one task only and by standardizing work procedures. The increasing use of toll-free lines, videoconferences, and e-mail instead of airlines for sales calls is an effort to automate and standardize, thereby decreasing the high cost of face-to-face selling. Transamerica Title Insurance Company has systematized and automated a service—property title search—that was formerly performed reliably by hand and only by a specially trained expert.

Citibank, one of the early driving forces in the ATM movement, was also a leader in the effort to balance hard and soft technology in the customer's favor in less visible realms. A classic example of the struggle between processing costs and customer satisfaction was reported in the *Harvard Business Review* in 1979. Citibank's operations experts spent 6 years unsnarling a foreign letters of credit system that at one point had accumulated a backlog of 36,000 customer inquiries and the worst customer satisfaction rating in the industry.[1] Applying both industrial engineering and advanced computerization techniques to the problem, a 30-step process was cut by two-thirds, while both customer and employee satisfaction ratings steadily improved. Today, in the World Wide Web era, such services are instantaneous.

The point of service industrialization, whether hard or soft technologies are being applied, is to make more services available and affordable to more people. The principles of automation and standardization strive to make rational much of the illogical service that is still practiced today. A perfect example is medicine. Today there is a swirl of controversy around the potential of grown and harvested replacement organs and the use of mechanical means to sustain life. This debate is testimony to the achievements of service industrialization—and to the quandary such success can bring about.

THE EMPLOYEE-CENTERED APPROACH

A second approach to the improvement of quality and productivity in service is, while not diametrically opposed to the industrialization approach, quite different in look and feel. Advocates of the *employee-centered* approach speak of it as being beyond the mere act of automating what can be automated and refer to its central thesis as "the intelligent use of human intelligence." Their favorite pastime seems to be conjuring up images of a service industry version of the old silent movie *Metropolis*, with service providers cast in the role of unthinking cogs in an oppressive, uncaring, machine-centered service system. Critics of the employee-centered approach see it as a surrender to the old myths equating service with servitude and a misplaced belief that advocating a labor-intensive view of work is the only way to ensure enough jobs for people in the future. Political and philosophical passions aside, it is also an approach with much to commend it.

The employee-centered approach is related to the "total quality" and "lean process" approaches to improvement that came into favor in manufacturing in the 1980s and 1990s. The central strategy is to push concern for quality and productivity improvement down in the organization to the place where the most should be known about the causes and remedies of the problem: the front line. The belief is that those nearest to the work are in the best position to solve the problems. As demonstrated at SAS and British Airways, this can be a very effective approach. However, the Scandinavians aren't the only ones to have seized on this strategy. In Japan, TQM and lean thinking have been applied successfully to service improvement by companies as diverse as Hotel Okura, Toyota, and MK Taxi. They have contributed to increasing consumer comfort, decreasing customer waiting time, and eliminating employee discourtesy. These examples are a good beginning. On the whole, Japanese managers are only just starting to catch on to the idea that service is an aspect of business in need of managing. But in those few Japanese organizations where service management is becoming an issue, the service improvement effort is decidedly employee-centered. In general, those efforts parallel closely the TQM efforts we have heard so much about with regard to the Japanese manufacturing effort.

It is interesting to note that there is a strong countervailing view in the Japanese management literature. Many managers and theorists are concerned that the TQM approach is not transportable to service management.

This view seems to revolve around three beliefs: (1) service does not lend itself to standardization and hence to control; (2) service quality is difficult to measure objectively; and (3) service employees tend to worry about trivial things, that is, they have a tendency to focus on solving the wrong problems with their self-defined efforts.

Japanese approaches, commonly referred to as customer satisfaction management, or CS management, tend to follow highly systematic models analogous to TQM. The first step in a Japanese service improvement program is usually some form of "management by policy." Senior management formulates policy and strategy relative to the value of service to the organization and the need for service improvement. Consultants diagram and analyze the service systems and processes. Middle management then proceeds to take up the issues of defining service, setting operational policy, and establishing the quantitative need for service improvement. The operational policy setting generally takes the form of encouraging employees to explore the causes of poor service and to take corrective action where possible. Service employees are told to focus their improvement efforts on the most important and pressing problems, and they are to set and attain a few select goals.

At the front-line level, the improvement effort begins by training service employees to work as a unit rather than as individuals in order to improve their performance. Management in turn promises to heed employee suggestions and recommendations for improving service performance. Frequently the wage system is modified to reward increased service efforts. All the efforts seem to emphasize pep-rally-like meetings where service employees are praised for their efforts and their collective determination to improve service.

In the United States there are many good examples of employee-centered service improvement systems. Honeywell Corporation, one of the big users of the TQM approach to manufacturing quality control in this country, has extended the effort to nonmanufacturing arenas. Quality improvement and involvement programs exist in engineering, personnel, and technical publications efforts. John Naisbitt reports that organizations as diverse as Inter-First Bank/Dallas, General Dynamics Corp., Standard Meat Company, and Miller Brewing have applied the TQM approach to service improvement. Service-focused quality improvement efforts have been reported in such unlikely places as the Veteran's Medical Center in Albany, New York.

THE CORE ELEMENTS OF SERVICE QUALITY
AND PRODUCTIVITY ASSURANCE

Whether the service quality and productivity assurance effort is employee-centered or technology-centered, it always includes four elements: involvement, measurement, reward, and follow-through.

Involvement. Involvement has a multitude of important meanings to quality theorists. First and foremost there is management awareness; this is what Philip Crosby calls "recognition by management that the [poor service quality] situation exists."[2]

Second is the matter of management commitment. Management must acknowledge and communicate the importance of service quality. The simple awareness and admission that service quality and productivity must be managed isn't enough, in and of itself, to start the ball rolling. A strong affirmation from management to the rank and file of the organization that the situation must change for the health and well-being of the organization is a must.

Third is management participation in deed as well as in word. John Simmons of the University of Massachusetts contends that one in three employee participation programs fails because employee involvement is viewed as a technique rather than a top-to-bottom way of organizational life. If management is excluded from the mandate to provide better service, no matter whether the approach is technology-centered or employee-centered, it is not likely to be viewed as serious.

This leads to the fourth and final sense of involvement—employee involvement. In the employee-centered approach this is usually not a problem so long as all the employees in the organization or functional unit are involved. But it is just as important in a high-technology approach to service management. The employees' participation here is more subtle, but nonetheless important. Involving employees in the process of changing the technology ensures that the employees will accept their role in relationship to the new technology, and that the new technology will be applied to the most important issues. The era of the systems analyst as the supreme expert who need not consult with the person doing the job, no matter how unsophisticated the job may be, is a thing of the past. The user is a fundamental and critical element in any new system. That importance is twice as great in a service management system.

Measurement.   There is a simple process that helps determine what we want to measure. It begins by identifying the customer's moments of truth, which we discussed in Chapter 3. It goes on to use the concept of the business proposition to help place organizational significance on the many ways the customer and the organization come into contact. The business proposition, which is the model of what the organization is trying to accomplish, involves a series of inferences about the relationship between customer experiences and organizational outcomes.

A commitment to service quality without a commitment to standards and measurement would be a dedication to lip service, not customer service. Only with customer-focused standards and customer-based satisfaction measurements can you create and manage dynamic, information-based service delivery systems that can be tuned and refined to changing customer expectations. As J. W. "Bill" Marriott, Jr., chairman of Marriott Corporation puts it: "Measurement of customer perception causes a lot of focus just where we want it, on the customer."

Setting standards.   When we work through the topic of standards in workshops, the discussion frequently turns technical over a basic values conflict. At some point, someone invariably groans that "customer satisfaction" scores are well and good, but my people don't see the customer. "We need real standards and real measurement if we are going to run this business right." In essence, the conflict turns out to be between internally generated standards and customer-centered measurement.

It's an understandable quandary. Setting standards and measuring performance in accordance with customer-centered values smacks of letting the inmates run the asylum. After all, aren't the organization's professionals best qualified to determine how to do whatever it is that they do? The answer is yes. And no. Like the myopia of catering managers planning coffee breaks around pastries and china patterns instead of telephones and restrooms, personal education and experience, company policies and procedures, and the habits developed over time all conspire to insulate the process of service delivery from the customer's perception of what is really desired.

Remember the formula for customer satisfaction mentioned earlier. It is not only the quality of the outcome, but also the customer's expectations and the customer's perception of the process leading from expectations to outcome that determine the ultimate quality of the service provided.

Knowing what to do and how to do it in a technical sense does not necessarily confer understanding of customers' wants and needs or customers' expectations of how they would like you to satisfy those wants and needs.

To see this conflict more clearly, consider the practice of medicine. "What could a patient possibly have to tell us about the practice of medicine that would be germane?" may be a typical approach of some professional practitioners from a lofty perch they've gained only after years of intensive and expensive preparation. "How could you possibly be practicing the healing arts without taking the patients' views into consideration?" is the seemingly militant consumerist response from the front lines. Each view is helpful only in defining the extremes.

No one questions the need for ethical standards and professional review in medicine. Nor do we contend that the civilians are qualified to judge compliance with those standards. A nondoctor is no more fit to judge the technical quality of a hernia operation than a nonmechanic is to judge the technical quality of adjustments to a car's fuel-injection system. The auto owner is, however, not only a competent judge of whether the tuned-up car is running well, but also the only relevant judge of whether the adjustments were worth the money paid for the service. Likewise, the hernia patient is competent to judge whether the relief sought has been obtained and in a way that met his or her expectations as a patient. Those judgments of outcome are relevant to the establishment of service standards. Lack of respect for those judgments is what brings mechanics and repair shops into ill repute and drags doctors and hospitals into malpractice proceedings.

The solution is to deploy and manage the organization's technical expertise in keeping with the customer's ever-changing definition of good service. It can be done. At Riverside Methodist Hospital in Columbus, Ohio, no one would think of letting patients pick up a scalpel or make a diagnosis. However, when two entire floors of the hospital were designated as a specialty center for women's health problems, the list of medical services to be offered and the setting in which those services were to be provided were both designed with input from the women in the community who might someday be the center's patients. At St. Luke's Medical Center in Milwaukee, Wisconsin, patients in focus groups were asked what made their stay most tolerable. The responses were the key to setting and updating nonmedical treatment standards.

In the financial field, Citigroup launched a concerted service improvement campaign in the late 1980s after it discovered a gap between the technical skills it had long considered to be good performance and the expectations and desires its customers believed were basic to good service. Likewise, First Union's formula for people-pleasing financial service was derived from first learning how customers define it and then measuring how well they believe the bank is providing it.

The subject need not always be approached so gingerly. For many organizations, standards are straightforward, easy to set, and integrated into the service strategy. When FedEx guarantees "absolutely, positively overnight" delivery, or Domino's creates a standard that states, "We'll be at your door within 30 minutes of your order" the tone for the measurement system is set.

Notice that useful, measurable standards tend to be expressed precisely. Moving the "Bear any burden, pay any price promise we make to our customers" service guarantee back into the organization can lead to problems if the customer-based measures are left behind. "You'll have the best sleep ever," or "You're gonna like our place," are slogans, not standards. If customers don't understand exactly what kind of service promise has been made, how will they know good service when they see it, or be able to evaluate what they get?

Nordstrom, L.L. Bean, and Lands' End along with their online counterparts all have clear satisfaction guarantees: If you don't like it, they'll take it back, no questions asked. Their customers don't have to worry that someone will decide that this particular return isn't allowable because the item is no longer on sale or that they don't have the sales slip and packaging, or the phase of the moon has changed. The standard is expressed in terms for the customer, not for internal organizational concerns like inventory control.

Setting standards that are neither firm nor customer-focused also tends to condone the view that there is a comfort level of allowable errors. Deluxe Corporation knows that sometimes it will make a mistake or miss the 48-hour deadline that is a part of its "48 hour turnaround, zero defects" service strategy. As a salve to the corporate ego, it would be easy to revise the standard from an absolute to a relative value—aiming to ship, say, 98 percent of all orders within 48 hours, then crowing because 99 percent were out the door in that amount of time.

In service, any error rate is a way of saying that it is perfectly all right to turn off, disappoint, and even lose a certain percentage of customers.

That's unacceptable logic to the superior service organizations. So Deluxe holds to the absolute standard because that is the definition of superior performance it wants its customers to expect and its employees to aspire to. It not only measures its rate of achievement against that standard but publishes the information in its annual report every year so everybody can know how well it is doing.

Frank McMillan, former director of quality for Shell Oil, puts the question in starker terms: "What is an acceptable error rate—what will you, as a customer, accept as acceptable failure—for airliner landings? Is 98 percent okay? 99 percent? Of course not. How about hospital nursery care. What is the acceptable rate for dropped babies: 98 percent? 99 percent? No. One hundred percent is all you will tolerate. Are your customers any less demanding than you are? I doubt it!" This quote should be on the desk of everyone charged with setting performance standards. High-quality service involves adherence to customer expectations, not a compromise between what the customer wants and what the organization is comfortable providing. 3M is one of a number of the companies we know well that defines quality itself as "conformance to customer requirements." That's where standards come from, and that is where meaningful measurement begins.

WHY THEY MEASURE

One of the most common characteristics of outstanding service providers is their dedication to measuring customer satisfaction and using the results to guide operations. They measure formally. They measure frequently—on average, monthly. And they attach important individual, work group, and organizational outcomes to the results.

Because the results of measurements are meant to be taken seriously, the most effective systems are those that produce actionable information. The object of the data quest is more than "smile ratings." If treatment at the front desk is considered a high-impact variable in a hotel—and it is— you can bet that Marriott, Hyatt, and Four Seasons are all getting regular readings on front-desk treatment from their respective customers.

Their way of asking the questions may vary, but the questions asked are very specific to their particular customer profile. There's nothing immediately useful to be learned from an open-ended, global query such as, "How was the treatment at the front desk?" Instead, a carefully crafted series of questions will probe into customer assessments of all aspects of the encounter: speed, accuracy, cordiality, helpfulness, completeness of information, response to inquiries, and any other moments of truth that build overall impression of quality.

Measurement results typically become the agenda for subsequent internal dialog and problem-solving efforts. After all, an organization's service quality measurement system is only as good as the service improvement discussions it prompts, and that's true at all levels in the organization. Many heated discussions are inspired by the results of a customer survey. As Tom Oliver, former FedEx senior vice president of sales and service, told us once, "If the customer believes he has a problem, he has a problem. Period."

While many service-centric companies use formal, highly reliable measurement systems, none relies solely on such systems for customer feedback. For example, Marriott's regular, scientific, third-party sampling and surveying is supplemented by a less formal, more open Guest Satisfaction Index (GSI) compiled from the in-room survey forms people voluntarily fill out and turn in. Because GSI data come in more frequently than the results of third-party, scientifically administered surveys, they are used as a rolling indicator of how a property is doing with guests. John Dixon, former general manager of the Marriott in Washington, D.C., characterizes his property's GSI as a "Reality check. It answers the question, 'Are we as good as we think we are?'"

GSI results are taken every bit as seriously as the results of monthly telephone polls. Regular ratings are posted in employee work areas. Meetings are held to discuss the scores and what they say about service quality. Written comments are posted for employees to read for themselves. And Dixon was a big believer in the value of combining the hand-written guest comments and the formal survey numbers into an overall picture of what guests are experiencing. "We dramatize and emphasize good results, the positive comments—they communicate the standard," he explains. "We use complaints and poor results to discuss improvement—they tell us how short we are of the goal."

Service measurements often benefit from a standard of comparison. One major Chicago-based specialty retailer regularly assigns its favorite market research company to track and analyze what customers think of the service in its stores. Then, to determine how that compares to service that's widely acknowledged as outstanding, the market researchers compare them to telephone surveys of Nordstrom customers on the West Coast. Comparing the internal measurements with the external data from half a continent away allows this midwestern retailer to benchmark the way its customers feel about it against satisfaction ratings from "the best of the best."

One measure of just how seriously the data being generated are taken by the service-centric is the important outcomes that increasingly are attached to the results. Information from the comment cards sent out by General Electric to follow up on major appliance service calls have salary impact for GE service technicians. Regular service quality surveys are basic to the decentralized style of management at Digital Equipment Corporation. Both United and Wheaton Van Lines confront and counsel agents and drivers rated less than satisfactory; those who cannot or will not clean up their acts are cut loose. At Longo Toyota in El Monte, California, negative feedback from customers gets salespeople called on the carpet, no matter how many cars they are selling. At FedEx, Marriott, and many others, pay and promotions can hinge on good customer feedback. And service quality is as important as profitability in the way managers of Pizza Hut restaurants are rated and rewarded.

The value of the information is only enhanced by spreading it through the organization. The more people in each functional unit of the company—be it a Wal-Mart store, a Club Med village, or an Embassy Suites hotel—know about the hit or miss ratio and what the causes of the hits and misses seem to be, the better able they are to improve their performance. Measurement for measurement's sake is pointless. As manufacturing quality guru Philip Crosby points out, "Building a better scale doesn't change your weight."

DETERMINING WHAT TO MEASURE

"Hey! How'm I doin'?" may generate useful feedback for a politician, but it hardly ever produces the quality or quantity of information needed to direct the creation of distinctive customer service. Likewise, knowing that from a random sample of 1000 recent customers we scored an average of 4.5 on a scale of 1 to 6 is nice, but not at all useful. It doesn't help us figure out how good or bad the customer considers 4.5 level performance or what we have to do to get a 6.

A number of market research specialists, prominent among them, the previously mentioned Berry, Zeithaml, and Parasuraman, have been trying to develop measurement systems that will be universally applicable to service quality and customer satisfaction. The Berry team's five factors (reliability, assurance, tangibles, empathy, and responsiveness) form what the team calls the ServQual measurement system. As a general litmus test, ServQual is an intriguing and useful measure. But the generic nature of any such universal index produces results that are unavoidably generic. And that can fall far short when what's needed is specific information that can be used to confirm or correct employee or unit performance. The more general the feedback, the less effective it is for such purposes. The really useful, specific, directly applicable information comes from talking to your particular customers, constantly and often at length, to determine what you are doing that is making them happy and what is letting them down.

Among the service-centric, we find that the measurement or service performance is a systematic effort that depends on no single measure to tell all. These organizations seem to wear both belts and suspenders, just in case. Technically speaking, they value "nonrepetitive, redundant" measures of their front-line performance, customer satisfaction, and service quality. Essentially they measure the same thing in a lot of different ways. The more information, the better, they maintain.

That reinforces our own bias that the most meaningful measurement reflects an organization's unique service strategy. That strategy, you'll recall, was originally devised from listening carefully to customers and identifying the moments of truth that have the greatest impact on their service satisfaction. Logically, then, the best measurement you can devise should mirror and validate the details of your service strategy.

One of us served as consultant to a medium-sized theme park in the upper Midwest, helping it evolve a measurement and feedback system for customer satisfaction and service quality. The premise of the founder was that the more fun people had in the park, the more likely they would be to come back themselves and tell others. Defining "fun" was therefore basic to measuring satisfaction.

The original operational model coalesced around four keys to guests having fun: friendliness, cleanliness, service, and show. We then tried to find the fewest questions we could ask, people exiting the park that would still reliably report on overall satisfaction and the four component factors. Though our scales were statistically correct, front-line workers and their managers smiled politely and, in essence, said, "That's nice. So what?"

We were puzzled at their lukewarm reaction, so we asked them about it. "What you have is nice for management, but it doesn't help us." They said, "When you ask about cleanliness, it would help to know exactly when and where they saw us doing good or bad." So we included detailed questions on clean restrooms, clean sidewalks, clean parking lots, and so forth. And where we had created general friendliness questions, we tossed them out and asked about employee friendliness by area and job type.

The refined measurement and feedback system may not have enhanced our statistical model, but because it increased the coverage of customer encounters, an interesting thing happened. Employees and supervisors suddenly weren't satisfied knowing they had achieved a 4.8 score on bathroom cleanliness. They insisted on knowing how things were perceived by shift, by type of restroom (men's or women's), and by time of day (early morning, midday, later afternoon, or evening). They simply couldn't get enough feedback.

From that sort of experience, we can draw two conclusions about measurement systems. First, the people on the front lines of the organization respond best to information relevant to their piece of the world, and they can tell you a lot about what will make that information relevant. Second, when people have relevant information about things they deem important and believe they can affect, they become very committed to using that information.

GUIDELINES FOR EFFECTIVENESS

Measurement can be a confusing area, primarily because of the statistical mystery and psychobabble some measurement experts drape about their craft. There are some statistical niceties to observe, but most involve sampling techniques—making sure you survey enough people and in the right way. Yet, as Professor Michael Scriven, an eminent research design and statistics expert, so aptly puts it, "Any statistical test you can't do with a simple hand calculator may be too complex to yield practical results."[3]

Here's a quick list of pointers to help you create a top-notch performance measurement feedback system:

- **Begin with your service strategy.** If it's well designed, you'll find a number of measurable promises in it. The service strategy should also suggest some less obvious measurements.

- **Measure frequently.** Once a month is a minimum. In 60 to 90 days, any customer and organizational performance information you now have will be stale. Domino's Pizza, for example, formally measures performance quality weekly.

- **Ask customer-based questions.** Tap both the customer's experience ("What happened to you?") and the customer's perception ("How do you feel about what happened to you?"). The customer's specific, personal experience and interpretations are far more enlightening than answers to open-ended, general questions such as, "On the whole, how was your stay?"

- **Ask fair questions.** Deal with the things your people can deal with. "Do you believe the federal government should step in" type questions may be entertaining, but they don't yield information people in your organization can act upon. Collecting production figures—number of customers served, number of interviews done—should focus on people-regulated processes, not machine-regulated systems that people are powerless to change or control.

- **Collect group and individual data.** Look for data that can be helpful to individual performers as well as work groups. The people who run the sale line in the dietary department need to know specifically how the sale went over as well as how the entire meal was received.

- **Benchmark yourself.** Collect information on the sales, market share, and customer satisfaction of your competitors at least three times a year. When J. C. Penney sends store managers out into the malls where its stores are located, they ask the same questions of Sears or Nordstrom customers and gather quantitative info on both their own stores and those of their competition.

- **Collect both quantitative and qualitative data.** Your measurement system should collect numerical ratings as well as customer comments. Both need to be analyzed and discussed. The specific comments explain the numbers. Both kinds of information are useful.

- **Make the results visible.** Displaying the results emphasizes their importance and destroys the notion that customer ratings are something held in confidence and not discussed with the front line or above a whisper. In the theme park mentioned earlier, customer satisfaction information was tracked on a giant graph painted on a 50-foot-long by 10-foot-high wall next to the time clock. At Marriott, front-desk results are posted where front-desk people can see them, restaurant service results where kitchen staff and servers will see them, and so on.

- **Make sure the results are employee-friendly.** Simple, straightforward averages and ratios work better than artificially compiled and weighted index scores. People are more likely to understand that "87 percent rated front-desk employees as cheerful and helpful" than "We received a 4.5 on our 10-factor, weighted average service quality index."
- **Make sure the results are believable.** If employees have seen the results collected, know how they are being compiled, and have evidence that it was their customers who gave the information, they're more likely to act on it. If the information comes down from on high, speaks of random sampling and anonymity, or in some way gives the impression that the results are abstract, employees tend to discount them. To make the data more believable, some companies successfully use their own employees to gather, compile, and post the data.
- **Make sure the results are used.** When customer satisfaction, performance, and service quality information is widely discussed, used for problem-solving meetings, and signals a celebration of success, people see that data as important. Simply posting numbers or sending out a complaint summary memo with an "FYI" on it doesn't really call for any significant action.

HOW GOOD IDEAS GO BAD

The goal of measurement is to gather information people can use to manage their efforts so that they do a better job of meeting the organization's customer service standards. When the feedback system doesn't work, it's often because the information gathered is being used incorrectly. It has stopped being feedback and becomes a chore, a threat, or something to be avoided.

Dr. Karen Brethower, an industrial psychologist and president of Connecticut-based, Executive Consulting, LTD, poses six questions for any measurement system that purports to help people improve their performance, but doesn't seem to be having the promised effect:

1. Is the information being used to embarrass, punish, or scold employees? If it is, it can be counterproductive in some surprising ways. One company used to give a "Rude Hog" award for the service rep with the lowest customer satisfaction rating. It wasn't long before employees were vying for it. The Rude Hog had become a badge of honor. Most systems designed to punish performance this way go wrong in a similar fashion.

2. Is the information about something that has no payoff for the people receiving it? Front-line people may be interested in sales volume, accounts opened, and so on, but if there is no personal relevance connected to the information, they clump it with other forms of corporate gossip and file it under "nonessential."

3. Is the information too late for employees to act on? By July, feedback about the service center team's April performance is too removed from the actions in the interim for employees to be concerned about or even remember much about the details of "way back when."

4. Is the feedback about something the people receiving it cannot influence? You can tell a 5-foot-tall person he's short, but nothing positive will come of it. Telling the mechanics how customers perceive the attitudes of salespeople in the dealership doesn't help either. But telling them customers perceive the service station as dirty and cluttered and their behavior as unprofessional can inspire some change.

5. Is the feedback about the wrong things? Salespeople can't help it if customers think the store is inconveniently located or isn't decorated in a warm and friendly way. But information that tells them they are closing 70 percent of the sales to customers who perceive them as accessible, warm, and helpful against only 25 percent to those who see them as cold and aloof—or can't find them at all—is right on target.

6. Is the information difficult to collect and record? Collecting and recording data can be a positive way to involve front-line people—

managers as well—in the nitty-gritty details of the business. But they won't do it if the procedure is hellishly difficult. Totaling and posting the volume of calls handled, customer feedback cards handed out, or sales made from proposals presented are manageable self-monitoring opportunities so long as they're relevant and nonintrusive.

Information.   Information is what management needs to control the business and what employees need to know so that they can be sure they are doing what is expected of them. When we talk of information, we are referring to three distinct things. The first is an objective—a statement of what the individual (or unit) is supposed to achieve; the direction his, her, or the group's actions should take, and the amount and quality of work to be accomplished. The second is feedback or information that can be used by the individual or group to confirm or correct the direction, quality, and quantity of the effort. Finally, there is information in the form of performance training in the knowledge and skills necessary to perform the job tasks in the first place. Without the flow of this information in the work unit, nothing much happens. People collectively and individually need to know how well they are providing the service they are expected to deliver if they are to have a chance at improving, or merely stabilizing, their performance of that service.

A lot of research has been done about the effect of feedback on performance. Working in a retail banking situation, Professor David A. Nadler has shown that by simply collecting information from customers and showing it to the employees of the branch, both employee attitudes and performance can be changed. Luckily it doesn't require a doctorate in industrial psychology to set up a usable feedback system.

A participant in a service productivity improvement workshop summed up an hour's lecture on performance improvement through feedback as well as the whole measurement and feedback dictum in about 25 words. "Let me see if I got all that," she said. "There are two things we have to do to begin to get better results: First, we have to have agreed-upon measurements for each department; second, we have to have a method of putting the measurements up where everybody can see 'em. That don't seem so tough."

Reward.   Reward, whether monetary or psychic, is critical to a service improvement program and to a smoothly running service operation in general. While there is considerable research that shows the power of pay for performance, it becomes increasingly difficult to establish and maintain purely piecework systems. In service it is sometimes nearly impossible. Just the same, service management must answer the question, "What's in it for me?" for the employees if management hopes to promote a high level of service delivery. The success of employee-owned organizations like United Airlines and United Parcel Service has not gone unnoticed. As a result, the concept of employee participation through ESOPs (employee stock ownership plans) receives serious consideration at compensation committee meetings these days. So do the more performance-based programs such as gain-sharing.

Money is an important and often overlooked part of the reward system of working for a living. If you don't think money is a motivator, just stop paying the people who work in your organization next Friday and see how many show up for work the following Monday. There are rewards beyond money that are important as well. Psychological gratifications ranging from being pleased by a job well done to recognition by others that one is performing well are all reward possibilities. The "rah-rah" sales rally has been out of vogue for a decade or so in the United States, but it has found a permanent place in the motivational tool kit of managers in Japan and western Europe. It also seems to be headed for a rebirth in this country as well. It has never been out in organizations with reputations for fierce employee loyalty such as Sun Microsystems, Harley-Davidson, and Hewlett-Packard.

What follows is a summary of a scene from the television version of the book *In Search Of Excellence*. This work ties the whole matter of motivation up in a package available for anyone who wants to carry it away and use it. The scene takes place in the lunchroom of the North American Tool and Die Company in Oakland, California. North American, a small machine tool company, is short on technology but long on ingenuity. The company has, through employee participation, decreased reject rates from 5 percent to 0.1 percent, increased sales from $1.8 million to $7 million, and increased profits by over 700 percent.

One of the keys to employee participation at North American is owner Tom Malone's dedication to the idea that everyone who works for the company and who contributes to its success should be recognized and rewarded. In this portion of the video, Malone is handing out what he calls jokingly "The North American Tool and Die Refrigerator Award."

The award is for a specific kind of employee behavior he wants to encourage and reward. One day as Malone was walking through the plant, he noticed an employee running in and out of the company lunchroom and carrying finished parts in and out of the lunchroom refrigerator. Malone quickly discovered that a number of parts being assembled for a customer order had been found too close to tolerance to be force-fitted. The employee, however, had figured out that if one part of the assembly was cooled in the freezer of the lunchroom refrigerator, the fit might work. And, in fact, it did. At the ceremony, Malone showered praise on the employee for his ingenuity and handed him a $50 check in appreciation of his effort.

There is an entire semester of applied psychology tied up in that little scene, but the wisdom can be distilled down to a simple principle: Pay attention to the day-to-day successes and failures of people. Acknowledge and reward both effort and the accomplishment of important goals. This principle is the strongest motivational tool a manager can carry.

Follow-through.   Follow-through is a management commitment to make a service management effort not simply a program but a way of life. Almost any motivational program can stir people up and gain commitment and effort toward a specific improvement goal for 90 days. There are hundreds of highly profitable, incentive motivation companies in the United States that have understood and taken advantage of this phenomenon. But isolated change and improvement programs tend to run their course and then to run downhill toward the performance levels that existed before the program. The difference between a program and continuous commitment is management.

In successful service conscious organizations, the demonstration of management commitment to quality of service is frequently embodied in the top person of the management team. When Bill Marriott, Jr., wanders the basement of the Marriott Hotel in Washington, D.C., checking the cleanliness of stored dinner plates, he may be demonstrating more commitment to the details of service quality than some of his employees are comfortable with. But none of them doubts that he cares about the quality of the experience guests have when they stay at a Marriott Hotel. When Rich Takata, president of CornerHardware.com, takes a turn answering customer complaints, everyone gets the message that customer satisfaction is important. And when Richard Rogers, president of

Syntex Corp., makes a point of having breakfast in the employee cafeteria every morning so he can be available to employees who want to see him, no one doubts that he places a high value on employees' ideas and opinions. It may be, as some skeptics contend, that the Marriotts and Takatas and Rogerses would serve their companies and customers better by spending that time on matters of a higher order. But it is also true that their personal appearances have an impact on the beliefs and values of their employees that would be hard to achieve through memos, directives, or underlings.

10

PROFILES IN SERVICE: WHERE SERVICE IS AN OBSESSION

> "Excellence is an art won by training and habituation. We are what we repeatedly do."
>
> —*Aristotle*

F OR NINE CHAPTERS WE HAVE pounded away at two distinct points. The first is that to achieve and maintain organizational success in the new millennium, it is imperative to become value-focused in your approach to the marketplace. Customers and consumers expect it, the necessity of developing meaningful competitive positioning demands it, and the profit and growth potential of service has never been greater. The second is that there are many examples of highly successful and respected service-conscious organizations you can model and learn from.

SOME ARE BORN GREAT...ALL OTHERS
WORK LIKE HELL

Some of these exemplary service companies have never known any other driving force. They were imbued with a strong service focus by the founder or founders from day one. In a sense, they are the born great. Other organizations have come to a service obsession later in their histories. The difference between starting out as a service-conscious organization and learning the trick after the fact can be considerable. Conversion, it seems, is always a more difficult accomplishment than simply having a priori knowledge and faith. Companies that have made that difficult transition have achieved greatness for themselves.

And some companies have had their service commitment thrust upon them. These include organizations that because of the nature of their business or because of the strong and obvious demands of their marketplace have learned to scramble—consciously or not—to serve and serve well their markets. There are lessons to be learned from all these kinds of companies, regardless of the route that has caused them to be distinguished from the rest of the pack by their success in running service-focused organizations.

In this chapter we will study four archetypal companies. All of them, by any measure, are fantastic at serving their customers of choice. Aside from their preoccupation with service, all four firms couldn't be less alike. Each is in a different industry. They are very different in size, scope, and circumstance. And yet that one element of similarity—an obsession with service—makes them more alike than different operationally and spiritually.

The first company we review is USAA, an organization founded in 1922 by a group of 26 U.S. Army officers gathered at a San Antonio, Texas, hotel. Why? Because as military officers who moved frequently, they had a difficult time getting insurance. They were considered transient and a risk. So the officers decided to insure one another. Led by Major William Garrison, who became the company's first president, they formed the United States Army Automobile Insurance Association. In 1924, when U.S. Navy and Marine Corps officers were allowed to join, the company changed its name to the United Services Automobile Association. By the mid-1950s, the company had some 200,000 members.

With customer retention at an unheard of 97 percent and as a provider of insurance and financial services to more than 90 percent of all military personnel, USAA tops the charts for awards and recognition for the quality of service and support it provides its members. The company's mission is crystal clear: to be the provider of choice of financial products and services for the military community.

The subject of our second case is Recreational Equipment, Inc. (REI). Based in Seattle, Washington, and founded in 1938 by Lloyd Anderson, his wife, Mary, and 21 other mountain climbers, REI currently has 55 outlets in 23 states. The nation's largest consumer co-op now has more than 1.6 million member-owners. Selling high-end gear, clothing, and footwear for those enamored of adventurous outdoor activities like climbing, kayaking, skiing, hiking, biking, and camping, REI has become a retail powerhouse that serves its brick and click membership.

Our third case is Bern's Steak House in Tampa, Florida, a remarkable study in getting service right for your customer. Started in the 1950s by Bernard Laxer, Bern's Steak House is now lauded as one of the most famous restaurants in the world. Laxer's goal? To find new ways to entice the public from all over the world to eat at his restaurant. And without question, those who do visit have a memorable and enjoyable evening. The unique characteristics of Bern's are numerous and include the world's largest wine selection, two dozen different caviars, and a 65-page dessert menu. Wait staff at Bern's are trained for more than a year before ever serving a customer. No detail at the steak house is overlooked, from the hand-sorted coffee beans to the organic garden used as the source for the fresh vegetables and herbs.

Our fourth case is a granddaddy of service excellence; Walt Disney World/Disneyland. In the wonderful world of entertainment, Walt Disney's kingdom is one of the biggest. Based in Burbank, California, the Walt Disney Company is the third largest media and entertainment conglomerate in the world, with operations encompassing movies, broadcasting, the Internet, and theme parks.

Disney's theme parks and resorts are the most popular in the world. Its Tokyo Disney Resort (operated by the Oriental Land Co.) draws 16.5 million people a year, while the Magic Kingdom at Walt Disney World in Florida is the number one park in the United States (15.4 million annual visitors). Its Florida complex also includes Epcot, Disney-MGM Studios, and Animal Kingdom, while its West Coast attractions include the Disneyland Resort and Disney's California Adventure. It also owns professional sports teams, the Anaheim Angels (baseball) and the Mighty

Ducks of Anaheim (ice hockey), as well as 39 percent of Disneyland Paris. Three lessons are illustrated by its tale: the value and impact of the service concept on long- and short-term planning, the value of the "key impact variables" concept on day-to-day operations, and the critical importance of employee involvement and job satisfaction on the success of a service-focused organization.

CASE 1: USAA

Look around for service excellence in the financial services industry, and you won't have to look far before you come across USAA (United Services Automobile Association). The San Antonio company has a tightly focused market niche: It offers insurance and an array of financial services to present and former members of the U.S. military and their families, exclusively. Even so, USAA has earned kudos from just about every quarter for its attention to the needs of its customers, as well as its employees.

Here's a short list of USAA's more recent awards and recognitions: one of the most admired companies in America on *Fortune* magazine's year-2001 list, a perennial on the magazine's "100 best companies to work for" list, and a rank of 217 on its *500* list; *CIO* magazine's top IT performer and one of its "100 leaders for the next millennium"; *Money* magazine's "best bank in America"; *Working Mother* magazine's "100 best companies for working mothers"; and *Worth* magazine's "reader's choice survey" for number one life insurance company, which rated USAA tops in *all 27 categories*.

It's no accident that USAA gathers "best of" awards more often than Tom Hanks wins Oscars. The company's mission is crystal clear: to be the provider of choice of financial products and services for the military community. With a few expansions over the years, that mission has remained constant since USAA was founded in a San Antonio hotel room in 1922 by 25 active-duty U.S. Army officers. Their specific purpose was to create an association that would fill the auto insurance needs of officers in the U.S. Army who were considered poor risks because they moved around so much.

Membership in the USAA was limited to active-duty army officers. Before long, the association widened eligibility requirements to include officers from other branches of the military. USAA signed up 1000 members in its first 14 months, a clear indication that it had identified a customer need.

USAA has grown substantially since then. It currently has 22,660 employees; 75 percent of them work at the San Antonio headquarters; and the balance work in offices throughout the United States and in Frankfurt and London. It ranks seventh among auto insurers and sixth among homeowner insurers; it has nearly $100 billion of life insurance in force; and its mutual funds have $42 billion in assets under management.

These days, USAA can offer its 4.5 million members a lot more than insurance. In 1996, when the association voted to expand its membership rules to include enlisted military personnel and their families, its product offerings expanded dramatically as well. USAA now offers its member-customers property and casualty insurance, life and health insurance, annuities, stocks and mutual funds, credit cards, banking services, travel services, Internet access, home security systems, and access to a wide selection of goods and services through its Web site usaa.com.

Chairman of the board Robert T. Herres, the retired Air Force general who served as CEO from 1993 to 2000, led USAA's expansion charge. In explaining the company's strategy in the mid-1990s, he eloquently and simply summed up its method: "First, you decide who you want your customers to be. Then you decide what they need and want. Then you figure out which of those needs you can meet, and then you do that better than anyone else."[1]

USAA sticks by those words of wisdom, working obsessively to serve the member-customers with whom it shares values, ethics, and traditions. The phrase, "We know what it means to serve," part of the USAA logo, is a continuous reminder that this is an organization that understands its customers. So it should come as no surprise that USAA insures nine out of ten active-duty officers in the U.S. military. The company also knows how to inspire loyalty: Its customer retention rate is 97 percent, and its employee turnover rate is just 7 percent. Dedication to service at USAA is clearly more than a mission statement; it's a mindset that is woven into every part of the operation with military determination.

Case in point: The desire to provide the best possible service to member-customers has driven USAA to develop the best possible technological tools for its customer-service people. In the 1980s the information technology unit devised an automated customer relationship management system that allows it to provide the specialized and personalized service that USAA's customers have come to expect. Members of the military move frequently, for example, so the system takes that into account. If a customer is transferred and can't contact the company for several months, USAA recalculates insurance rates retroactively; any savings for the period are credited to the customer. A state-of-the-art telecommunications system—one of the world's largest automated call distribution systems with 20,167 phones—enables customer service employees to help customer-members when they call, rather than put them on hold, pass them around, or abandon them in a telephone tree without hope of rescue.

Perhaps most important: USAA treats its customers no better than it does its employees. The San Antonio headquarters features restaurants, convenience stores, fitness centers, playing fields, a dry cleaner, and a post office. Most employees work 4-day, 38-hour weeks. They have access to on-site child care (facilities that are accredited child development centers) as well as rides to work in company-sponsored vanpools.

USAA's commitment to employees truly shines in its training and education offerings. Long a champion of training, USAA uses both traditional classrooms and technology to ensure that employees receive just-in-time and just-enough training. Employees average 90 hours of professional training annually; some 2500 employees were enrolled in college courses and 3500 in insurance-industry courses, all at company expense.

Invariably, interviews with USAA employees and customers end up exploring the family feeling people get from the company. Employees have it, even though they work on the huge San Antonio campus with 17,000 other people. It's not surprising that customer-members, who seem to be the obsession of every one of those USAA employees, feel part of the family, too. As one long-time customer said, "I know it sounds hyperbolic, but there's a sense of family with USAA. I get barraged by entreaties from various insurance companies, but USAA's mailers always seem to say, 'We're here to serve you.'"[2]

Is it any wonder USAA is a perennial winner on so many "best" lists?

CASE 2: REI

Be it click or mortar, this outdoor gear retailer's customer education, service support, and interactive shopping experiences set it apart. Step into any store of Recreational Equipment, Inc. (REI), and you enter not just a retail setting but a supersized simulation, a sort of virtual reality experience without the pesky headgear. Care to see if that GoreTex parka really is waterproof? Expose it to an honest-to-goodness downpour in REI's rain forest room. Curious as to how those cross-country skis will glide on real snow? Try them out on snow made by the staff on site. Want to see how that mountain bike handles under authentic conditions? Take it for a spin on an elaborate indoor track replete with hills and obstacles. And of course there's REI's signature two-story climbing wall to test rock-climbing gear. It is as creative an example of experience engineering as exists outside of a theme park today.

This "try before you buy" approach is just one part of Seattle-based REI's distinctive customer service strategy. Couple it with a hiring philosophy that puts bona fide outdoor gear experts and adventurers on the front lines doling out advice to customers, and mix in an award-winning Web site with unparalleled customer education and community-building features, and you've got a service formula that has long formed an impressive competitive barrier around REI.

Founded in 1938 by 23 Pacific Northwest mountaineers who sought reasonably priced climbing equipment, REI is run as a customer cooperative. It has 1.8 million active members who pay a $15 lifetime membership fee. In addition to benefits like special discounts on gear, repair service, and adventure trips, the fee entitles members to a patronage dividend at the end of each year, based on a percentage of how much they've spent with REI during the year.

Management believes that the cooperative structure not only helps create more loyal and involved customers, but it enables REI to keep a tighter focus on customer needs. REI gets to know its member-customers—their demographics, buying habits, and purchase histories—on a level that few other companies do. This is an intimacy that paves the way for precise target marketing and effective cross-selling.

REI conducts customer satisfaction phone surveys of its member-customers four times yearly, and shares the results with all company employees. In 2001 the company hired a mystery shopping firm to begin testing its retail stores for their customer service acumen.

Culture, selection, and training pave the way.   REI's service excellence begins with management's insistence on hiring salespeople who not only have a passion for its product line, but also have the hands-on experience to back it up. If a customer walks into the Seattle store, for instance, and asks whether someone has climbed Mt. Rainier or even Mt. Everest, any number of hands will likely go up. Customers rarely have to worry about stumping the REI sales corps.

"We do a lot of outreach to outdoor recreation communities to recruit our people, going to cycling or hiking clubs to find people who come equipped with substantial experience in their particular outdoor sport," says Mike Foley, a senior public relations associate at REI. "We believe when a customer visits an REI store, their experience will be unique based largely on how our employees educate them about the gear or adventures."

The same hiring criteria extend to REI's e-commerce site (www.rei.com). A customer phoning the site's toll-free number with a question, or sending an e-mail query, will benefit from the same level of "been there, done that" experience from sales reps.

Given REI's product line and reputation, many of these job candidates come calling on the company rather than vice versa, thereby keeping recruiting costs low. For many, the job is simply an extension of the outdoor lifestyle.

Despite the staff's prepackaged expertise, REI still continually trains staff members to stay current on its vast and diverse product offerings. Major REI vendors like Columbia or Patagonia, for instance, regularly host on-site training seminars on the ins and outs of their products. But REI knows that one of the best forms of training is staff that regularly uses and tests the gear, using that personal experience to help educate customers.

Going multichannel: rei.com takes off. With such crowd-pleasing interactive experiences beckoning from physical stores, what led REI's leaders to believe they could lure customers just as effectively to computer screens to shop? Senior leaders saw the World Wide Web as a tool for tapping markets where the company had little or no retail presence and for overcoming some of the limitations of existing paper catalogs. Management understood that the Web wasn't really about technology, but about surrounding customers with valuable information, convenient access, and varied shopping preferences.

While other companies may be paralyzed by the thought of an e-commerce site cannibalizing other parts of their business, REI believed that a multichannel strategy could broaden its business reach. REI's mantra became "to deliver any product, at any time, to any place, and to answer any question." Going virtual paid quick dividends. REI's Internet business unit has grown steadily, with 2000 sales of $92 million, a 125 percent increase over 1999's $41 million figure. The unit also includes REI-Outlet.com and REI Japan.

True to management's vision, REI now takes plenty of online orders from customers who drive by its landmark Seattle store every day. The success underscores that today's winners increasingly are those who learn to successfully marry physical and digital worlds.

Setting e-service standards.   REI also owes its e-commerce success to some 60 years of retail experience, which includes a successful catalog business, an established product fulfillment infrastructure, and a weighty brand. Yet simply moving a catalog business to the Web hardly guarantees success. REI customers keep using the Web site because of its simple, easy-to-navigate design, hassle-free product ordering, relatively low shipping costs (subsidized by the company), reliable product delivery, an unparalleled library of how-to product information, and access to chat rooms and community forums that enable customers to swap tips on gear or adventure trips with other users.

Shopping convenience also is a big factor. Foley says some 30 percent of REI.com orders arrive between 10 P.M. and 7 A.M. Pacific Standard Time, when retail stores are no longer open.

A customer listening campaign discovered that customers of REI's Web site expected even faster product delivery service than its catalog buyers. So REI ratcheted up service standards and now regularly ships 95 percent of its orders within 24 hours of receipt. It will soon be able to process orders within an hour after arrival.

In addition, Web customers also have access to a live "text chat" option, where they can type in a question while logged on and have it quickly answered by a customer service e-rep. Given permission, the rep can even assume control of the customer's browser and direct him or her to relevant or requested Web pages.

The Holistix Performance Index placed REI.com in the top 1 percent of 300,000 sites tested for page download and server response time in November 2000, one of the busiest months of the year for e-commerce sales. In addition, *Forbes* magazine named REI.com the Internet's top outdoor gear and apparel site in its 2000 "Best of the Web" issue.

There's yet one more way that REI has set itself apart from other click-and-mortar businesses. Rather than spinning off the rapidly growing REI.com to reap the rewards of an IPO, management believed that remaining one company and not creating a barrier between physical and virtual environments would serve customers far better. This decision benefits customers in a number of ways. For one, any customer can return an item purchased online or via catalog to an REI retail store for refund. This is not something all click-and-mortar operations offer. There's nothing quite as frustrating and seemingly illogical as having to box up and mail a product thousands of miles away when a sister retail store is a 10-minute drive away.

Customer education as a loyalty factor.   As mentioned earlier, a chief way REI adds value and creates loyal customers—not to mention breeds vocal advocates—is through its customer education and community-building efforts. REI's retail stores have long dedicated meeting room space for informational clinics. The company connects with community groups and recreational clubs not only to provide training in the use of its gear, but also to host unique adventure opportunities for current or potential customers.

On the Web side, the "Learn and Share" section of REI.com provides visitors with expert guidance on everything from fly-fishing to climbing a mountain to how to choose a kayak. Some 400 online clinics and how-to informational articles are available on the site. Most of those articles aren't written by copywriters but by product users on the REI staff. As a result, the articles read more like educational pieces than sales pitches. Web customers can access live chat rooms and community bulletin boards where they can share information about their favorite trips or experiences using REI gear—even look for trip partners.

These kind of custom aspects of e-commerce offerings not only can add enormous value but provide another compelling reason for customers to return to a site.

Technology drives service improvement.   Another way REI combines physical and digital worlds for customers' benefit is through use of Web-based kiosks in its retail stores. The kiosks, providing a direct in-store link to REI.com, serve a handful of purposes. For one thing, REI merchandise isn't always in stock in every store. So a customer who doesn't find an item in stock can log onto one of the self-service kiosks (which have access only to REI.com) and order from the Web site's extensive collection. The site offers some 78,000 items, far more even than REI's gargantuan Seattle store. Items can be delivered to homes or the store for pickup. "The kiosks have been particularly effective in our smaller stores, where customers wonder if we have an item, and sales staff can look it up on the kiosk and say yes, we do, and place a special order if needed," says Foley.

If a customer wants to compare the features of certain kayaks or multiple sleeping bags or configure a car roof rack to carry an assortment of bikes, skis, or canoes, he or she can access the Web site via kiosk, create a chart, and print it out for use in-store.

Second, the kiosks offer more detailed information, such as product specs, than even REI's amply educated staff could ever memorize about the vast product line. Employees can use the Web site as sales support to find information on less popular or more complex items, passing that knowledge on to customers.

REI's cash registers also are Web-enabled. Cashiers, who often get plenty of questions from customers about store merchandise, such as where to find add-on items, can look up and even place an online order for customers at the point of sale, with the customer paying for it on the spot.

CASE 3: BERN'S STEAK HOUSE—A STUDY IN MEMORABLE SERVICE

Bern's Steak House in Tampa, Florida, is a remarkable study in getting service right for your customer. Touted in John Mariani's *America Eats Out* (Morrow, 1991) as an American original and one of the most famous restaurants in the world, owner Bern Laxer's credo seems to be "fulfillment through excess," and his results vindicate his theory.

Located in an odd "cat-in-the-hat" assemblage of buildings in a nondescript part of town, Bern's serves up remarkable meals and memorable dining experiences. The menus alone are a feast.

True to the name, Bern's features beef; serving six cuts of beef from Delmonico to porterhouse, trimmed of all nonedible parts, available in any thickness, broiled to any of eight degrees of doneness, and with or without a charred exterior. The goal: a meal tailored to each diner's wishes.

Other highlights include: The appetizer menu features five tartars and two dozen caviars. Seafood is always fresh—the kitchen has a 7200-gallon holding tank that keeps 2300 pounds of live fish. Spices are ground fresh each day. Bern's grows its own herbs and sprouts, marinates its own olives, and bakes its own breads and crackers. Vegetables come from the restaurant's own organic farm, and of course, they blend, roast, and grind their own coffee from 11 select varieties of bean.

The wine list has 8000 entries and the wine cellar (an insulated, temperature-controlled warehouse) contains approximately 500,000 bottles of wine ranging in price from $20 to $10,000. There is a separate by-the-glass menu of 200 selections. Dessert is served apart from the dining room, in a 250-seat building of intimate sound proof alcoves where diners can select from a 65-page list of desserts and coffees and 385 dessert wines and spirits including some of the rarest cognacs, Armangnacs, and sauternes in the world. And of course, there is a choice of 16 possible musical backgrounds.

One might expect a dining experience of rare haughtiness and snob appeal. But Bern's is nothing if not civil and approachable. Diners are characteristically Floridian casual, and black-jacketed waiters carefully pace their performance to the comfort level of their charges. No one, it seems, walks away from an evening at Bern's feeling underfed or unappreciated.

Key to the stunningly flexible service experience is the training regime owner Laxer has instituted for the wait staff. The hiring criteria are simple—intelligence, no previous restaurant experience, and a low-key, self-assured, enjoyable personality—and the forbearance and perspicacity of a saint. Wait staff training begins in the kitchen, where waiter trainees learn and work every station and routinely serve KP duty during a 2 to 3 month stint.

During a guided tour of the kitchens and wine rooms a waiter confided, "I peeled more potatoes in this kitchen than I ever did in the army." Trainees then move on to a stint at the vegetable farm and graduate to dining room wait assistant, with time out to apprentice in the dessert enclave and understudy in the wine room under one of the restaurant's sommeliers.

After 18 to 24 months of assisting and learning, waiters graduate to red-jacket status, wherein they wait tables solo but always under the watchful eye of the room captain and dining room manager Paul Rainey. Eventually, trainees are adjudged ready to be tested, and they sit for a 3-

We Do Things Differently Here

Because we learned early that if you want to be the best at something, you can't worry about the cost. Or the "trouble." That's why

Our waiters train one year with us, working at almost every station in the restaurant, workshops, and on the farm, and then train for another 8 to 12 weeks in the dining rooms before they wait on you by themselves. And then still wear red jackets for perhaps a year before we feel that they are fully knowledgeable to answer your every single question properly.

And we devote the space equivalent to some 100 dining seats just to offer you the widest selection of wines in the world—by the glass as well as by the bottle.

And use only freshly-squeezed juices and great quality liquors to prepare your cocktail; even though you may never see the labels or see us squeeze the juices.

And fly in fresh caviar regularly.

And bring you only live seafood whenever possible by building a 2500-pound live fish capacity in our kitchen and on our roof (and invite you to select your own if you wish while it is swimming).

And buy veal bones to help us make better onion soup even though we have (and use) hundreds of pounds of our own beef bones.

And import—and sprout in our kitchen—cress seeds from England just to add one small flavor ingredient to your salad.

And marinate our olives for at least one month in pure olive oil, herbs and spices; even though you may scarcely notice one on your salad.

And grow what we can on our own farm, organically—without pesticides or other toxic materials—and pick your vegetables ripe and fresh as frequently as possible.

And peel your tomato before serving it.

And age your steak as long as we do.

And broil your steak with far-healthier lump charcoal instead of super-convenient briquettes.

And then cut and trim and weigh your steak only after you have placed your order (with 62 choices to cut, a bit more labor is required than if we just served you several pre-cut steaks).

And make garlic butter for your steak the old-fashioned way—by peeling lots of garlic and blending it with 100% sweet cream butter.

And use hundreds of pounds of 93 score AA unsalted fresh creamery butter weekly in the kitchen.

And have our sour cream and cream cheese specially made for us.

And prepare all our vegetables either to your order or in very small quantities.

And bake your potato to order (and throw it out if it is baked a shade too long).

And completely prepare and fry your onion rings so that they come out of the fryers just as your steak comes off the broiler. And carefully double-drain every single order of fried foods we serve you—a fresh paper towel is used for every single order.

And hand-sort our green coffee beans to eliminate every single defect before we roast (up to 10 different beans separately), and *then* blend our American, espresso and Turkish coffee beans each day in our kitchen.

And use four separate grinders so that each different coffee and each different blend is freshly ground only to your order—the $\frac{1}{2}$ teaspoon *powdered* coffee to top your cappuccino, the three *fine* teaspoons for your Brazilian snow, and the three *medium-fine* teaspoons for your espresso coffee—for example. (We also brew your coffee strong and believe that only heavy whipping cream is good enough for it.)

And make all our own ice creams, sherbets, pies, pastries, hot fudge, whipped cream, breads, crackers, etc. ourselves, so that we might use more exciting ingredients throughout.

And import products like special liqueurs and flavors from all over the world just to produce a unique dessert.

And. And. And.

Perhaps you begin to see—we really *do* do things differently here.

Because we mean it when we say we want you to have a most memorable evening when you dine with us—each time you come.

BERN'S STEAK HOUSE
TAMPA, FL

FIGURE 10-1   Bern's Steak House philosophy

hour, 200-question oral examination of the restaurant menus, wine lists, and service protocols, conducted by the senior dining room staff.

In the end, graduate waiters are assigned a room of the restaurant and a name. All members of the dining room staff are referred to by a single name, and names are often retired with the waiter.

Waiters, many of whom have professional degrees and are second careerists, are so adept at creating an individualized dining experience—complete with a kitchen and wine cellar tour if requested—that it is difficult to describe a single standard ambience. If you like your dining quiet, intimate, and romantic and your wait staff unobtrusive, no problem. If you're entertaining friends and are intent on impressing your guests with the uniqueness of Bern's, simply suggest to the waiter that your friends are "first timers" and would love to hear the Bern's story. The wait person will swing easily into a performance persona.

In an era when waiters and waitresses routinely act as if it is their duty to let diners know they are simply being tolerated, and, save for some nasty accident of fate, their roles could well be reversed, Bern's is a useful reminder that welcoming civil service is neither a dead art nor a valueless commodity. It is a treasure to behold. It starts with a vision and lives in the details.

CASE 4: WALT DISNEY COMPANY

On Interstate 4 southwest of Orlando, Florida, a gold and purple building fronts the highway. It sports a very large sign with but a single word: "Casting." It's the Walt Disney World personnel office. It is an eloquent testament to the Disney approach to service management; it starts with finding (and retaining) good people for a show that has been running to a packed house since 1971. The Disney theme park management handbook makes this point. After listing two almost mirror-image sets of standards for the treatment of "guests" (customers), and "cast members" (employees), we find this eloquent summary of management "magic" of Disney:

> We believe that guests will receive the quality of treatment we expect them to receive, when members of the cast receive the same quality of treatment.

More than 45 million people will visit Walt Disney World in Orlando in a typical year; another 20 million will set their sights toward the original Disneyland and new California Adventure, in Anaheim, California. Walt Disney World theme parks claimed the top 7 spots in theme park attendance for the year 2000—with nearly 75 million total guests. If Scandinavian Airlines has 50,000 moments of truth a day, Disney has 10 million. Now ask yourself this: How does a company build a world reputation for service like this, and a thriving worldwide business using essentially the same 18-year-olds that we can't get to clean their rooms?

What Walt Disney invented in 1955 was a new, never before seen business: the modern amusement park. The rides may be designed for kids, but don't kid yourself—this is adult entertainment. Disney people constantly talk about "the setting," the sight and sound and touch and sensation that each attraction is designed to deliver. "You don't build it for yourself," they remember Walt saying. "You know what the people want and you build it for them."

At Disney, people talk about "keys" that "unlock" the product. It starts with the concepts of *show* and *efficiency*. The former involves the sights and sounds, the look and feel, the overt and implied messages of the various entertainment experiences inside the parks. The latter is the way equipment and operating systems are designed and deployed within each area. Together they feed into a concept of *safety*—the safety of the guest is an absolute, uncompromisable standard. One of the outcomes of applying these three design elements is Disney's reputation for courtesy. The company believes that quality service is more easily obtained when the setting supports a good show that is efficiently provided and safely managed. Employees are more able to focus on customers when everything else is working effortlessly and as planned. On the other hand, interference with any of the three basic keys reduces or diverts attention from service quality.

People have off-beat ideas at Disney. When they design an attraction for the park, they "imagineer" the entire experience—not just the mechanical parts of a ride, but what you see and hear and sense all around you. If you happen to go through the parks in the off-season, for example, when the crowds are thinner and most of the lines are shorter, you'll find it still takes you about half an hour to get on Space Mountain. It makes no difference how open the walkways may seem, there's always a line at Space Mountain. The reason for this becomes clear when you've finally wound your way around and down the blue-lit corridors to the platform where they're loading the little rocket cars and you notice that they're running the ride at half capacity. They could run through faster, but then you wouldn't have time to look and talk and read the signs telling you that pregnant women and people with heart conditions can bail out at the convenient exit over here. And if you get through it more quickly, you would not get the full effect of the experience the ride is designed to deliver.

Disney has the lowest employee turnover in the theme park business: 15 percent in an industry where more than 100 percent per season is not uncommon.[3] At the management level, it's about 6 percent. Selection plays a big part in that. In a sense, Disney "de-recruits." It makes it clear in its recruiting and employment materials that the parks are a demanding environment and that the only way to move up is to start at the bottom. There is no doubt in the minds of applicants that the standards are tough and uncompromising and that personality quirks must be subordinated to the entertainment experience and public image they are expected to project.

Whether inside an attraction or on the grounds of the park, everybody is considered to be "on stage" and is charged with keeping the "set" neat and clean. In the Disney parks everybody picks up paper. And everybody is on a first-name basis, as befits a large, friendly family. A few years ago, the annual report pictured Michael Eisner, the high-powered CEO who has reinvigorated Disney since he came on board in 1984, making the rounds in Walt Disney World without a name tag. Now at Disneyland and Walt Disney World, if you work for the company, you're supposed to wear a name tag any time you're in the park. Sharp-eyed employees spotted Eisner "out of uniform," and they let him know about it. They weren't afraid to beard the top dog in the Disney menagerie over something as mundane as a name tag because at Disney rank may have its privileges, but it also has the same responsibilities that everybody else has.

Selection is a science at Disney. No one gets hired after a first interview. It takes at least two personal screenings by two different interviewers. Post selection, the first day and a half on the job is spent in a program called Disney Traditions, a full-fledged course in the history, philosophy, ideals, goals, and values of the Magic Kingdom. From there, it's time for on-the-job training—which may take 2 days to 2 weeks, depending on the complexity of the job (there are more than a thousand different types of positions in all) to be done.

New employees who don't work out are seldom fired. Instead, the Disney way is to assume that somehow they've put that person in the wrong position, and they'll try retraining and reassigning for a long time before giving up on someone. Those who do work out can gain the opportunity to do a number of jobs within their department and cross-train for new responsibilities that keep them growing and moving within the Disney family. It's one of their retention keys.

The training investment is ambitious and constant. Disney spends 4 days training the kids who push the brooms and dustbins around the park. Four days! How long can it take to teach someone to sweep up spilled popcorn and candy wrappers? A couple of hours? The rest of the training time is spent teaching those lowliest of cast members the answers to the questions that guests are more likely to ask of the sweepers than of the brightly smiling, freshly scrubbed guest relations ambassadors provided for that purpose.

"Where's the nearest place to get pizza?" "What are the names of the Seven Dwarfs?" "What time is the 4 o'clock parade?" "If I'm standing here in line for Space Mountain and it says it will be 45 minutes before I get on the ride, how long will it really take to get on the ride?" Disney has found through paying attention to its customers that the people with the brooms are five times more likely to be asked these questions than the people ostensibly provided for that purpose. So instead of having them send the guest over to a person with the official responsibility, they teach them the answers. That's part of the setting: friendly people who are ever ready to help you. And that, in turn, empowers these workers to truly think of themselves as full-fledged members of the Disney cast and to do things for guests in the park.

Training isn't restricted to just one job. Ride the Jungle Cruise long enough, and even the sanest and tamest of people may want to feed themselves (or perhaps an occasional small and obnoxious passenger) to the artificial crocodiles. To guard against that kind of burnout, Disney rotates its cast members around to different attractions or gives them a chance to move into the retail shops for a while.

It also gives them opportunities to move up. Hosts and hostesses, the basic front-line troops who run the rides and have the most extensive public contact, become "lead" hosts and hostesses. From among the leads come the assistant supervisors and the supervisors.

Disney also recognizes the importance of allowing its front-line people to get "offstage" when pressures mount or fatigue starts to set in and there's no negative consequence for taking advantage of that safety valve. Everybody (at least everybody at Disney) knows that dealing with the public all day is a hard job, and sometimes you get a little frazzled on the front line.

As the show business metaphor suggests, getting offstage is a tactic that allows a cast member to retreat from the public eye momentarily and recharge the mental and emotional batteries. Disney managers know how to spot the signs of stress and tension in their people, and occasionally (though you have to be paying attention to actually see it happen) one will suggest that a worker take a break for a few minutes while he or she fills in and keeps things running smoothly. Since supervisors came from the front line, they're prepared to do the job without a bump or hitch being visible to the guests.

There is one misconception about Disney. Others have written that Disney has a requirement that every year park executives, almost all of whom have come from the front lines, *must* spend so many days working in front-line jobs at one of the parks. That's not true. They're only *allowed* to work so many days a year in the park.

The vision hasn't changed substantially since Walt Disney himself was walking the streets of the Magic Kingdom. Once asked whether his ideas would survive him, he replied: "Well, I think by this time my staff, my young group of executives, and everyone else are convinced that Walt is right. That quality will out. And so I think they're going to stay with that policy because it's proved that it's a good business policy. Give the people everything you can give them. Keep the place as fun as you can keep it. Keep it friendly, you know. Make it a real fun place to be. I think they're convinced and I think they'll hang on after ... as you say ... well ... after Disney."

The Disney parks aren't a static memorial to Walt Disney's original conception, however. Since Walt Disney World opened in 1971, several additions have been made to the Florida complex: Epcot in 1982, Disney-MGM in 1989, and Animal Kingdom in 1998. The original recently opened Disney's California Adventure in 2001, a high-tech thrill ride bonanza.

For years the most universal complaint about the parks has been the long waiting lines. And while Disney imagineers and improvement teams have worked wonders at making the waits seem shorter, the complaint has persisted until 2000 with the invention of FASTPASS. FASTPASS allows guests to make appointments for certain rides and certain attractions. This innovation is, of course, now sweeping the theme park business.

Given the high visibility of the Disney parks and the number of people who wander the parks worldwide, it's no surprise that the question "How do you do that?" has been frequently asked. In response, Disney University offers seminars in the Disney approach to leadership to "outsiders" on a regular basis.[4] And there is indeed much for an outsider to learn from looking behind the stage. Dr. Thomas Connellan, author of *Inside the Magic Kingdom*[5] (an outsider's view of the Disney management magic) says that there are many lessons a business can take away from studying "the Disney way." Among them are:

- Pay fantastic attention to detail. Disney leaves nothing to chance.
- Everyone walks the talk. No one is exempt from the philosophy.
- Everything walks the talk. No object is allowed to stray from the image.
- Customers are best heard through many ears. Everyone is a listener.
- Reward, recognize, and celebrate.

Where or what is next for the Disney service management magic? The sky's probably not really the limit. After all, Disney has been making films and TV shows about the moon and beyond for years. Can a theme park be far behind?

11

Teaching the Elephant to Dance

"A competitive world has two possibilities for you. You can lose. Or, if you want to win, you can change."

—*Lester Thurow*

A QUICK RECAP

WE LIVE IN A SERVICE ECONOMY and an increasingly service-centric society. Service, in one form or another, now accounts for almost 80 percent of the jobs in the United States. Other developed countries have experienced similar trends in the past 20 years. After a distraction or two in the mid-1990s, savvy organizations are again becoming serious about the quality of the customer's experience and finding ways to improve it.

Furthermore, we have concluded that a high-quality service orientation is a powerful competitive weapon. When indifferent or downright shoddy service is an all too common experience for customers of many businesses, organizations that demonstrate a significant commitment to their customers' needs readily distinguish themselves from their competition. Their commitment to quality service is an essential part of their business strategy, not just a frill or a "nice to have" feature. We contend that businesses that do not demonstrate a significant commitment to the needs of their customers will be left further and further behind. Quality of service is once again a top-management issue.

Evidence from a number of successful organizations points to the concept of *managing the moments of truth* as the philosophy that drives service management. Service management is more than establishing a complaint department or "putting somebody in charge of service." It's a top-down, whole-organization approach that starts with the nature of the customer's experience and creates strategies and tactics to maximize the quality of that experience. Making a commitment to service management means turning the whole organization into a customer-driven business entity, which is a very tall order.

However, organizations that have accomplished it are easy to spot. They tend to share certain internal characteristics:

1. They have a strong vision and an articulated strategy for service that is carefully developed and clearly communicated.
2. They practice visible management.
3. They "talk" service routinely.
4. They have customer-friendly service delivery systems.
5. They balance high tech with high touch; that is, they temper their systems and methods with the personal factor.
6. They recruit, hire, train, and promote for service.
7. They market service externally to their customers.
8. They market service internally to their employees.
9. They measure service and make the results available—and consequential—to everyone in the organization.

ALL TOGETHER NOW: 1—2—3—KICK

How tough is it to reorient a large organization into a customer-driven business? We compare the job to teaching an elephant to dance. Many of the same challenges are involved. Before an elephant learns to dance—

or a large organization changes its ways—two things must happen: First, somebody must show that it's possible for this pachyderm to pirouette; and, second, the elephant must be motivated to make it happen.

Service management offers a way to create and communicate a vision of service. It offers a way to make that vision a reality in the day-to-day business. It is indeed a way to make an organization a customer-driven enterprise. It is the way to teach the elephant to dance, or at least improve the odds that it will want to learn.

Despite great diversity among outstanding service organizations, there is a common thread that makes them more alike than different: They have a distinctive service orientation. A service-driven organization has an understanding of its customers, a clear service strategy, customer-oriented front-line people, and customer-friendly systems for delivering service.

TOTAL QUALITY SERVICE: AN ACTION MODEL

In the first edition of this book, we offered a general prescription for implementing a total service management way of doing business, in the form of five key steps. Since that time, we have become ever more firmly convinced of the need for those five critical processes. Further, we have come to view them as a kind of comprehensive change management framework, which can help the leaders of a service enterprise keep their attention focused on the strategic direction and define the critical actions needed to implement it. We call this five-part change management formula the Total Quality Service, or TQS model.[1]

Outstanding service organizations have mastered five critical processes that lead to superior customer value. The basic TQS model, in its overall conceptual form, is simply the unification of these five action elements. Each of the five areas has its own specific methods and practices. Each deserves a great deal of attention and study because it offers a wealth of possibilities for making a quality initiative successful.

The TQS model is more a discovery than an invention. It is a perception that emerged from the study of the philosophies, leadership approaches, and business practices of a large number of outstanding customer-committed organizations, which all seemed to have these five basic things in common. And these common elements seemed to form the basis for a new worldview about business, customers, and quality. For the current discussion, we can summarize the five basic action elements.

Market and customer research. Outstanding service organizations understand the very basic needs, instincts, life situations, problems, and buying motivations of their customers. They see their customers as unique people, not as market units. They know what critical elements of value will win and keep their business.

It takes two kinds of research to understand your customers: research on the market and research on the customers themselves. *Market research*, in this connotation, is the investigation of the structure and dynamics of the marketplace you propose to serve. This includes identifying market segments, analyzing demographics, targeting critical market niches, and analyzing competitive forces.

Customer perception research goes at least one step beyond conventional market research. It attempts to understand the expectations, thoughts, and feelings of the individual customer toward the service product and service provider. It attempts to discern one or more critical factors in the customer's perception of the total experience. This enables you to come up with a *customer value model*, which is a set of criteria that drive the customer's choices between you and your competitors.

Many large organizations do excellent market research. Many, however, do little or no customer perception research, or do it ineffectively. Many middle-sized or small organizations do virtually no research at all. It is safe to say that probably a majority of business organizations do not have an adequate understanding of the critical subjective factors that influence their customers' perceptions of value.

Strategy formulation. Outstanding service management organizations have cast their lot with the principle of customer value. They have developed, evolved, or designed business approaches that win and keep customers by offering value. They know clearly what business they are in, what their missions are, what their core values and beliefs are, and what strategic approaches they have to take to succeed through customer value. They understand how to subordinate technology, operations, methods, and organizational structures to the overarching demands of a customer value business strategy.

Frequently, becoming fully customer-centered or improving service quality demands repositioning the organization itself. This requires its leaders to review various aspects of the competitive strategy and possibly even to rethink the vision, mission, core values, and basic direction for the enterprise. They must reexamine the total value package they bring to the market, down to its very fundamentals. They may, in this process, confirm their current concept of their customer relationship, adjust it slightly, or completely revolutionize it.

Education, training, and communication. The top performers are skilled at communicating the customer value message to everyone in the organization. They understand and accept the magnitude of the investment required to develop and maintain the collective human knowledge, capability, and commitment necessary to deliver outstanding customer value. They know how to create and maintain healthy information cultures—the collective know-how that comes through shared values, shared beliefs, shared facts, and shared performance. They have learned how to win and sustain employee commitment to the spirit of service and the values that make it real.

We know of no outstanding service organization that does not use an intensive, continuous, dedicated process of educating its people about their customers, about quality, and about their roles in delivering superior service. The methods of education, training, and communication play a central part in helping everyone understand the customer's needs and expectations; the vision, mission, and values of the organization; and the strategies for winning and keeping the customer's business. This is a critical process in getting the organization moving along the Total Quality Service track, and it remains critical in sustaining its commitment.

Process improvement. Outstanding organizations are good at changing themselves and becoming the kinds of organizations they need to be to meet their business missions. They will not tolerate the kinds of bureaucracy and organizational craziness that cripple so many of their competitors. They have a commitment at all levels of leadership to continuous quality improvement, and they actively seek ways to make their organizations work better on behalf of the employees as well as the customers. The effort to make the organization's systems customer-friendly must be perpetual.

It is essential to continually examine, question, and revise if necessary every process, procedure, policy, rule, or work method. In an effective service-committed organization, all systems owe their existence to the ultimate objective of delivering customer value, either to the external paying customers or to the internal customers who contribute their part to the ultimate objective. All systems are on probation all the time. All are eligible for revision if they do not add value.

Assessment, measurement, and feedback.   The excellent service performers understand that information empowers people, and they go to great lengths to help people know what their customers want and need and how they are doing in meeting those wants and needs. They also make sure people get feedback, recognition, and appreciation for the contributions they make to customer value. They have aligned their internal reward processes with the business purpose, to make sure that people do indeed receive personal value when they commit their energies to delivering customer value.

The only way to guide the efforts of the people in any organization toward Total Quality Service is to give them feedback about their progress. Every organization needs a carefully thought out approach for measuring customer value and the critical organizational processes that create it, a way to share this information with its people, and a way to react constructively to its meaning. This has been one of the most confusing aspects of quality improvement for many people. Making all standards and measurements customer-focused helps a great deal to clear up the measurement issue.

Figure 11-1 shows these five action areas united into a wheel model, with the goal condition of Total Quality Service at the center. Taken individually, each of these five areas has its own appeal. Each could be an appropriate starting point for an organizational quality initiative. But the secret to superior quality is in combining these action elements into a unified approach that works. This is what makes TQS a change model; it is a prescription for becoming the kind of enterprise that can achieve and sustain the dynamic state of affairs characterized by Total Quality Service.

Let's use a nautical metaphor for putting all five action elements of the TQS model together into perspective. If Total Quality Service is the ideal, ultimate, never-to-be-arrived-at destination, then the TQS approach is the journey. Customer research serves as the compass, strategy formulation provides the navigational chart, education and communication put the wind into the sails, process improvement provides the rudder that keeps the ship on course, and measurement and feedback tell

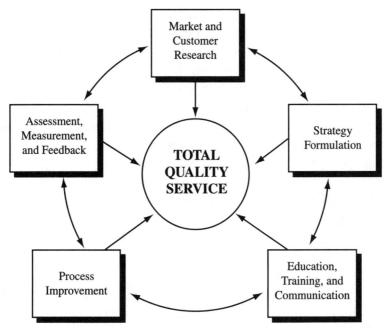

FIGURE 11-1   The Total Quality Service (TQS) model

the captain and crew when and how to change course. It is the effective interplay of all five factors that keeps the ship sailing properly on its journey.

With this wide-angle view established, let's focus on a definition of Total Quality Service and see how it transcends the old distinctions between product and service.

Total Quality Service
A state of affairs in which an organization delivers superior value to its stakeholders: its customers, its owners, and its employees.

This implies a business philosophy, a form of leadership, a collective spirit of service, and a way of operating that embraces quality and customer value as its guiding principles.

If you examine this particular choice of words, you can see that it implies a goal condition to be sought, not any particular method of operating. Methods arise to help achieve the goal, not to become ends in themselves.

It uses the customer's response to value delivered as the basic litmus test of its success. It forces us to pose the question "Have we created and delivered real customer value, as evidenced by the customer's reaction to what we've done?" It proceeds from the view that customers who receive superior value will reward the organization with their continued patronage.

And it recognizes the needs of the organization as well as the needs of the customer. Total Quality Service requires that all stakeholders get their needs met. You can deliver great customer value but go out of business because you're not operating cost-effectively. And if the employees aren't receiving value as members of the organization, you can't sustain their commitment.

Any state of affairs can change. As J. Willard Marriott, Sr., founder of the Marriott Corporation, said many years ago, "Success is never final." There is nothing anyone can do to guarantee that an organization will maintain a state of Total Quality Service forever. Marriott believed it was harder to remain an outstanding service company than it was to become one in the first place.

Few managers will admit that they are attached to bureaucratic methods, and almost all of them would agree that there is a need for creative new approaches—in the abstract, that is. When the time comes to change their own ways of doing things, however, they often remain firmly attached to their customary habits and procedures. This is when top management can play an important role. If executives remind managers at all levels of the importance of the service strategy and kindly but firmly encourage them to support it in practice, even confirmed bureaucrats can break through fossilized habits and replace them.

Teaching the elephant to dance—or implementing a service management program in a large organization—demands a strong education process, as well as continual persuasion. Management must offer visible and consistent support for the service concept, embracing the role of preacher and teacher and spreading the gospel of service to front-line people.

As the service management process matures, the organization's support systems must align with the service concept. Here are some questions that will help you check for alignment: Does your recruiting and hiring process attract people who can fulfill service roles effectively? Does the new employee orientation program instill the service strategy from the start? Does all communication from the company preach the same gospel that the chief executive preaches? Do training programs advance the cause of effective service? Does your performance planning system reinforce the goals of the service management program? Does your appraisal system provide feedback to employees about the effectiveness of their efforts?

LESSONS LEARNED

In the first edition of this book, we closed this chapter with a short list of ways to do it wrong, descriptions of the traps we'd seen managers fall into while they reoriented their organizations to service quality. Fifteen years of aiding and abetting organizations have taught us a few more things about making a "service focus" part of a culture and not simply a fad of the month.

As Thomas Edison learned when he was working on the light bulb: There are more ways to get it wrong than to get it right. Here are six hard-won lessons worth considering as you journey toward building a winning service focus for your organization.

1. **Economic pressure is an important motivator.** Service has more impact on an organization's fate than most people realize, and the day-to-day quality of that service is worse than we care to admit. To begin reversing the downward spiral of service, you must have a clear and understandable economic reason for changing direction. Many organizations don't take action until the barbarians—and the bill collectors—are pounding at the gate. That's usually too late. Fear of failure is a strong focusing force, but it kicks in only when radical measures are required to save the company. An environment of panic makes it difficult—not impossible, but difficult—to rally employees behind an effort to revitalize a neglected service ethic.

   A better course of action is to create clear economic or financial measures of service impact and keep them in front of everyone. What sorts of measures? The cost of a lost customer, coupled with customer turnover, is one example. The cost of handling customer complaints is another. A Pennsylvania-based catalog company tracks customers who fall into three categories: "at-risk" (likely to defect), "advocate," and "loyal." The number and ratio of customers in each group gives the company several useful measures. The most important metric, though, is the record of customers' movement among these categories.

2. **Management involvement is critical.** If service improvement is to become a strategic focus and not just a program, it must start at the top. Most organizations try to manage service from a defensive posture, delegating responsibility down the line as far as possible. But individual line managers have limited control over service quality; there are more moments of truth that affect service quality than a single line manager can control. A senior manager needs to be accountable for the big picture of service quality, the complete customer experience chain, and be authorized to do whatever it takes to make the customer experience smooth and seamless.

3. **Five mistakes characterize most failures.** Time and again, we've seen the same five errors keep a service focus effort from succeeding. They are:

   - **Not understanding the customer's needs.** One senior manager faced with the reality that his organization was woefully shy of current customer intelligence protested, "Really now. We don't need a lot of fancy research, do we? I mean, we're customers too, aren't we? Don't we know what customers want?" The short answer is no. Although you can know what the organization wants customers to want, marketplace reality is a fading photograph. There are many ways to collect data; our message is, just do it. Keep the customer's voice clear, relevant, unfiltered, and up-to-date.

   - **Failing to set standards.** Don't make the mistake of telling your people to "Get out there and do good!" in the misguided belief that service is intangible and therefore unmeasurable. "You'll know it when I see it" isn't good guidance. Yes, service is a real-time, artifact-free activity, but customers can describe successful and unsuccessful service delivery. That's a good beginning. Standards—being able to specify what good, bad, and great service looks like—are prerequisite to asking people to deliver it.

   - **Allowing substandard performance to go unchallenged.** It's tempting to sidestep those "Yes, you did. No, I didn't" conversations that can occur when you deal with the intangibles of service. It's easier to take an employee's or line manager's word that everything is A-OK and that an incident or this week's low scores are an aberration. But as we've amply demonstrated, the cost of shoddy service—even solitary incidents—is too high to allow it to go undiscussed.

- **Not communicating with customers and employees about service.** You know about this one if you know the old adage about alligators and swamps in need of draining. When people become too bogged down in details, they lose sight of their mission. Management must keep both employees and customers apprised of what good service looks like and how well the organization is delivering it.

- **Promising the customer more than the organization can deliver.** This error runs the gamut from grandiose to subtle. You can spend lots of money advertising a capacity you don't have and make thousands of customers irate at your failures. Or you can conduct telephone surveys asking customers about their most recent visits to the service bay of your auto dealership and fail to do anything about the complaints they share with you. Either way, you're promising and not delivering.

4. **Employees can help or hinder.** Your employees can work for you or against you. They are your first market; if you don't sell them on a world-class service focus, you won't consistently deliver it to customers. Employees need to see the importance of changing. And there has to be something in it for them to change the way they approach and relate to customers. They need time and support. Training in new skills only "takes" with patient coaching and a clear understanding that changes in job performance will be personally and organizationally worthwhile. Involving your people in the change (allowing them to feel some ownership, as in, "I helped invent this") lowers their anxiety level and increases their commitment. Feedback systems, improvement monitors, and personal payoff also help. A lot.

5. **Building alignment reduces friction.** Management's top priority is to align people with the service strategy and then empower them to work on the customer's behalf. How top people spend their time tells the rest of the organization what is really important. As Will Rogers noted, "People learn more from observation than from conversation."

As we've seen, alignment starts with a clear, concise, understandable, actionable, measurable service strategy. Taking time to discuss the implications of the service strategy with everyone in the organization is an enormous investment, but it is the most important one you can make. Likewise, your adherence to the precepts of the new strategy, which is the only convincing proof of your commitment, is critical. That proof can be as simple as your willingness to support the cleanliness value in your service strategy by picking up trash when you see it or as complex as your disposition of individuals, departments, or divisions that are incompatible with your new strategy.

6. **Complacency kills.** As we've asserted previously, the longer you're in a service business, the greater the likelihood that you don't understand your customers' needs. The department store manager who has a heated, reserved, parking stall; who comes into the store through the executive entrance; and who takes lunch at the club, may not have a clue what customers and employees experience in his or her store. Even a manager one step removed from the action should beware of this kind of "all's well" complacency.

At some point, the service management program ceases to be a program at all; it becomes the organization's basic orientation. Getting to that point, however, requires a large investment in time, energy, money, and creative thinking. Organizations that make that investment most effectively, we believe, will be the ones that thrive and grow.

12

SERVICE TOMORROW: WHAT CAN WE EXPECT?

"Who the hell wants to hear actors talk?"

—*Harry Warner, Head of Warner Brothers Studios*

HOW WELL DID WE PREDICT TODAY?

PREDICTING THE FUTURE isn't really all that risky, in most cases, because people seldom remember predictions, and even less often do they consciously compare the today they're experiencing with the tomorrow somebody else predicted yesterday. The supermarket tabloids like to publish psychic predictions at the end of each year, about asteroids hitting the earth, alien landings, and Hollywood marriages. But none of them review last year's predictions for accuracy, and their readers don't seem to notice.

In this book, however, we don't have the benefit of mnemonic immunity, because the predictions we made in the first edition are still there in black and white, staring us in the face. It seems we have little choice but to begin the discussion of the future of services with a review and scoring of our original predictions.

Most of our specific predictions actually hit the mark, or came pretty close; however, one of the biggest and most general predictions seems open to question. The opening line to the first edition's version of this chapter said:

> We look forward optimistically to the next decade: Services of all kinds will get better and better.

Immediately following that, we said:

> Will service be as important a part of our economic tomorrow as it is today? No. It will be *more* important. By all indications the increasing shift from industrial America to service America, the demand for more and better services, and the increasing number of service jobs will make us all much more service-conscious. This will happen not only in the United States but also all around the developed world.

Probably most experts would agree that services have become a more prominent part of economic thinking and more important to the United States and other developed economies. However, it is arguable whether services of all kinds have really gotten better. Some seem to have gained, some have probably remained about the same, and others have probably lost ground. Actually, we don't—so far—have the means to measure and compare services across a broad range of economic sectors, so evaluating the prediction is largely a matter of opinion and argument.

Many business people in other countries will declare without hesitation that service in America, in general, is superior to service in virtually all other developed countries. Many Americans, however, are quick to dispute that assertion. And, on an individual basis, one person's favorite airline is another person's nemesis.

So, we can probably score one "yes" and one "maybe" for those two macropredictions. And a third prediction, we believe, unfortunately came true for the most part. We said:

> Probably only 10 to 15 percent of the players will really be able to swing their organizational cultures around to make them truly customer-driven. The other companies will continue to invent slogans, hoping that the right advertising message will do the trick. As the service philosophy becomes more and more fundamental to doing business, the other companies will gradually figure out how to do it, too.

So, the status report seems to be: Yes, service is more significant economically than before; no, it's probably not significantly better overall than before; and no, most companies have not, in general, succeeded in building strategic customer focus into their corporate DNA.

On a more specific level, we correctly predicted that the new wave of deregulation would present a host of new competitive opportunities for new firms, and challenges for established firms. In particular, we predicted serious challenges for AT&T, as a consequence of its break-up and loss of monopoly status. The same applied to the broad financial services industry, with banks acting like brokerage houses and brokers trying to impersonate bankers.

We correctly predicted the high-tech/high-touch character of the proliferation of services, that is, the notion that:

> For every automatic teller machine that does away with an interpersonal transaction, there may be an increasing personal involvement in, say, automobile repair.

We correctly predicted a big increase in demand for temporary help services in a wide range of industries and occupations. We also correctly predicted a big rise in demand for child-centered products and services, from education, to fashion, to books, to electronic gadgets and many others.

We also correctly predicted the upheaval in the health-care industry, with hospitals feeling ever greater pressure due to shorter patient stays and competition from the doctors they'd long considered their business partners. We also correctly predicted the forcible reorganization of health-care economics at the hands of governments and HMOs, and the resulting pressure on the incomes of physicians.

However, we had nothing at all to offer about the Internet and the huge wave of energy and resources going into the Internet, the Web, and online delivery of services. This means we completely missed the online investing phenomenon, for example, and its cyclonic effect on the traditional Wall Street wirehouses. We never thought about it; in fact it wasn't even on our radar screen at the time. As so often happens in forecasting, the most significant outcomes are not necessarily the ones you got right or got wrong, but the ones that never even occurred to you.

THE STRETCHING SPECTRUM OF SERVICES

Looking forward, into a business environment that will be ever more complex, diversified, fluid, and rapidly changing, it's both easy and difficult to guess what will happen. One thing that probably will happen is that the pace of innovation will increase, as smaller and more agile firms search constantly for new and different ways of creating value. Such rapid innovation is probably the biggest single competitive threat to the megafirms that dominate but generally cannot or do not innovate. Ironically, the minnows occasionally get to gang up on the big fish that's been eating them one by one.

We will probably also see a continued stretching of the spectrum of services, from the most commoditized delivery schemes such as fast food, gasoline, and convenience stores, to the ever more exotic levels of personal, high-value, technology-enabled services. At the bottom end of the food chain, factors such as human contact, variety, novelty, individuality, ingenuity, and surprise will count for little, as customers have been conditioned to accept the minimum value for the minimum price. At the other end of the spectrum, those same values will be all-important.

Associated with this widening spectrum of value creation models, we will probably see a continuing trend on the part of megafirms toward using information technology to depopulate the customer interface and reduce the associated costs. As the very large firms—banks, airlines, brokerages, financial services firms, insurance companies, telecom companies, and Internet service providers—become increasingly distant and impersonal toward their customers, the smaller and midsized firms will probably move closer toward personalized, value-added services which can differentiate them in the face of ever more brutal financial competition.

There is one important "jump ball" in this David-Goliath scenario, which is difficult to predict and which does not lend itself well to simple generalizations. That factor is the appetite of customers—in large numbers—for added value, in proportion to their willingness to pay for it. As the largest firms move more and more toward price competition and economic pressure methods to force out the mid- and small-sized competitors, will they succeed in conditioning customers to "think cheap"?

A good deal of evidence suggests that customers, overall, do not seem to have fixed attitudes about the question of value versus price. In some cases they will pay substantially more for an enriched value package; in other cases they simply won't. There has always been a kind of three-way tug-of-war involving the customers, the "simple but cheap" providers, and the "fancy but pricey" providers. There does not seem to be any one single equilibrium point that's valid across all service sectors.

ACHIEVING SYNERGY WITH TECH AND TOUCH

Using the now-familiar tech versus touch comparison, we might be more productively engaged by trying to sketch out the kinds of options that service suppliers will be able to choose from and show how the integration of high-tech approaches with high-touch approaches can strengthen the value package of any one player. As in previous discussions, we use the term "high tech" to signify high *technique* in general, that is, the use of resource-intensive delivery systems not limited to digital or electronic technology.

Consider the simple view offered by Figure 12-1, which we might call the tech-touch decision space. Not only is it possible to place a wide variety of value packages, or business models if you prefer, into the various quadrants of this simplified strategic space, but it is also possible to speculate on the kinds of new value concepts that might fill in the unexploited areas.

As an example—a tired, but useful one—consider a classical low-tech/low-touch service, namely fast food. At the extreme, it would be

Touch	Low Tech	High Tech
High	Food catering Personal services Financial planning Fitness coaching Interior design	Concept restaurants Ultra "physicals" Cruise vacations Cosmetic surgery Hybrid online services
Low	Fast food Self-serve markets Gasoline ATMs Taxis	Wireless web Online software Online education Remote investing Digital homes

Low   **Tech (nique)**   High

FIGURE 12-1   High-tech/high-touch options

quite easy and perhaps plausible to transform the typical burger store into a completely self-service model, much like a throwback to the Automat of the 1950s. At present, all the typical counter clerk does in a chain-style burger restaurant is take the customer's order, relay it by a set of push buttons to the cooks on the assembly line, collect the payment, and hand the food to the customer. All that remains in this model is to have the customers push the buttons and swipe their own credit cards or ATM cards, or insert cash. The food could easily slide down a chute. If the clerk is not expected to add any real value, why not complete the job of transforming the burger shop into a vending machine?

The typical branch bank probably falls into the high-tech/low-touch quadrant of the model, although it's really mid-tech at the most. In a similar line of thinking, if the bank's owners really want to steer customers to the ATM outside or to the bank's Web site, and don't expect the tellers and other inside workers to contribute any differentiating added value, then it would be rather simple to complete the transformation of the branch bank to a vending-machine model.

Note the *implied value judgment here*: The mere physical presence of a human being in some kind of service delivery episode does not make it a high-touch episode. The person has to act, in a human capacity, to supply some kind of energizing or differentiating form of nonroutine value. Handing over a sack of burgers or rubber stamping a deposit slip does not qualify as a high-touch element of service in our system of definitions.

In the third quadrant, low tech/high touch, one can easily imagine various highly "personal" services in which human competence, empathy, compassion, and diversity of interaction carry the primary value. Small business operators have always provided this kind of value—dentists, personal physicians, hairdressers, accountants, therapists, fitness coaches, and many others. It's another question, and an interesting one, whether large firms can successfully field service packages in this quadrant. Can you deliver a highly personal service with a large and complex operation? Hospital operators like to believe they can, but the cases in which these operations truly outperform small, entrepreneurial operators seem few and far between.

And what of the fourth quadrant, the tantalizing promise of high tech *and* high touch? For the more affluent and service-minded health-care consumer, this might include things like the "super physical," that is, the intensive, in-depth health appraisal. Such a value package, delivered by leading institutions like the Mayo Clinic in Rochester, Minnesota, and Scripps Clinic's Center for Executive Health in San Diego, California, includes not only the complete series of standard medical tests, but more intensive monitoring of body physiology, fitness testing, nutritional and psychological counseling, an in-depth review by a physician, and a comprehensive written report. Some programs even include metabolic testing and evaluation of cellular nutritional status. Contrast this to the typical HMO physical, which is usually a series of screening tests intended only to identify warning signs of developing medical problems that might prove costly for the provider to treat if they're not detected early. The "report" usually comes in the form of a doctor's pronouncement: "You're fine. You should lose a little weight."

Perhaps this discussion should focus a bit less on trying to predict what kinds of specific services might emerge in the next 5 to 10 years and more on a rationale for inventing them. If your firm offers a value package that sits squarely in one of the four quadrants just discussed, it might be a good idea to examine the possibilities in the other corners. Can you replicate all or part of your value package at a point higher or lower on either of the two scales—tech or touch? Should you concentrate only on one configuration, or can you use your existing infrastructure to diversify your service presence? Will the same set of resources—people, talent, know-how, information, intellectual property, or physical facilities—support two or more distinct value packages?

These design choices (tech, touch, or both) take us back to earlier discussions about the need to reconcile technological values such as speed, efficiency, cost reduction, and standardization with human and personal values such as empathy, respect for the individual, autonomy, sense of community, and novelty. People tend to accept, apply, and appreciate the value of technological resources to the extent that those resources support and amplify the values they cherish. They "resist" technology—in the vocabulary of the techo-priests—to the extent that they see it as undermining those values, or, at a minimum, doing nothing to advance them.

Common sense models like the multichannel customer interface pioneered by direct marketing firm L.L. Bean and others, which includes a combination of online Web-based information supported by instant access to a person, either by phone or keyboard to keyboard, have a greater chance of appealing to a broad range of consumers than the early "digital customer" psychology.

The fundamental truth to be faced in designing new service models is simply this: You won't know if they will be successful until you try them out on real customers and those customers buy them. There is no magic formula for cranking out a new service concept. There is, however, almost infinite room for innovation, and thinking carefully about a synergistic combination of tech-service and touch-service offers interesting and important opportunities for finding the rare model that can become a hit. If you're looking for ways to differentiate your enterprise from its competitors, this kind of thinking may help you find it.

2

SERVICE AMERICA II: DOING BUSINESS IN THE NEW MILLENNIUM

13

The New Business Landscape: Globalism, Hypercompetition, and Technology

"Chance favors the prepared mind."

—Louis Pasteur

ARE BUSINESSES REALLY GIVING CUSTOMERS WHAT THEY WANT?

THERE'S A PECULIAR SORT OF MYTHOLOGY woven into much of the thought process of Western business. One hears it often in the kinds of expansive discussions that take place over dinner or drinks when executives get together. It's the mythology of competition.

In its simplest form, it says "If your firm is not willing to, or capable of, giving customers what they want, somebody else will do it, and you'll be left behind." It's a noble and heroic pronouncement, but it's very often wrong. Competing based on customer value is often a more complex proposition that it first seems.

Although it's true that a reasonably free market environment invites competition and innovation and that customers have an awesome capacity to make choices, it does not necessarily follow that suppliers will invariably deliver what the customers want or would like. While the doctrine of Darwinian selection seems to apply fairly well to price competition, it's a questionable premise when it comes to quality or other aspects of value that could involve trade-offs against price.

Do airline passengers, for example, want to be herded about like cattle, made to pay price penalties for changing their plans, and lied to when things go wrong? If so many people want outstanding service (and presumably some of them are willing to pay higher prices for it), why is it that no major U.S. airline is in the service business? Why is the product so commoditized and undifferentiated? Why is competition in that marketplace driven primarily by price? And why is the so-called high-value product, that is, a first-class ticket, priced as much as five to ten times higher than the standard ticket? Is it really worth that much more? Or, could it simply be that airlines use the first-class cabin as an overflow area, with frequent flyer upgrades serving to increase the average ticket price on a flight-by-flight basis? Theoretically, anybody who's dumb enough to pay full fare for a first-class ticket is willing to subsidize the bargain prices charged to the coach passengers and those who buy last minute Internet tickets at fire-sale prices.

The choices available to customers of a certain industry may have more to do with the shared ideology of the competitors than any magical process of natural selection among innovative service products. Jan Lapidoth, one of the chief intellectual architects of Scandinavian Airlines' dramatic turnaround in the early 1980s, observed "One of the products that all airlines offer for sale, including us, is actually an inferior product. Nobody wants to talk about it, and no airline wants to do anything about it. What is that inferior product? It's the center seat."

Does anybody want to ride in a center seat? If not, why do airlines still have them? Why don't they discount the price for a center seat, giving the passenger an incentive to accept a lower-quality service experience? Why not hold a special lottery, or lucky draw, just for center-seat riders? The answer is fairly clear: So long as people put up with it, why bother to do anything about it? How many passengers refuse to board or ask for refunds because they got a center seat? Many grumble, but few rebel.

How many surveys of typical computer users—that is normal civilians, not geeks or "power users"—show people asking for more and more exotic or specialized features in their software? How many people really want to mail-merge a business letter with an address list located on a Web site somewhere? How many people plead for software products that have to be replaced whenever the suppliers decide they need more money? On the other hand, how many people report that they'd pay more money for an operating system and workable software that didn't crash and destroy their data? And, as long as the PC has been on the desk, doesn't it seem strange that a person has to use a screwdriver to disassemble the thing in order to add a new gadget like a modem?

Indeed, the proliferation of products and choices in computer-related industries probably has much less to do with consumer demand or interest and everything to do with the ideology of the people who run the companies and make the products. Customer choice or desire counts for little when the prevailing ideology is technology-focused rather than customer-focused. Presumably, any major firm that chose to offer products with significantly greater customer appeal might get ahead of the others. On a practical level, however, very few of them seem interested in bucking the prevailing ethos.

In the computer sector, the single renegade company has always been Apple Computer, whose Macintosh product continues to set ever higher standards of functionality and aesthetic appeal. Apple, however, is trapped in a technological cul-de-sac by the dominant Windows operating system, which guarantees the Apple will never attain more than a modest market share. No other computer supplier has shown the slightest interest in consumerizing the PC.

The health-care industry is another extreme example of a "mindset" industry, like airlines, computers, and many others. Many, and probably most, physicians and hospital operators still insist on treating their customers—sorry, "patients"—like compliant children. Most hospitals still operate like factories, with the patients moving like raw material through so many processing stations. Patient education, one of the top-rated values of most health-care customers, is a hit-or-miss proposition in most medical facilities. Despite the rhetoric about "patient care" and slogans like "We're your partner in health," doctors as a group are still widely perceived as lousy listeners who are more motivated by production than by problem solving.

We could pick a number of other industries to abuse and accuse of operating from an arrogant or self-serving mindset, but the point is the same for all of them. When the dominant suppliers in a line of business are unwilling to offer real choices to their customers, the customers usually end up accepting what's on offer. Sure, there can be the occasional renegade who rethinks the whole value proposition, but those certainly tend to be the exception.

The ironic aspect of this service inertia is that *all the industries just mentioned, and many others, are absolutely ripe for innovation, often of the most basic and exciting kind.* A bit of imagination could turn up enormous opportunities to make the experience of staying in a hospital more valuable, less onerous, and much more personally rewarding. The computer industry, notwithstanding its narcissistic self-image as the source of all innovation, is remarkably slavish and imitative in its mindset. Most of its innovation centers on making its products obsolete and unworkable as quickly as possible and finding new ways to bamboozle customers into buying the next ones off the line, not in meeting real needs.

Think of any industry—air travel, automobiles, banking, education, entertainment, finance, health care, hospitality, information, insurance, retailing—and you can see how its main players have drifted into a production mindset of giving the customers what they will settle for, not what they might find valuable, interesting, exciting, durable, or cost-effective.

This could be one of the great undiscovered truths of the new age of service: The best is yet to come. Why should we confine ourselves to what we know how to do? Why not go around to the customer's side of the relationship and see things with new, innocent eyes? Why not dare to rethink the value proposition itself? Why not engage our customers, and prospective customers, in a cooperative search for new and better ways to create value?

It's often said that the perfect is the enemy of the good. But it's also true that the good enough is the enemy of the better. In this era of globalism and hypercompetition, following the same old stereotypes can be a ticket to mediocrity. Maybe we're facing a period of unprecedented opportunity for innovation and value creation; maybe we just have to recognize it right in front of our faces.

DAVID AND GOLIATH: YOU GOTTA DO IT BIGGER OR DO IT DIFFERENTLY

Although the problems and opportunities facing small and midsized firms are very different from those facing the megafirms, you'd never know it from reading much of the literature of business and management. Most books on management tend to gloss over the differences. Reading publications like *Business Week, Fortune, Forbes, The Wall Street Journal*, and *The Economist*, one could easily get the impression that there are only about 100 companies on Earth, all of them booking $10 billion or more in sales.

The truth of it is that most business is not megabusiness, but small business; indeed, even microbusiness. And a lot more of it is minibusiness, firms in the range of $10 million to $100 million. Firms with dozens or hundreds of employees are much more common than firms with tens of thousands.

Many of the heroic pronouncements of business writers seem ideally suited to arouse the hormones of executives and managers of megafirms, but their value for small and midsized firms can be highly questionable. Issues such as advertising, brand building, competition, channel building, supply chain management, and capital formation may mean little to the small niche player who is not serving a market measured in tens of billions of dollars.

Over the past two decades, most developed countries, and the United States in particular, have seen an unprecedented wave of mergers, acquisitions, and coventures among megafirms. The year 2000 alone saw the creation of the world's largest media conglomerate, AOL-Time Warner; the world's largest oil enterprise, Exxon-Mobil; and a number of largest and second-largest firms in the banking, pharmaceutical, publishing, and telecommunications industries. In the United States, especially, airline mergers have reduced the competitive field to a handful of big carriers, plus a menagerie of near-death smaller players struggling to keep up.

This progressive David and Goliath scenario means that smaller firms will have to struggle ever more mightily to find their places without falling under the feet of the giants. In the Christian Bible, young David killed Goliath with a pebble launched from his sling. In business, however, Goliath usually wins.

The world's largest retailer by far is Wal-Mart, a behemoth approaching $200 billion in annual sales, which has been steadily putting pushpins into the map of urban, suburban, and rural America, and increasingly moving internationally as well. And just about every new store it opens imposes a death sentence on one or more small local retailers, including clothing shops, houseware stores, hardware stores, music stores, bookstores, and others.

In the David and Goliath scenario, you get two basic choices: you either do everything bigger and better than the rest, or you do it differently. How can a small, independent bookstore, music store, or hardware store compete with a megabrand store that has seemingly infinite capital with which to stock a vast range of products in great depth, advertise heavily, discount aggressively, and lose money for a year or more until the competitors have died off? It can't. Its only real choice is to find a position of its own—a value proposition or a variation on the delivery of value—which it can develop, perfect, and defend.

To oversimplify a bit, if you're a Goliath, you compete with capital; if you're a David, you compete with finesse. One of the most interesting examples of a small chain store that has demonstrated this type of value-based competition is SuperQuinn, the Irish firm that operates some of the most remarkable food stores anywhere. Founded in 1960 by Feargal Quinn, who recognized the coming of self-service as a commercial concept in Ireland, the 13-store chain concentrates on delivering an outstanding and *ever-improving* customer experience.

From ultrafresh food to appealing visual presentations to homemade sausage and fresh-baked bread, to fruit displayed in order of ripeness, to signs that tell the buyer which local farm produced the eggs or the lamb chops, a SuperQuinn store is a marvel of intelligent retailing. In weekly customer focus groups, Feargal Quinn, his sons, and executives keep asking their customers one question: "How can we get more of your business?" And the customers can't wait to tell them.

When asked whether the giant chain food stores could implement his methods, Quinn shakes his head and says, "They could, but they don't think they can. We've had one group of executives after another come over here, from the big American chains, and all up and down the continent. They leave shaking their heads, and saying, 'We could never do it that way. We're too big. He's got only thirteen stores, and that makes the difference.'"[1]

Quinn has little patience for the homogenized approach to mass management employed by many large firms. He says, "I always feel sorry for any firm when a numbers man takes over as chief executive. I can tell right then that the firm is headed downhill."

Actually, there are more SuperQuinns in the marketplace than one would tend to think, at least based on a casual scan of the general business press, which preoccupies itself far too much with the clashes between Goliaths. It can be done, and it is being done every day, in every country.

THE POSTCAPITALIST MODEL: OUT WITH HIERARCHIES, IN WITH HETERARCHIES

One significant trend that has been shaping the strategic options of many service organizations, large and small, is the deconstruction movement, which is essentially a shift from classical capitalist structures to what Peter Drucker calls the postcapitalist way of doing things. The long-accepted corporate pyramid model has been giving way to a host of alternative structural concepts, most of which tend to look more like networks or molecules than like hierarchies. The new term of art is *heterarchies*, that is, resource arrangements not based on formal subdivisions of power and authority, but based on reciprocal and mutually beneficial relationships among autonomous players.

The classical capitalist theory of organizations has always dictated that a successful firm would be one which progressively acquired larger and larger chunks of capital—things like manufacturing plants, real estate, airplanes, railroad cars, ships, mines, TV stations, and telephone lines—and then used those capital assets to generate revenues and profits. The postcapitalist theory calls for *having access* to those assets as needed, but not necessarily owning them.

The owner of a physical asset has the obligation to protect and preserve it, to maintain and modernize it as necessary, and to assume the risks associated with its future obsolescence. Those who simply "rent" capital, that is, pay to gain access to it without having to own it, carry no such risks. They have greater flexibility to change and evolve their style of operating, without being married to a capital structure they can't easily change. More and more, service organizations are choosing to operate as knowledge-based enterprises rather than capital-based enterprises.

This postcapitalist shift has led to greater use of outsourcing, partnering, and strategic relationship building. A company that sells fashion products, such as clothing, jewelry, cosmetics, and other lifestyle products, really has very little need to own physical capital. Its key asset is its market concept: the brand name, the type of style it promotes, the ability to attract suppliers within its category, the ability to negotiate relationships with real estate operators, and a whole range of associated know-how and skills. It can rent or lease all the plant and equipment it needs to bring its products to its customers.

Meanwhile, the provision of physical capital, at a price, has become a huge service industry in itself. Mall operators provide retail space for merchants, who need only preoccupy themselves with marketing. Leasing firms acquire and lease out buildings, aircraft, ships, railroad cars, oil drilling rigs, construction cranes, and a host of other expensive assets to operators who simply put them to use.

Here is a case in point: In 1998 Nortel Networks, a Canadian supplier of high-performance Internet networks, decided to shift out of capital-intensive manufacturing. It began selling off as many as 15 manufacturing operations which it had previously used to supply itself with electronic components and circuit boards. The company then signed long-term purchase agreements at favorable prices with the major manufacturing firms that bought the plants.

Nortel's executives believe they can get components and assemblies more cheaply with this system than they could previously by making them, because the suppliers can maintain economies of scale and inventory management on a larger scale. Further, they believe, those firms can concentrate solely on keeping up with the state of the art, without having to divide their attention between product design, manufacturing, and marketing.

As business becomes ever more global and boundaryless, more and more firms need to examine their relationships to capital. This steady deconstruction of the traditional capital-intensive corporate hierarchy has created a new style of competition and cooperation: "coopetition" as some like to call it. Relationships among firms are becoming much more diversified and multifarious as more and more of them simplify their operations and concentrate on their so-called core competencies.

What these changes mean to the large firm is the need to rethink the boundaries and channels for competition and customer access, as well as the range of options for suppliers, partners, and marketing coventures. What it means to small or midsized firms is much more of the same. A more diversified structure of competition and cooperation within any industry can favor the small firm just as much as the large one. It opens up more opportunities for them to ride along in the wagons of the larger players and gain access to customers they might not otherwise have had.

If you're in the mood to rethink your business model and reconsider the role of your enterprise in its environment, you could do well to look for new connections. Create new avenues of access to your customers by leveraging the assets and avenues owned by other players. And, of course, make sure you know the difference between a competitor and a customer. In the changing business landscape, yesterday's customer could become your competitor, and yesterday's competitor could turn out to be your customer. Organizational structure, especially in service enterprises, should be merely a means to an end, evolving over time as necessary, not a fixed decision for all time.

14
CHAPTER

BUSINESS AT THE CROSSROADS: HIGH TECH OR HIGH TOUCH?

"The concern for man and his destiny must be the chief interest of all scientific inquiry. Never forget it amidst your diagrams and equations."

—*Albert Einstein*

THE THIRD WAVE: PROMISES AND PERILS

IN HIS 1970 BOOK *FUTURE SHOCK*,[1] futurist Alvin Toffler postulated that human civilization was moving into the third of three great waves of change. The first two of his hypothetical waves, agriculture and industrialization, had made profound changes in human society and its structures. The third of these great waves, a period defined by knowledge, information, and global consciousness, would, according to Toffler, bring changes every bit as profound as the first two.

That Third Wave which Toffler foresaw is well upon us. We have entered a period of unprecedented change, upheaval, and uncertainty. The old rules for doing business are coming into question, and the new rules aren't yet completely clear. More and more enterprises are having to think longer and more diligently about the new environment and having to look for new explanations of what's going on.

In the two decades following the 1980 appearance of Toffler's book, *The Third Wave*,[2] many of his predictions came true, or began to take form. The rapidly accelerating pace of change of all types—social, political, technological, and commercial—has increased the level of stress on individuals, communities, institutions, and enterprises. The advent of cheap and abundant information, global communication, and the concept of "knowledge at a distance" have all contributed to a kind of iconic environment of shared symbols, a media mentality, and a cultural chop suey of mixed values, views, and agendas.

Oddly, however, the more widely the icons of the popular culture are shared, the more the differences and subdivisions of the society become apparent. The increasing mobility of populations and the ever more prolific flow of information have contributed to an atomization of society. Shared information and shared symbols have not had the effect of standardizing or homogenizing attitudes and values, particularly in countries such as the United States where the so-called information revolution has unfolded most rapidly.

Futurist John Naisbitt has pointed out what he calls the *global-tribal paradox*,[3] namely that:

> **The more global we become in our consciousness,**
> **the more tribal we become in our behavior.**

This paradoxical combination of shared experience and individualized values and priorities has created real dilemmas for many businesses, especially those trying to operate across geographic, national, and cultural boundaries. For example, Federal Express, one of the most highly regarded of American businesses, stumbled badly when it attempted to conquer the European market for time-sensitive delivery in the early 1990s.

The company set up headquarters in Belgium, intending to attack the entire continental market in one great campaign. Trying to follow a concept they called "pan-European marketing," the firm's strategists applied a "one size fits all" approach, failing to discern the social, cultural, and political differences that shaped the various markets and submarkets they had in their gun sights. Despite the firm's great notoriety, reputation for quality, and brand identity, pan-European marketing flopped. After an investment of over $200 million, the firm had made remarkably little progress in cracking the various entrenched fortresses, and finally threw in the towel. Top management decided to back out of the campaign and concentrate on becoming the dominant transporter of material across the Atlantic, yielding the competitive turf to the established players.

Similarly, Scandinavian Airlines System, under the leadership of its charismatic chairman Jan Carlzon, stubbed its toe when it decided it could create a "global travel services" enterprise, by linking airlines, hotels, and various other hospitality firms around the world. Presumably, a business traveler would remain in the care of some participant or another in this enterprise from the time he or she left home, all through a transnational itinerary, and all the way back home. It didn't work.

Part of SAS's grand design was an attempt to resurrect the moribund American carrier, Continental Airlines, through a marketing and operating coventure and by infusing the "customer care" culture of the Scandinavian operation into the psychologically depressed culture of the Texas-based company. The highly publicized Frankenstein story never worked out. The cultural magic didn't happen, the economic rationale began to unravel, and by the time SAS had invested several hundred millions of dollars in the concept, it's board of directors finally pulled the plug.

The Third Wave is indeed a wave of paradoxes, and that realization can go a long way toward helping executives understand it and understand its influences on the possibilities facing their enterprises.

Apparent contradictions often exist side by side. One-stop shopping (the concept of buying everything from one place) works sometimes and fails at other times. Wal-Mart, for example, offers a huge array of products. At the same time, however, many people still shop at specialty and subspecialty stores that offer cosmetics, housewares, clothing, and personal articles. If it were as simple as it seems, we'd eventually have nothing but chain stores selling goods to us. Megamarkets and micromarkets may seem mutually contradictory, but they exist side by side nevertheless.

In a country like the United States, millions of people see and hear many of the same celebrities, watch the same movies and TV shows, hear much the same music, and buy many of the same toys and fad products. Yet the American commercial culture is defined much more by its diversity than by its uniformity. Magazines, for example, target ever more specific sectors of the population: brides, computer fans, feminists, runners, skateboarders, wood-carvers, and countless others. There are magazines targeted to gays, and others aimed at lesbians; there are ethnic identity magazines aimed at blacks, and others aimed at Latinos. The famous mass circulation magazines of the mid-century such as *Life*, *Look*, and *Saturday Evening Post* all disappeared, giving way to niche publications.

The coming of digital information technology, which some experts consider the primary defining factor of the Third Wave, has amplified and compounded these social, cultural, and commercial differences. No discussion of the Third Wave, or indeed of contemporary business trends, could possibly be complete without a consideration of the effects of cheap and abundant information. While the various electronic gadgets and distribution systems may come, go, and evolve, the defining truth of the information revolution is not the technology itself, but the things technology makes possible and renders impossible.

TECHNOLOGY: SERVANT OR MASTER?

Any proper review of technological effects on business should include a wide range of technologies, not just information technology. For the record, we note that advances in many technologies, such as food production, medical transplants, pharmaceutical medicine, genetic engineering, materials science, and energy production can all have profound effects on the options and opportunities facing business enterprises. Given the limited space we have here, however, we feel it is most advisable to concentrate on the implications of digital technology, because of its sheer prominence in current business thinking.

The topic of technology, and especially its proper use in human experience, seems to involve an increasingly uneasy tension between two ideologies. Advocates seem to array themselves across a wide spectrum of belief, ranging from the narcissistic technonazis, who see no end to the dominance of digital values, to the defensive technophobes, who want no part of any of it. We must eventually come to some state of peaceful coexistence between humanist values and digital values; however, that rapprochement may be a decade or more away.

In recent years the Internet and all things digital have outranked virtually every other long-running story in the minds of news broadcasters and publishers. Journalists joined with makers of computers and software, as well as those who promote Internet services, in a kind of semiconscious collusion to popularize the PC/Net phenomenon. This "gee whiz conspiracy," with the popular press in the role of cheerleader, has developed an almost messianic obsession with selling the benefits of digital technology to T. C. Mits (the "celebrated man in the street") and to T. C. Wits as well. Before we become entranced with the idea that "technology will revolutionize service businesses," let's get a realistic grip on what's really happening.

In its earliest days, the Internet was hailed as "the great democratizer." It would level the effects of social status, economic conditions, and political clout. It would put even the tiniest businesses on an even footing with the mighty giants. Now, even its most rabid promoters admit that it will have exactly the opposite effect. It will exaggerate the disparity between the haves and the have-nots. Notwithstanding the politically correct ads showing an adorable little black girl somewhere in Africa logging on to the Web, the poor and the bewildered will not be lifted out of their economic circumstances by the computer or the Internet. They are stranded in a very different paradigm.

The big surprise of the so-called digital divide may be that it is rapidly becoming more ideological and psychosocial than economic and technical. Many technical experts, digital philosophers, and Internet ideologues who preach and write about the wonders of technology refuse to acknowledge that there is an ideological gap. The digital divide, they seem to believe, is merely an unfortunate—and temporary—economic chasm that separates the haves from the have-nots. Some of them even maintain that the divide will be self-repairing, as technology itself will eventually empower the have-nots to compete with the haves for resources.

But consider that two-thirds of the humans on the planet have never heard a dial tone. Nearly half have no access to electricity or running water. In all likelihood, not more than 10 percent of the world's population will be economically eligible for the Internet in the next two decades. The idea that all we have to do is "give 'em computers" is a projection of a distinctly American, upper-middle-class worldview onto all peoples of the world. It smacks of the Great Society all over again—the cyberequivalent of "Let them eat cake."

The protest movement against the digital doctrine has, so far, received relatively little airtime. The popular press, broadcasters, and business writers seem to take it as an article of faith that digital technology is ultimately good. Of course, there may be the occasional unanticipated consequences, but there is little room in their discourse for the nagging metaquestions: Will digital technology benefit everyone equally? Will it dehumanize relationships and the discourse between humans? Will it make us unacceptably dependent on a new priesthood, the software makers whose ideology may not match mainstream values? These are exceedingly complex questions which are seldom good material for news stories.

Futurist John Naisbitt's book *High Tech, High Touch*,[4] protests at some length about the mindless push toward dehumanizing technology in virtually all dimensions of commerce and in the way we relate to our institutions. Unfortunately, he and his cowriters offered little more than a prolonged rant, with few real examples or cases, and almost no prescription for change.

Digital gadfly Clifford Stoll had considerably more to offer in his first book *Silicon Snake Oil*,[5] which argued that "geek" values are being forced on the general public, most of whom are not competent to evaluate the implications of a digital-everything world. His second book, *High-tech Heretic*,[6] argues cases more specifically. He is particularly concerned about notions such as books and libraries becoming obsolete and being replaced by digital access devices, and the mindless rush of school administrators using scarce public funds to fill their classrooms with computers.

Social and political activist Ralph Nader has also expressed very strong views about what he considers the mindless push of technology, motivated more by the commercial interests of the technology industry than by careful thought about the values and choices involved.

We believe there is a developing ideological conflict, and possibly a generational conflict that will increasingly polarize various interest groups within the developed societies, and particularly in America over the next few years. It will mean a collision between humanist values and digital values, as expressed by the members of two apparently disparate value systems and even subcultures. A growing constituency, including members of the U.S. Congress and other legislatures, feels that the market dominance of technology megafirms like Microsoft, and the disproportionate influence of the technocratic subculture the firm epitomizes, will pose ethical, moral, and social problems as the development of digital technology follows its own arcane agenda. Others, less alarmed about the fate of society, seem content to let the digital agenda play itself out, confident that the marketplace and the pace of progress will somehow sort it all out.

In any case, these complex questions form the inescapable backdrop for the strategic thought processes business leaders will have to face more and more seriously as time goes by. Technology will always be a mixed blessing. The question for every executive team is: How can we control, or at least influence, the mixture for our own enterprise? From what package of values, beliefs, and expectations shall we proceed in betting our chips on the human and technological events that will shape our options in the near future and over the longer run?

E-COMMERCE AND THE DOT-COM DELUSION: FANTASY VERSUS REALITY

The years 1997–2000 will probably go down in U.S. history as the period of digital mania, perhaps on a par—some will say—with the Black Plague that swept Europe in the fourteenth century. Others will remember it as the golden age of the Internet—a time of infinite possibilities, unbounded confidence, and fabulous fortunes. To business people in other developed economies, it was something like watching a Disney movie from afar.

It was, indeed, a mania in just about every possible sense of the word. There seemed to be something in it for everybody. The geeks discovered business, venture capitalists discovered the geeks, the popular press discovered the Internet, and the general public discovered Internet stocks. It produced, by virtually any measure, one of the greatest transfers of wealth that Western economies had ever seen.

In record time, a whole new industry formed, in a sort of sociocommercial Big Bang—the Internet industry. Thousands of small companies materialized, out of nothing at first, financed out of the personal savings of entrepreneurs who dreamed of making vast fortunes with the new "Internet business model." The buzz quickly spread, and many of the start-ups found themselves pursued by venture capitalists eager to cash in on what they had heard was a sure thing. An epidemic of "pure

Internet" businesses broke out, with ever more amazing public offerings of stock on the share markets.

In one of the most astonishing examples of the human capacity to suspend disbelief, "dot-com mania" swept through the American culture like a wildfire. People with virtually no knowledge of stock market investing flocked to online brokers, eager to bet their chips (in many cases, their entire savings) on the fabulous "story" stocks such as Yahoo!, Amazon, America Online, and a host of hardware firms such as QualComm, Cisco Systems, Intel, and, of course, the perennial favorite Microsoft. The popular press cheered on each new round of emotional excess, touting the dot-com darlings as the sure-fire winners in the New Economy. The mantra of business journalists became, "The tech sector is what's driving the growth of the American economy."

Meanwhile, the best-capitalized of the dot-com firms, most with no more than a Web site as their value package, began to spend money like drunken sailors. Internet companies did business with one another. Dot-com marketers had to buy computers, hire Web site developers, find software programmers to set up their "e-commerce solutions," buy expensive Web servers and telecommunication switches, and, of course spend millions of dollars buying banner ads on the leading "portal" sites like Yahoo!, AltaVista, Excite, and America Online.

Early in the development of dot-com mania, both of us began to ask "What's wrong with this picture?" What was wrong was that a profitless industry had appeared, virtually out of nowhere, kept alive by the cash supplied by innocent—and ignorant—investors. The economic village formed by the Web site entrepreneurs and all of the suppliers who took their money—correction: their investors' money—lived in its own little economically incestuous world. Money flowed in, but profit did not flow out. So long as venture capitalists, amateur investors, and journalists bought the New Economy story, the mania rolled on, almost with a life of its own.

But eventually, the story began to unravel. Internet companies were burning through investor capital at alarming rates, and few of them showed enough sales productivity to justify further investments. Despite the breathless press stories about the phenomenal growth of online commerce—in percentage terms, of course—the fact is that online sales accounted for only a few percent of total retail sales, even in the United States. That remains the case today. Once the awful truth began to leak out—that few if any of the e-commerce darlings had any hope of ever making a profit and that most of them were doomed to close—amateur investors and Wall Street traders alike began running for the exits.

In a series of disastrous downdrafts, the U.S. stock market expressed the reality of the New Economy: There wasn't one. Share prices for stocks like Amazon, Yahoo!, AOL, eBay, QualComm, Cisco, and a host of others dropped like stones. As valuations fell by as much as 80 and 90 percent, more than a trillion dollars in valuations evaporated A few optimistic analysts and promoters bravely predicted a comeback, but it never came. The Internet mania was dead.

Unfortunately, Internet-only companies had doomed themselves to unprofitability very early in the rush, by adopting a fanatical giveaway mentality. The idea was to forget about actually selling anything on your Web site—at least not selling it for anything like a profit margin—and just get as many people as you can to visit your site. When they come, you can sell them to other people who want to advertise their products. This was called "aggregating eyeballs," the basis of the so-called portal approach, and only a very few firms ever made it work.

They got most of their ad revenue from the many smaller Web wannabes who spent their investors' capital trying to build "attention share." Unfortunately, very few Internet-only companies actually sold enough of anything to cover their advertising and operating costs. As they went out of business and stopped buying advertising, even the major portals felt the pain.

Anyone who would contend that the Internet constitutes an industry, by any reasonable definition of the word, would have to concede that it was, is, and probably always will be a red-ink industry. Considering the unknown amounts of personal capital poured in by millions of Web site operators hoping to make a profit, losses like the nearly 2 billion dollars racked up by Amazon alone, and the hundreds of millions of dollars burned up before many of the better-funded start-ups burned out, we could only characterize the Internet "industry," charitably, as an economic sinkhole.

Here's a peculiar fact: Many of the geeks who rabidly promoted the Internet and all forms of e-business were the same ones who screamed bloody murder in the mid-1990s when America Online announced it would give its customers access to the Internet at no extra charge. They lamented that allowing hordes of civilians into the Internet would just clutter up the place with a bunch of newbies and nuisances.

In one famous but now forgotten incident, an American couple who were both lawyers posted (arguably) the first ever cyberadvertisement on a chat board, promoting their legal services for aliens threatened with deportation or loss of status. The outcry was immediate, manic, and mean. Not only were they excoriated on bulletin boards all across cyberland, but they had to be punished for this unthinkable transgression of the cyberculture. Everything is free, remember? Nobody does business here. They received tides of junk mail, bogus magazine subscriptions, and unwanted credit cards. They saw their personal data posted on bulletin boards and received e-mail threats of physical violence. This is apparently the same group of nice folks who now tell us the future of the society is in e-commerce.

In the business sector, dot-com mania spawned a whole new set of ethical dilemmas. Entrepreneurs got together with venture capitalists and stock underwriters to launch businesses that had no hope of long-term viability. Investors rushed in like eager sheep, parted with their fleece, and were left with worthless shares while the insiders walked away with their cash. Almost all of the so-called Internet millionaires were actually stock market millionaires. It was about adding valuation, not value in the marketplace.

The message to young people thinking about starting businesses became: Forget "built to last" and learn "built to flip." More and more, companies are created with the sole purpose of taking them public and then "flipping" them. The quaint idea of building a going concern that would deliver long-term shareholder value was nowhere in the equation. The new cyberhero was not the entrepreneur who worked hard to build a viable firm but the one clever enough to promote it, flip it, and then move on to the next one before the bills came due.

Established firms were in many cases at a disadvantage vis-à-vis unprofitable digital-mania firms who could use their hyperinflated share prices to acquire other firms without putting up cash. This put enormous pressure on executives of all firms to employ PR gimmicks and accounting tricks to try to inflate their own share prices to unsustainable levels.

Ironically, most of the old rules still apply, to the consternation of many new-economy guerrillas. The Internet will evolutionize business, not revolutionize it. In fact, it's more than likely that the companies who take best advantage of online technology will be the established leaders in the so-called old economy—retailers, publishers, catalog marketers, banks, and all the rest.

Mark Twain, possibly one of the best marketing consultants in history, lived during the time of the California gold rush. He advised, "When everybody is out digging for gold, the business to be in is selling shovels." Actually, very few independent miners made fortunes digging for gold; most went broke. Selling shovels was indeed more profitable than digging with them. Curiously, one of the few millionaires to emerge from the gold rush period was a Jewish immigrant named Levi Strauss, who made heavy-duty work clothes out of denim and sold them to miners as fast as he could make them.

E-commerce will be recorded as the big failure story of the first decade of "M2"—the 2000 millennium. Successful companies will, of course, continue to use online technology to simplify and integrate their operations, interlocking their systems more and more with those of suppliers, partners, and customers. Business-to-business marketplaces seem likely to flourish, due to their obvious efficiencies and advantages of speed. And most established companies will aggressively extend their market reach through online technology. However, the heart of the e-commerce story, as promoted by the press, namely the Internet-only company, will eventually be seen as virtually a total failure.[7]

Barry Diller, chairman and CEO of USA Networks, which includes the Home Shopping Network, confessed to having learned an expensive and brutal lesson about Internet marketing:

> For a period of time the idea that speed is everything had currency. Speed has always been important, and in many situations you certainly want to move more quickly than the next fellow and build a service as expeditiously as possible. But making it *the* rule in the business process is wrong. You need to listen to nuance; there are important things that you recognize when you're not speeding for speed's sake. A lot of companies were out there running a race where the winner didn't win anything. We got caught up in that for a time.
>
> We said, "Oh, my God, we have to establish online retail businesses really quickly—a jewelry store, an outlet store, more." We entrusted the development to a group of people, and they blew through tens of millions of dollars. Finally we realized that if they kept going they would have spent over $100 million, and we said, "Are you out of your minds?" They said, 'Well, you said you wanted it quickly.' Yes, we did, but at what cost? How fast you should move depends on how much money is at stake. These people couldn't understand this—it hadn't even occurred to them. We just shut it right down.[8]

THE DIGITAL MOAT: DIGITIZE THE CUSTOMER AT YOUR OWN RISK

Many organizations, and most large ones, are making what we believe to be an important mistake in one particular use of information technology, namely the *electronic customer interface*. Beginning in the mid-1990s, many firms, particularly in the United States, began installing automated telephone "menu" systems which would route customer calls through a series of decision points to the proper department. Some, such as AT&T, even began using digital speech-recognition technology to try to figure out how to route the customer's call by having a synthesized voice ask for a spoken response and then deciphering the possible options from the caller's statement.

Still others have attempted to manage customer calls completely by automatic response, with no human contact of any kind. Karl Albrecht shares a recent experience:

> I recently had occasion to call a San Diego city department to arrange for an inspector to visit my home and verify that some remodeling work met with city building code requirements. When I called the proper telephone number, I was dragged through a procedure in which I keyed in various elements of information by pushing buttons on the telephone pad, including the permit number I had been given. After I had completed my task, a computerized voice announced the date on which the inspector would visit. Then the computer hung up the phone.
>
> I was both impressed and appalled by the experience. Confirmed digital citizens will no doubt smile approvingly at this latest triumph of technology. Others may experience a sense of dismay in knowing that one more large organization, in this case a city government, has decided that human contact is too costly and not a worthwhile investment of its resources.

There is a clear and probably unstoppable trend on the part of large organizations, toward using information technology to depopulate the customer interface and reduce the costs of managing customer relations. Banks do it, insurance companies do it, telephone companies do it, local utilities do it, airline companies do it, and so do many, many others. We believe this is a pernicious and destructive trend for several reasons.

First, it's a clear statement to the customer that says, "We're too busy to bother with your particular idiosyncrasies, so we're handing you over to the computer. You will be allowed to do whatever it's been programmed to do." It tells the customer that standardization, efficiency, and cost savings are more important than any feelings or special needs the customer might have. It also says that any variation in the customer's need or problem that doesn't fit into the software algorithm is not important and will simply not be tolerated. In the case of the city inspector, the computer simply announced the date of the inspection. One might have expected a human to verify that someone would be home on that day and to negotiate a more suitable date if not.

It's as if the executives of many companies have decided to build a kind of digital moat around their organizations, to keep the customers at a comfortable distance. By refusing to have a human being answer the telephone, not only do they save money, but they avoid having to interact directly with an upset customer or one who has a complicated or time-consuming problem. The computer cannot—yet—hear and respond to the anger, frustration, or apprehension in the voice of the caller. Furthermore, since nobody knows which customers are disgruntled and which are satisfied, it can be assumed that all customers are basically happy.

It's abundantly clear that many people find this digital barrier offensive, off-putting, and often frustrating when it prevents them from completing their missions. Yet, just as most people have accepted the proposition of doing part of the service employee's job themselves, such as operating the automated teller machine and filling their own gasoline tanks, most will probably passively accept the digital customer interface. Indeed, what choice will they have, if this becomes the standard? What number do you call to tell someone the computer gave you lousy service? Where do you go to complain about the complaints department?

One significant effect of the digital moat will likely be for many of the largest organizations to utterly abandon the proposition of winning their customers by any kind of added-value service or human touch. They will gain cost savings in the customer interface at the expense of the customers' perception of their firms as nameless, faceless, uncaring, standardized automatons. They will sacrifice virtually all possibility for competitive differentiation. Can one computer answer the telephone more quickly than another? Can one computer bore the caller better than another with mindless music and advertising diatribe while he or she is on hold waiting for the next available computer to take the call?

Another effect of the digital barrier will be for companies to limit their possibilities for follow-on selling by sales people with direct access to customers. Even customers who call to get problems solved are often the best prospects for additional sales, if they get satisfactory results.

This tendency to digitize, standardize, and depersonalize service interactions with customers will probably turn out to be a mixed blessing for many large companies. At the same time that they are driving down their costs with information technology, they will be dooming themselves and their service products to the status of standardized commodities, which will be under constant threat of replacement by other, cheaper information processes. When a person can call a computer and purchase automobile insurance without ever speaking to a human being, how can the firm hope to differentiate its value package from those of its competitors? When banking has become a purely standardized process of conversing with a computer, either by telephone or by online computer access, what makes any bank different from another? In this standardized, digitized world, the only competitive weapon will be a cheap infrastructure with plenty of cash flow with which to battle other low-cost, anonymous competitors.

Not surprisingly, new and inexperienced firms in the pure information industries, such as Internet service providers (ISPs), depend heavily on the digital moat to distance themselves from their customers and keep their operating costs as low as possible. With over 4000 ISPs in the United States alone, all trying to lure customers with lower and lower prices, many simply do not want to face the fact that their customers need and want something more than an online sign-up procedure and automated e-mails every time a problem arises.

Curiously, Internet service and Web site hosting are industry sectors that could benefit greatly from customer-oriented differentiation of their service packages. We may see more and more attention paid to the customer's state of mind as they realize that simply connecting two computers is not necessarily a high-value service.

For the smaller firm, the big-company trend toward digitizing customers may present special opportunities for competitive advantage. By creating a customer experience that is unique, differentiated, and valuable, the more service-oriented firm may be able to mark off a part of the playing field that the digital Goliaths are not interested in, or capable of, dominating. It remains to be seen whether jaded consumers would respond favorably to a renewal in personalized, individualized service, especially when the largest providers are all pushing toward commoditized products at ever lower prices. However, it makes little sense for the smaller firm to resort to the digital moat as a cost-reduction option, since it typically enjoys very few others, and could well be passing up its best avenue for differentiation.[9]

WEBONOMICS: WHAT IT WILL AND WON'T DO

The Internet, the Web, e-commerce, the New Economy, information technology, or IT, the "online thing"—whatever you choose to call it—will present at least as many challenges as opportunities for business leaders, especially over the next decade. If there's one lesson to be learned from the digital mania of the late 1990s, it is this: It ain't that simple, and it ain't that easy.

Far too many executive teams are unnecessarily intimidated by the bewildering hodge-podge of digital jargon, and far too many of them have abdicated their strategic responsibilities to groups of whiz kids who know lots about technology but very little about people or about business. In the "old days," the computer department did its job just as the other functional departments did, and it took its direction from top management. In the "new days" of the chimerical New Economy, the inmates are too often running the asylum.

Armed with a priestlike social status within the organization, bags of the company's money, and the arrogance that only youth and ignorance can display, many of these digital hoodlums have laid waste to corporate strategies and their associated cultures. Many have succeeded in little else but freezing out the customers, turning their companies into vending machines, and blowing through astonishing amounts of money.

If we're going to restore adult supervision and also make intelligent use of digital technology, then company leaders are going to have to face up to their own individual responsibilities to understand—at least in strategic terms—what digital technology means to their enterprises.

We use the general term *web technology* (in the broader and more general sense than the World Wide Web) to denote the global commercial use of online technology, and the vernacular term *webonomics*, which is the coming together of information technology and business strategy in the context of the interconnected global commercial structure, as a shorthand form for all of the various labels previously mentioned. To help business leaders take back their organizations after the Internet hangover wears off, we offer the following brief appraisal of the threats and opportunities posed by the Online Age.

- **Assertion 1.** The aggressive application of web technology is constructive, disruptive, and destructive, all at the same time. The changes in process and infrastructure that it makes possible often go further and wider than its architects anticipate or intend. It can destroy businesses, lines of business, and industries, while creating others. The ignorant or clumsy application of such strong measures can have Frankensteinian consequences.

- **Assertion 2.** Becoming an "Internet business" is a lot like buying an elephant for a pet and putting it in your back yard: You get more than you bargained for. Many entrepreneurs, small business operators, and not a few executives of larger firms have discovered that many of the "too good to be true" business models come at a surprisingly higher price than anticipated. The rules of the macroeconomic system must be taken into account.

- **Assertion 3.** Designing a good Web site is the least important, and least challenging, part of applying web technology to an established business. Too many start-up teams have learned the hard way that a Web site is not a business, although it can be an effective business tool. The trick is to figure out how web technology, as one component of an integrated value creation strategy, fits into the overall business model.

Reduced to its most basic truths, web technology does only two things. First, it creates more and better connections between people and enterprises. Second, it enables the flow of more information, faster and more abundantly. At the level of business processes, industries, economies, and societies, it makes possible changes depending on how intelligently—or diabolically—it is employed.

At the webonomics level, the widespread and aggressive use of online technology has seven major effects, each with its own unique benefits, side effects, and potential business implications. They are:

1. **It makes information cheap (like it or not).** If you're an investor, a market researcher, or a physician, you can get a wealth of information fairly quickly, often for no more cost than your time (which, however, may not be insignificant). The widespread availability of cheap information of all kinds could eventually have incalculable effects on the overall efficiency of our economies and on the costs of doing business. On the other hand, if you're the one who invested heavily in

creating the information that others now give away, you may not be so happy about the cheapening effect of the Web economy. For example, if you're a music producer and you've put up several million dollars to bring a new album to the market, seeing it given away for free on Web sites may not particularly warm your heart.

2. **It reduces or reallocates operating costs.** Replacing your customer contact employees with a software system presumably cuts or eliminates labor costs, once you've paid the cost of the software development, installation, debugging, and maintenance. On the other hand, maybe sales aren't as high as they were when the helpful sales reps (remember why we called them that?) were pushing the products and encouraging customers to buy. We should also remember that customers don't come for free; you have to pay to get access to them. Did we eliminate all of those costs, or simply reallocate some of them to other categories? Costs don't always magically disappear; sometimes they simply migrate.

3. **It diversifies the creation of value.** Web technology makes, or presumably will make, some things possible that were never before possible. Remote medical diagnosis, for example, could have profound effects on health care in poor countries and could revise the economic paradigm of third-world disease. Knowledge at a distance, arguably the real core premise of the Third Wave, has enormous implications.

   The electronic book, for example, will presumably enable some readers to carry a whole miniature library with them and to download other books at will, whereas the Gutenberg model contains only "frozen" data. The e-book can also eliminate the costs of printing, shipping, warehousing, shelving, and disposal when the book is no longer popular. On the other hand, it also eliminates the ambience, human contact, and selling pressure of a retail bookstore. Those expensive brick-and-mortar operations might actually be delivering more value than we think, notwithstanding the views of those who favor e-books as the new model and look forward to the total demise of the printed word.

4. **It liberates or redeploys physical capital.** If Dell Computer Company and others can manufacture computers one by one, to the exact specifications of individual customers, presumably automobile companies and other manufacturers can do the same. The

pre-Web model called for batch manufacturing of products against an estimated level of demand, and stocking them somewhere, such as on car dealers' lots. The webonomic model calls for just-in-time construction as well as ordering. Inventory carrying cost is a significant expense factor for virtually all retailers. CEO Michael Dell says, "Inventory—stock on hand—is the physical embodiment of bad information." Clearly, the reduction of inventory in the pipeline and in holding facilities releases capital for other purposes. On a more profound level, webonomics fans like to talk about substituting information for physical matter, as in the case of eliminating a branch bank building and replacing its processes with online technology. While this may seem appealing in many ways, we also have to think about the broader consequences and ask whether we are really eliminating something or just displacing it.

5. **It destroys or reallocates profits.** It's wise to remember that your profit is somebody else's cost, so cost reduction often becomes profit reduction when the falling dominos travel the whole length of the chain. For example, price-shopping software, long used by travel agents to get the best fares for their clients, has found its way onto the Internet. Price-shopping engines, using software robots called "shopper bots," systematically examine Web sites of suppliers of particular products or services and make a ranked list of prices. Industrial market sites, known as business-to-business (B2B) exchanges—put sellers into intense competition. An individual supplier may book a higher volume of business by getting access to a larger number of prospective customers, but the "auction" paradigm that dominates B2B systems tends to drive prices and profit margins down to painful levels.

Consider a less exotic example: The local newspaper is becoming less and less valuable, and indeed obsolete, as a source of information about job opportunities, as Internet sites spring up to bring employers and job seekers together. The employment section of the paper is clearly living on borrowed time, as a source of revenue for the publisher. Similarly, local newspapers and publications like *The Wall Street Journal* are providing less and less value by publishing yesterday's stock prices, when up-to-the-minute prices are available free on countless sites. The profit associated with those services is either being destroyed or reallocated; it's difficult to determine which.

6. **It redeploys middlemen.** Some Internet fans like to predict that intermediaries of all kinds are doomed in the webbed economy. Many of them probably are: Brokers, agents, and some retailers have experienced direct and indirect threats to their livelihood as a result of webonomic changes. On the other hand, one can argue that the application of web technology can just as easily create new kinds of intermediaries as get rid of the old kinds. To paraphrase Mark Twain, "Recent reports of my demise are highly exaggerated." In the purest sense, Internet portal sites such as Yahoo! and America Online serve as intermediaries by aggregating information and providing a navigational service to those who don't know where to look. Auction sites provide the same service. Business-to-business marketplaces bring buyers and sellers together. One of the many early myths of the Internet was the "many to many" proposition, the idea that everybody can just go online and find everybody else. With over 30 million registered Internet domain names, there is much more digital debris than valuable information. Middlemen will be just as important as ever before, but they won't necessarily be in the middle of the same kinds of relationships.

7. **It creates more and shallower relationships.** The semi-infinite number of possible connections made possible by the web structure of information means that friends and strangers can keep in touch, with roughly the same degree of intimacy. More connections mean more contacts, but the limits of time and attention tend to mean that many of these contacts are more superficial and perfunctory than ever before. In our occupations, we keep in touch with clients, publishers, and conference promoters in various countries. Some of them have become close friends through personal contact. Others, not yet met, have become acquaintances through online contact. Web technology enables many people to establish more and shallower relationships, although it is questionable how well it can promote real intimacy. Notwithstanding the reports of couples who meet on the Internet and even get married there, the ideological premise that the Internet or the Web constitutes any kind of real human community can only be based on an impoverished definition of the term. Certainly, people can become acquaintances, colleagues, and even to some extent friends, by some interpretation of the term. But unless we're prepared to redefine the concept of

relationships, it's difficult to see how web technology can enhance real human intimacy.

In considering the promises and possible consequences of web technology for your enterprise, keep in mind that major technological innovations don't happen in isolation. They take place within an extended context: They have enablers, they have consequences, and they often have side effects. Doing business in the real New Economy calls for much more than putting up a Web site. We believe that executive teams now have the daunting—and refreshing—opportunity to return to first principles and to rethink their business models, with the advice but without the undue ideological influence of the techno-priests.

Today's enterprise leader needs to consider the firm's basic business model in the context of web technology, and then consider web technology in the context of the business model. It's not a matter of "getting an Internet strategy." It's a matter of building a success model for one particular, unique enterprise and having the intellectual courage to implement it regardless of the fads and fantasies being preached in the surrounding environment.

It's been said that the early bird gets the worm, but the second mouse is more likely to get the cheese. It's more important to be running in the right race than to outrun everybody else in a race to the wrong finish line.

15

What's an Executive to Do?

"A vision without a task is but a dream; a task without a vision is drudgery. But a vision and a task are the hope of the world."

—1730 inscription on a church in Sussex, England

THE SERVICE REVOLUTION WE PREDICTED so confidently in the first edition of this book turned into a service *evolution*, and arguably a slow one at that. Looking beyond all the slogans, campaigns, and hoopla, it seems that real lasting change in Western management practice has been agonizingly slow. We've discussed what we believe to be the reasons for that at some length, and we've offered a model for change management that we know works. And, we stand by our belief that the service management paradigm is one of the most coherent and durable to have emerged in the past several decades, one that will ultimately outlive the fads, movements, and Internets.

THE ETERNAL TRUTHS OF SERVICE

For the benefit of executives who are determined to concentrate the focus of their enterprises on strategic customer value, we nominate certain durable lessons which have emerged from this uneven success story. We sum them up as follows:

1. **Customers seek value, not "customer service."** We've abandoned the obsolete term "customer service," which connotes the trivial, be-nice, smiley-faced attempt to pacify customers. Potential buyers want a total *value package*, which includes product, price, support, information, and a whole set of contingencies unique to their interests.

2. **Small miracles don't count.** If you think delivering customer value translates into bottom-line results, think again. There is now clear evidence that small differences in *customer-perceived value* have little direct impact on customer preference or repurchase behavior. Your value package must be significantly better than the others to win the customer's business.

3. **You can't fake customer focus.** All the advertising slogans, campaigns, buzzwords, and motivational programs can't mask the contradictions between the real focus of the business and the *value proposition* sought by the customer. The litmus test of customer focus is fairly simple: Is the entire organization, including its work culture and leadership culture, set up to deliver a superior customer experience? Nothing else counts.

4. **Most heroic "customer focus" programs fail.** Our studies show that the "fizzle factor" for most big-deal organizational campaigns is over 70 percent. It's an easy bet that the typical campaign will fade and die within the typical organizational attention span, which is about 6 months at most. Sorry if this sounds pessimistic, but truth is truth, and we must deal with it.

5. **You don't get customer focus if the leaders don't want it.** Many CEOs and senior executives who rattle off the obligatory sound bites about customer focus haven't a clue what it really means, and if they did, they'd want no part of it. It's still a relatively rare executive who understands what *strategic customer focus* demands of him or her, and knows how to model it to the organization.

6. **The way your employees feel is ultimately the way your customers will feel.** As customers, we sense and respond to the culture of any enterprise we do business with. Whether it's the neighborhood café, the telephone company, or the government agency,

the core attitudes and beliefs of its culture seep out, sending a sub-jective message about their attitudes toward us. Strong and healthy cultures send strong and healthy messages to their customers.

7. **You can't bottle attitude.** The spirit of service is one of the most fragile and perishable of all corporate assets. If not supported by the leadership, the spirit of the culture soon regresses to medioc-rity. This is why one-time motivational campaigns seldom succeed. It takes continuous personal attention from the leaders of the organization to build and maintain the kind of morale, energy, commitment, and focus needed to deliver outstanding value.

8. **The manufacturing model won't cut it.** We're in the throes of a paradigm transition, which will eventually replace the traditional, introverted Western industrial management model (based on the factory) with a more strategically focused model of value creation and open organizations that interact more fluidly with their envi-ronments. The early attempts to apply manufacturing designs such as TQM and ISO 9000 to service quality were an embarrassing failure, as we predicted as early as 1992. We still have a lot of unlearning to do and a lot of new learning to put in its place.

9. **Words speak as loudly as actions.** We're moving toward a new vocabulary of business. The language used throughout the organization not only signals the mindset, but conversely it forms the mindset. The new language of service management signals concepts like *strategic customer focus*, *strategic partnering*, *customer-perceived value*, *value proposition*, *customer value model*, *customer value package*, *service culture*, *key value drivers*, *critical value-creating practices*, and, of course *service leadership*.

10. **Success is never final.** The old idea of "customer loyalty" is mis-guided and dangerous. The most you can do is win a degree of cus-tomer preference, which is always temporary. Keeping the edge is at least as difficult as getting it. Some well-known companies have enjoyed a "golden age" of popularity with their customers, only to lose it and slide back into the competitive swamp. It takes a single-minded determination to create better customer value than your rivals, and to keep the focus of the organization on what works and what wins, no matter what.

We close this second edition with a few key reminders. Please take out one of your business cards, write the following four reminders on it, and keep it in your wallet for frequent reference.

REFOCUS ON THE CUSTOMER

The idea of creating value for customers never really goes out of style. What person in an organization would argue that the customer's perception of value doesn't count and has no impact on the success of the organization? Certainly there may be phases or periods of time or fad concepts or even disasters that distract the attention of the leaders and the employees. But long term, like value in the stock market, customer value always comes back.

Are you still conducting market and customer research on a regular basis? Are you sharing the findings with managers and employees throughout the organization? Do they understand what customer value is in your line of business, and do they know how to deliver it? Do the executives and managers speak the language of customer value, or do they speak the cold, detached language of financial results?

Do you have a workable system for measuring customer perceptions of value, and do you share those results throughout the organization? Do the executives and managers have regular contact with actual customers, or do they hibernate in their offices and hide behind their stacks of paperwork? Do you conduct focus groups and other kinds of customer listening procedures, asking your customers how you can win and keep more of their business?

Call it *customer consciousness*. Do it.

REINVENT THE SERVICE STRATEGY

Maybe it's time to review your service strategy. What is your core benefit premise, that is, the customer value proposition on which you base your business model, the design of your service systems, and the operation of the enterprise? Does it make sense? Do all of the leaders in the organization understand it and take it seriously? Do the employees understand it and take it seriously?

Is it time to rethink the business model or realign the priorities to get closer to the mark? Does the service strategy reflect the critical truths of the customer value model? In other words, are you focused on delivering what the customers have told you they want to buy? Is it time to consider reinventing the business or the business model or possibly the value package that implements the business model? Do you need to consider moving out of certain lines of business or moving into others? How can the use of information technology enable you to do things you might not have been able to do before? Can you use technology to radically improve the customer's experience or to deliver service more effectively?

Call it *strategic focus*. Do it.

TAME THE SYSTEMS AND USE THE TECHNOLOGY

It's probably time for systems psychotherapy; that is, a comprehensive review of your service delivery system and an audit of its capacity to deliver on the service strategy. Evaluate the five kinds of system intelligence: performance, corrective, exception, recovery, and extra value. Diagram the various cycles of service, blueprint the key patterns of delivery, and figure out the cycle costs involved.

Look for evidence of system craziness or lack of intelligence; you're sure to find enough of it to keep you interested. Look for wasted time, money, and energy, especially the customer's. Look for duplication, unnecessary procedures, unnecessary paperwork and red tape, and habitual malfunctions. Be a customer for a day and shop your business— anonymously, of course. Experience what typical customers experience, and ask yourself how pleased you are with the value you receive.

Talk to the front-line employees about customer value; find out what they think it is. What priorities are they actualizing in their daily work? Are those priorities supported by the critical elements of the customer value model? What obstacles, if any, do they see to delivering outstanding value? How good do they think the service is? How do they think it might be improved?

Call it *realignment*. Do it.

REENLIST THE PEOPLE

Maybe you're in close touch with the managers and working people of the organization; maybe you always have been. Or could it be that too many crises, too many priorities, and too many brushfires have distracted the leaders of the enterprise and put them out of touch with the culture?

How well do you understand the employees today? Who are they? What do they want? What do they seek in their jobs and careers? What are their priorities? What frustrates them, inhibits them, or demotivates them? How would you describe their morale? Are they switched on, switched off, or just glowing at half wattage?

How well do they understand the vision and mission of the enterprise? How well have you communicated the strategy and focus to them? Have you given them the training and support for the job knowledge, skills, and attitudes they need to deliver outstanding customer value? Do they know what the priorities are? Do they feel they have the freedom and entitlement to think for themselves and to find better ways of doing their jobs? Do they work together as a team, for both external service and internal service?

How do they perceive the quality of work life in the organization? Do they have competent supervision? Do they see opportunities to learn and grow on the job? Do they feel they can get ahead on merit and move up to a better job if they do well in the current job? Do they think fair play, justice, and equal treatment are real values of the organization? What is the grapevine saying?

If you're not entirely happy with your answers to these and other, similar questions, maybe it's time to get back in touch. Maybe it's time for a time-out. Maybe the executives and managers need to take a break from the battle lines and wander out into the organization and catch up on the culture. Maybe you need to listen more, hear more, and make some notes. Become part of the culture again. Recognize faces and remember names. Meet newcomers. Offer encouragement, sympathy when necessary, and praise whenever possible. Get the energy up and get the heads all pointing in the same direction.

Call it *leadership*. Do it.

ENDNOTES

INTRODUCTION

1 Articles in *Quality Digest* included Albrecht, Karl, "The Last Days of TQM?" November 1992; "ISO 9000: A Great Leap Backward," August 1992; and "Is TQM Dead?" April 1994.

2 Zemke, Ron, "Bashing the Baldrige," *Training*, February 1991, pp. 29–39.

CHAPTER 1

1 U.S. Bureau of Labor Statistics.

2 Ackoff, Russell, Paul Broholm, and Roberta Snow, *Revitalizing Western Economies*, San Francisco: Jossey-Bass, 1984, p. 2.

3 U.S. Department of Commerce, Economics and Statistics Administration, "Service Industries and Economic Performance," March 1996, p. 5.

4 *The Wall Street Journal*, January 9, 1985.

5 Tuchman, Barbara, "The Decline of Quality," *The New York Times Magazine*, November 2, 1980.

6 U.S. Census Bureau, "1997 Sources of Receipts and Revenues, 1997 Economic Census," issued August 2000, pp. 13–15.

7 U.S. Office of Consumer Affairs in Cooperation with Chevrolet Motor Division General Motors Corporation, "Increasing Customer Satisfaction Through Effective Complaint Handling."

8 Goodman, John, "Basic Facts on Customer Complaint Behavior and the Impact of Service on the Bottom Line," *Competitive Advantage*, June 1999, pp. 1–5.

9 Famulla, Rainer, "Insights into Andersen Consulting Financial Services Customer Index," April 2000.

10 Goodman, John, "Basic Facts on Customer Complaint Behavior and the Impact of Service on the Bottom Line," *Competitive Advantage*, June 1999, pp. 1–5.

11 Shelp, Ronald Kent, et al., *Service Industries and Economic Development*, New York: Praeger Publishers, 1985, p. 3.

12 Ibid.

13 Levitt, Theodore, *Thinking About Management,* New York: The Free Press, 1991.

14 Ibid.

CHAPTER 2

1 Peters, Tom, and Robert Waterman, *In Search of Excellence*, New York: Harper & Row, 1982, p. 17.

2 Normann, Richard, *Service Management: Strategy and Leadership in Service Businesses*, originally published in Swedish, translated into English by John Wiley & Sons, 1983.

3 Carlzon, Jan, *Moments of Truth*, Cambridge, MA: Ballinger Publishing, 1987.

4 Ritz-Carlton Hotels Company received the Malcolm Baldrige National Quality Award in 1992 and 1999.

5 For example, Connellan, Thomas, *Inside the Magic Kingdom: Seven Secrets of Disney's Success,* Austin, TX: Bard Press, 1996.

6 Zemke, Ron, and Dick Schaaf, *The Service Edge: 101 Companies that Profit Through Customer Care*, New York: New American Library, 1989.

7 Buzzell, Robert D., and Bradley T. Gale, *The PIMS Principles: Linking Strategy to Performance*, New York: The Free Press, 1987, p. 107.

8 Reichheld, Frederick, and W. Earl Sasser, "Zero Defections: Quality Comes to Services," *Harvard Business Review*, September–October 1990, pp. 105–111.

9 Parasuraman, A., Valarie A. Zeithaml, and Leonard L. Berry, "SERVQUAL: A Multiple-Item Scale for Measuring Consumer Perceptions of Service Quality," *Journal of Retailing*, vol. 64, no. 1, Spring 1988, pp. 12–40.

10 Pine, B. Joseph, and James H. Gilmore, *The Experience Economy: Work Is Theatre and Every Business a Stage*, Boston: Harvard Business Press, 1999.

CHAPTER 3

1 Connellan, Tom, *Inside the Magic Kingdom: Seven Keys to Disney's Success*, Austin, TX: Bard Press, 1997, pp. 20–21.

2 Bell, Chip R., and Ron Zemke, *Managing Knock Your Socks Off Service*, New York: AMACOM, 1992, p. 77.

3 Connellan, Tom, *Inside the Magic Kingdom: Seven Keys to Disney's Success*, Austin, TX: Bard Press, 1997, p. 41.

CHAPTER 4

1 The first known appearance of the Platinum Rule was in Albrecht, Karl, "The Platinum Rule," *Quality Digest*, April 1994, p. 19.

2 For a detailed explanation, with examples, of the customer value model, see Albrecht, Karl, *The Only Thing That Matters: Bringing the Power of the Customer Into the Center of Your Business*, New York: HarperBusiness, 1992, p. 124.

3 Peterson, Robert, comments made at a J. D. Power & Associates 1991 Customer Satisfaction Symposium, March 1991.

4 Zemke, Ron, and Tom Connellan, *E-Service: 24 Ways to Keep Your Customers When the Competition Is Just a Click Away*, New York: AMACOM, 2001, p. 40.

5 Bain & Company and Mainspring Communications, "Retailing Survey," Boston: MA, December 1999.

6 Goodman, John, "Basic Facts on Customer Complaint Behavior and the Impact of Service on the Bottom Line," *Competitive Advantage*, June 1999, pp. 1–5.

7 Ibid.

8 U.S. Office of Consumer Affairs in Cooperation with Chevrolet Motor Division General Motors Corporation, "Increasing Customer Satisfaction Through Effective Complaint Handling."

9 Brady, Diane, "Why Service Stinks," *Business Week*, October 23, 2000.

10 Goodman, John, "Basic Facts on Customer Complaint Behavior and the Impact of Service on the Bottom Line," *Competitive Advantage*, June 1999, pp. 1–5.

11 Berry, Leonard, "Improving Service Quality in America: Lessons Learned," *Academy of Management Executive*, vol. 8, no. 2, 1994.

12 *The Service Edge* (Newsletter), April 1993, as excerpted with permission from *Hospitals Magazine*.

CHAPTER 5

1 Porter, Michael E., "What Is Strategy?" *Harvard Business Review*, November–December 1996, pp. 61–78.

2 Treacy, Michael, and Fred Wiersema, "Customer Intimacy and Other Value Disciplines," *Harvard Business Review,* January–February 1993, pp. 84–92.

CHAPTER 6

1 This model was originally presented in Karl Albrecht's book, *The Only Thing That Matters: Bringing the Power of the Customer Into the Center of Your Business*, New York: HarperBusiness, 1992, p.176. It was later extended to the strategic planning context, i.e., strategic customer focus, in his book, *The Northbound Train: Finding the Purpose, Setting the Direction, Shaping the Destiny of Your Organization*. New York: AMACOM, 1994, p.128.

2 Dychtwald, Ken, *Age Power: How the 21st Century Will Be Ruled by the New Old*, New York: Tarcher/Putnam, 1999.

3 DeBruicker, F. Stewart, and Gregory L. Summe, "Make Sure Your Customers Keep Coming Back," *Harvard Business Review*, January–February 1932, p. 92.

4 Albrecht, Karl, *Brain Power: Learn to Develop Your Thinking Skills*, Englewood Cliffs: Prentice-Hall, 1980, p. 236.

5 Shostack, G. Lynn, "Designing Services That Deliver," *Harvard Business Review*, January–February 1984, p. 135.

6 Normann, Richard, *Service Management: Strategy and Leadership in Service Businesses*, New York: John Wiley & Sons, 1984, p. 15.

7 Albrecht, Karl, *The Only Thing That Matters: Bringing the Power of the Customer Into the Center of Your Business*, New York: HarperBusiness 1992, p. 223.

8 For readers not familiar with the American criminal justice system, a "Miranda warning," named after the defendant in a landmark civil-rights case, is an obligatory warning police officers must give to arrested suspects before questioning them to ensure that they understand that they have the right to remain silent and be represented by an attorney and that any statements they make can be used against them in court. On television police shows, this is called "reading them their rights."

9 U.S. Office of Consumer Affairs in Cooperation with Chevrolet Motor Division General Motors Corporation, "Increasing Customer Satisfaction Through Effective Complaint Handling."

10 Zemke, Ron, *Managing Knock Your Socks Off Service Recovery*, New York: AMACOM, 2000.

CHAPTER 7

1 Sathe, Vijay, "Implications of Corporate Culture: A Manager's Guide to Action," *Organizational Dynamics*, Autumn 1983, p. 8.

2 "Benchmarking Study of Electronic Customer Service," March 2000. Published by the International Customer Service Association and e-Satisy.com, Chicago, IL, October 2000.

3 Schlesinger, Leonard, and James L. Heskett, "The Service Driven Service Organization," *Harvard Business Review*, September–October 1991.

4 Development Dimensions International is a consulting firm based in Pittsburgh, PA. Taken from DDI Web site, www.ddi.com.

CHAPTER 8

1 For a more detailed discussion of the art of story telling as the world's oldest teaching technique, see "Storytelling: Back to a Basic," by Ron Zemke, *Training*, March 1990, pp. 44–50.

2 Personal experience of Chris Lee, a Minneapolis business writer, and follow-up report, "NWA Settles Snowstorm Suit for $7.1 Million," *Minneapolis Star Tribune*, January 10, 2001.

3 From *The Service Edge* (newsletter), September 1991, p. 5.

4 From *The Service Edge* (newsletter), July 1991, p. 5.

5 Ken Summers, senior vice president of Human Capital Associates, a Colorado Springs consulting firm that specializes in lean manufacturing and six sigma implementations, tells this story to illustrate what happens when an organization's systems are not aligned with its customers' values. In this case, the hospital's systems destroyed his trust in its competence.

6 From *The Service Edge* (newsletter), July 1993, p. 4.

7 Personal experience of Kathy Ridge, president of Ridge Consulting & Training, Charlotte, North Carolina, which first appeared in *Managing Knock Your Socks Off Service*, by Chip Bell and Ron Zemke, New York: AMACOM, 1992, pp. 85–86. This is a good example of how bad systems prevent the best-intentioned people from serving customers. "You can take great people, highly trained and motivated, and put them in a lousy system and the system will win every time," says Geary Rummler, president of the Rummler-Bache Group.

8 Anderson, Kristin, and Ron Zemke, *Tales of Knock Your Socks Off Service: Inspiring Stories of Outstanding Customer Service*, New York: AMACOM, 1998, p. 12.

9 Ibid., p. 47.

10 Ibid., pp. 58–59.

11 From *The Service Edge* (newsletter), April 1992, p. 5.

12 "Heavy Duty," *Minneapolis Star Tribune*, January 3, 2001.

13 Anderson, Kristin, and Ron Zemke, *Tales of Knock Your Socks Off Service: Inspiring Stories of Outstanding Customer Service*, New York: AMACOM, 1998, pp. 16–18.

14 Ibid., pp. 49–51.

15 Fister, Sarah, "E-Commerce Meets E-Service," *Training*, June 2000, p. 42.

CHAPTER 9

1 Matteis, Richard, J., "The New Back Office Focuses on Customer Service," *Harvard Business Review*, March–April 1979, pp. 128–142.

2 Crosby, Philip, *Quality Is Free*, New York: McGraw-Hill, 1979, p. 173.

3 Michael Scriven is a professor at Claremont Graduate University, Claremont, CA.

CHAPTER 10

1 Henkoff, Ronald, "Growing Your Company: Five Ways to Do It Right," *Fortune*, November 25, 1996, pp. 78–87.

2 Brewer, Geoffrey, "The Customer Stops Here," *Sales & Marketing Management*, March 1998, pp. 30–38.

3 Henkoff, Ronald, "Finding and Keeping the Best Service Workers, *Fortune*, October 3, 1994, pp. 110–122.

4 If you'd like more information about the Disney approach to leadership, people management, or service quality, contact Disney University Seminars, P.O. Box 10-093, Lake Buena Vista, FL 32830-0093. Telephone: 407/824-4855.

5 Connellan, Tom, *Inside the Magic Kingdom: Seven Secrets to Disney's Success*, Austin, TX: Bard Press, 1997.

CHAPTER 11

1 The TQS "wheel" model first appeared in Karl Albrecht's book, *The Only Thing That Matters: Bringing the Power of the Customer into the Center of Your Business*, New York: HarperBusiness, 1992, p. 70.

CHAPTER 13

1 Quinn, Feargal, *Crowning the Customer*, Dublin: O'Brien Press, 1990.

CHAPTER 14

1 Toffler, Alvin, *Future Shock*, New York: Random House, 1970.

2 Toffler, Alvin, *The Third Wave*, New York: Morrow, 1980.

3 Naisbitt, John, *The Global Paradox*, New York: Morrow, 1994.

4 Naisbitt, John, with Nana Naisbitt and Douglas Philips, *High Tech, High Touch*, New York: Broadway Books, 1999.

5 Stoll, Clifford, *Silicon Snake Oil*, New York: Doubleday, 1995.

6 Stoll, Clifford, *High-tech Heretic*, New York: Doubleday, 1999.

7 Portions of this section are excerpted from "Digital Backlash," by Karl Albrecht and Ron Gunn, published in *Training & Development*, November 2000.

8 "If I Knew Then What I Know Now," eCompany; online news report, America Online, March 2001.

9 Portions of this section are excerpted from "The Digital Moat," by Karl Albrecht, first published in *Harvard Business Review–Japan*, December 2000.

INDEX